The Making of *Hoosiers*
Second Edition

The Making of *Hoosiers*

How a Small Movie from the Heartland Became One of America's Favorite Films

Second Edition

Gayle L. Johnson

For everyone who believed in me

Copyright © 2016, 2010 by Gayle L. Johnson

All rights reserved. No part of this publication may be reproduced, distributed, or transmitted in any form or by any means, including photocopying, recording, or other electronic or mechanical methods, without the prior written permission of the author, except in the case of brief quotations embodied in critical reviews and certain other noncommercial uses permitted by copyright law.

Printed in the United States of America

ISBN-13: 978-1536968491

ISBN-10: 1536968498

Cover design by Alan Clements

Cover images by iStockphoto and Fotolia

For more information on *Hoosiers*, visit the book's companion website, The *Hoosiers* Archive, at http://hoosiersarchive.com.

Contents

Preface	**1**
Chapter 1 The Inspiration: The 1953–54 Milan Indians and Hoosier Hysteria	**3**
Selling Hoosier Hysteria in Hollywood: The Search for Financing	16
Chapter 2 Setting the Scene: Location Scouting and Extras Casting	**21**
A Town Transformed	26
Extra, Extra! Casting the Townspeople	28
Outfitting and Styling the Extras and Actors	32
Chapter 3 The Starting Lineup: Casting the Main Roles	**35**
Handpicking the Huskers	40
Chapter 4 Tip-off: Filming Gets Under Way	**49**
Cameras Roll in New Richmond	55
School Days in Nineveh	61
Chapter 5 The Second Half: Filming Continues	**67**
Courting Fame in Knightstown	68
The Season Opener: Oolitic	79
Norman's Last Chance: Lyons	81
Running the Picket Fence: Dugger	81
Cedar Knob Game	85
Sectional Game	86
Regional Game	88
Other Filming Locations	92
Opening Credits	92
The Town Meeting	92
Home Scenes	94
Hospital Scenes	97
Additional Scenes	98
Returning to New Richmond	99
The Reality of Living Your Dream	101
Chapter 6 The Last Shot: Filming Winds Down	**103**
Hinkle Hassles	105
Going into Overtime in Knightstown	113

Chapter 7 The Final Cut: Editing, First Screenings, and Marketing Strategy	**115**
They Cheered and Laughed: The Test Screening	120
Changing Release Dates: Distribution and Marketing Strategies	121
Sneak Previews for the National Press	124
Chapter 8 Endgame: The Movie Premieres	**127**
The World Premiere	128
Sneak Previews in Indiana	131
The Toughest Audience: The Indiana Rollout	131
Everyone's a Critic	132
Two Experts: A Coach and a Player	134
The Milan Reaction	135
NCAA Controversy	136
Hoosiers Heads West	137
The National Rollout	138
Box Office Returns	140
Critics' Comments	141
Writing	142
Directing	143
Acting	143
Chapter 9 Postgame Wrap-up: The Years After the Movie's Release	**147**
The Deleted Scenes Resurface	155
The End of One-Class Basketball	158
Attracting Productions to the Hoosier State	160
An Ongoing Partnership	163
Back Home Again in Indiana	164
Reflections	167
Chapter 10 Legacy: *Hoosiers*' Lasting Appeal	**171**
Factors in the Filmmakers' Favor	172
Authenticity	174
Objectivity	176
Story Quality	176
A Focus on Characters and Their Relationships	177
Straightforwardness of Motives	177
A Hint of Mystery	178
Responsibility	178
Humility	179
Respect for Others	179

The Comfort of Nostalgia, Tempered by Serious Themes	180
The Art of Minimalism	180
Literalism Versus Symbolism	182
Quality of Acting	183
Gene Hackman	183
Barbara Hershey	185
Dennis Hopper	185
Supporting Actors	187
The Three Main Characters	188
Coach Norman Dale	189
Shooter	192
Myra	193
Relationships Between the Main Characters	195
Norman and Shooter	195
Norman and Myra	197
Myra and Shooter	199
Other Characters	199
The Huskers	199
Jimmy	200
The Townspeople	201
The Movie's Themes	202
Basketball	202
A Community Tradition	202
A Unifying Force	203
A Constant	204
A Path to Healing	204
The Thrill of Victory	205
The Agony of Defeat	205
Issues of Race	206
Redemption and Second Chances	208
Forgiveness	209
Giving and Receiving Grace	209
A Simple Matter of Faith	210
Reaching Your Goal and Achieving Your Dream	211
Initially Resisting but Ultimately Embracing Change	211
Personal Change	212
Societal Change	213
Teamwork and Self-Sacrifice	213
Family and Community	214

Small-Town Life	215
Religion	216
Three Key Scenes	217
Dealing with Jimmy's Early Absence	217
The Town Meeting	218
The Final Huddle	219
Other Interpretations	220
Lessons in Leadership and Management	220
Gender Issues	221
Making a Personal Story Universal and Relatable	222
Epilogue	**225**
Images	**227**
Acknowledgments	**245**
Image Credits	**246**
Notes	**247**
Chapter 1	247
Chapter 2	251
Chapter 3	254
Chapter 4	258
Chapter 5	262
Chapter 6	268
Chapter 7	270
Chapter 8	272
Chapter 9	275
Chapter 10	280
Epilogue	286
Index	**287**

Preface

"Oh, I wish I could be there!" —*Shooter*

"Bodies needed" announced the headline of a brief newspaper item on December 1, 1985, about the making of the movie *Hoosiers*. Filming was drawing to a close, with only the state-finals game left to be shot. Fifteen thousand fans were needed to fill Hinkle Fieldhouse in Indianapolis—and I longed to be one of them. All year I had been following with great interest the story of the movie that would attempt to portray the almost-fanatical devotion to basketball known as Hoosier Hysteria. Screenwriter/producer Angelo Pizzo and director David Anspaugh were native Hoosiers who built careers in Hollywood and then returned to their home state to make a movie about a topic close to their hearts.

Everything I knew about the movie came from newspaper articles. They were brief and infrequent at first but became more detailed and numerous as the year progressed. From perusing these accounts I sensed this movie would be something special—something important. And I wanted desperately to be at the filming of the final game.

Hoosiers was about much more than just basketball or small-town life in the 1950s. Pizzo wisely centered his story on themes of second chances and redemption, of dreaming big and seeing those dreams come true. This enabled the creation of a movie with wide appeal. In fact, *Hoosiers* has been called one of the most inspiring films of all time. But just as inspiring is the story of how this film came to be.

Novice scriptwriter Pizzo and first-time feature director Anspaugh had to overcome other people's skepticism and their own self-doubt. But they weren't alone in their quest. They successfully enlisted the help of others along the way—first just a few, and then a few hundred, and eventually a few thousand. And the support and acceptance of the people of Indiana became a vital component of the filmmakers' and movie's success.

Unfortunately, I never made it to the shooting of the final game; I lived too far away. But the compelling story of the movie's production stuck with me. This book takes you on the journey that was the making of *Hoosiers* and examines the reasons for the film's vast and enduring popularity. When I think of the *Hoosiers* team who succeeded beyond their wildest dreams, it's not the Hickory Huskers I have in mind—it's David Anspaugh and Angelo Pizzo.

1
The Inspiration: The 1953–54 Milan Indians and Hoosier Hysteria

"No school this small has ever been to the state championship!" —Shooter

Probably the biggest misconception about the movie *Hoosiers* is that it is based on a true story. It would be more accurate to say that this iconic 1986 film was *inspired in part by* the Milan Indians basketball team. In 1954 Milan became the smallest high school in Indiana history to win the boys' one-class four-stage state tournament. Everyone in Indiana knows the story; it's been called the Milan Miracle. Said *Hoosiers* screenwriter and producer Angelo Pizzo, "Every year right before tournament time, the newspapers would bring it out again. Coaches would use it as inspiration: 'You too can overcome the odds against being a small school.'" In fact, he said, "In a certain sense it was like a classic mythological tale." And this story would become part of Pizzo's inspiration for his first screenplay.

Pizzo grew up in the 1950s and '60s as the oldest of eight children in Bloomington. He went by the nickname Andy—a moniker he would keep until his mid-20s. Bloomington was the home of Indiana University and was the setting of the Academy Award–winning 1979 movie *Breaking Away*, which included a storyline about IU's Little 500 bicycle race. Pizzo's grandfather was a Sicilian immigrant, and his father was a pathologist, coroner, city council member, and Democratic State Representative.

Living only two blocks from the old IU fieldhouse probably made it inevitable that Pizzo would become a college basketball fan. He often watched the team practice and rebounded free throws for players such as Walt Bellamy, Herbie Lee, and Gary Long. Pizzo didn't play much basketball himself, though, because his lack of speed, size, and agility made him more of a fan than a participant. So he played baseball instead. Mickey Mantle was his boyhood hero.

Not surprisingly, the future filmmaker also was a movie aficionado. He relished westerns and epic, larger-than-life films with noble, courageous characters that swept him away into another world. Some of his favorites included *Ben-Hur*, *El Cid*, and *Lawrence of Arabia*. Anytime he didn't come home in the evening, his parents knew he was probably at either the Princess Theater or Indiana Theater, watching the same movie repeatedly. His mother sometimes took him to foreign films made by directors such as Ingmar Bergman and Luis Buñuel—the kinds of motion pictures kids rarely view. "I had many nightmares based on *The Seventh Seal*!" Pizzo recalled.

At University High School, Pizzo went through a rebellious, antiauthoritarian period. In the fall of his junior year he was temporarily suspended from school because he had allowed his hair to grow over his ears. He didn't participate in extracurricular activities and graduated near the bottom of his class. Pizzo struggled with feelings of insecurity and lacked confidence. "I felt success would never happen to me," he said. "I never believed in myself. I sort of kept going in some weird way, taking one step after the other with this weird blind faith."

In 1966 Pizzo enrolled in IU. Even though he was admitted on academic probation, he earned straight A's his first semester. He would have liked to study filmmaking, but neither IU nor any other Indiana school offered a major in film. Also, although that academic topic intrigued him, Pizzo actually considered it impractical, because he couldn't imagine making a living at it. So he pursued his other main interest by majoring in political science. Pizzo thought he might attend law school and eventually work for the State Department or a senator. He pledged the Sigma Nu fraternity, mainly because he wanted to go to parties and meet girls. At Sigma Nu he befriended social chairman David Anspaugh, who was from Decatur, a small town near Fort Wayne and the Ohio border.

As a kid Anspaugh had played Little League baseball and spent every Saturday at the Adams Theater, consuming films such as *The Ten*

Commandments. "That was the temple," he said of the Adams. "That was where I really fell in love with movies." At Decatur High School Anspaugh played basketball but was better known as a successful football quarterback, leading his team to an 8–0–1 season his senior year. He also was a record-setting pole-vaulter. He was class president his freshman and sophomore years, served on the student council, worked on the yearbook, attended Hoosier Boys State, and was named to the senior honor roll. At IU Anspaugh started out studying business, but he found his classes unengaging—a fact reflected by his poor grades. So he switched his major to secondary education. Whenever Anspaugh drove between Decatur and Bloomington, he always had a camera with him, and sometimes he stopped to photograph the flat, barren landscape. He wondered if he would find a way to use these images to express himself as an artist someday.

As frat brothers and roommates, Pizzo and Anspaugh discovered they both had a love of basketball and movies. They took a film-related class that fell under the category of comparative literature. "I think [it was] called 'Film in Society,'" Anspaugh said. "In addition to the class, [we] screened a lot of movies, at least once a week. We were also encouraged to go to screenings outside of class. I was introduced to a lot of foreign films that I had never seen growing up in Decatur." They viewed many of these movies at Bloomington's Von Lee Theatre. Anspaugh received a hand-me-down 16mm camera from his father, a portrait photographer. He used it to shoot rallies, protests, concerts, and football games. And in 1968 Anspaugh and Pizzo served as extras in the Paul Newman flick *Winning*, filmed in part at the Indianapolis Motor Speedway. They wanted to get as close to the moviemaking action as possible.

Anspaugh and Pizzo during IU's 1967–68 school year.

Although at the time neither Anspaugh nor Pizzo planned to become a filmmaker, they often discussed movies they would like to make if they could. They tossed around the idea of creating a film about how much basketball means to people in Indiana and how it's interwoven with the culture. They wondered what it must have been like to be a hometown basketball hero in the postwar era, before Elvis and the Beatles, before TVs and interstates. Pizzo said, "We decided there was a movie in there somewhere. We imagined being the ones to make it."

After a couple years in Sigma Nu, the two friends found themselves at odds with the fraternity's leaders and many of its members, who openly disparaged Vietnam War protesters and condemned recreational drug use. Feeling increasingly uncomfortable with what seemed like an oppressive atmosphere in the house, Anspaugh and Pizzo left Greek life behind and began associating with other freethinkers.

By the time Pizzo graduated from IU in 1971, U.S. involvement in Vietnam and the tumultuous nature of the late 1960s had created what he termed "a sense of rage and vulnerability" in his generation. The new graduate found himself disillusioned with politics, disenchanted with the government, and disdainful of the system. He applied for and received conscientious objector status and prepared to be sent to an alternative-service assignment. But his draft lottery number wasn't called, and with no backup plan, Pizzo felt lost and restless. As he put it, he was "searching for a sense of self, a goal, a direction." His father advised him to identify what he loved and then figure out how to make a living at it. Pizzo was still passionate about movies, having amassed over 150 books about film. So he enrolled in the University of Southern California to study film history, theory, and criticism, with the goal of earning a doctorate and becoming a professor.

One year, when Pizzo was on Christmas break from USC, he attended a high school basketball game at Bloomington South, and all those memories of Hoosier Hysteria came flooding back. "The energy in that place—it blew away any rock concert," he said. "[People were] out of their seats, off the ground. I thought if I could ever capture this on film, it would be special." So he outlined a possible plot for one of his classes at USC, but, he said, "it got a withering review. They said, basically, 'It's a cliché story, David and Goliath; we've seen it a hundred times. There's nothing unique about it; it's really boring.'"

During his third year of graduate school, Pizzo took an internship on *The Mary Tyler Moore Show* during its final season. MTM Enterprises president Grant Tinker told Pizzo about a producer, Philip Mandelker, who was developing a TV series called *The Fitzpatricks*. He needed someone to do research for the show, about a steelworker and his family living in Flint, Michigan. But when Mandelker's assistant quit, Pizzo assumed that role instead. He decided to take a break from school, with the intention of returning in a few months. The job "was hard work, 14 to 15 hours a day," he said. "But I figured that this was my chance to find out what making films was about." *The Fitzpatricks* aired only ten episodes. But by then Pizzo had learned so much by immersing himself in the industry that he no longer saw a need to go back and finish his doctoral thesis on the genre theory of film criticism. After working at Warner Bros. Television, Pizzo moved to Time Life Films. There he developed TV movies of the week, eventually becoming vice president of production for feature films. During this time, he became somewhat dissatisfied with his role of advising and supporting writers, directors, and actors. He felt envious of and one step removed from them, because it seemed that they were the ones who did the real work.

On March 30, 1981, Pizzo attended the NCAA basketball Division I championship game at The Spectrum in Philadelphia, where he watched his alma mater, IU, defeat North Carolina. The victory spurred him to again revisit the idea of making a movie centered around Indiana high school basketball—this time because he found himself at a crossroads in his career. Time Life had recently disbanded its film production unit and paid out Pizzo's contract. "I was devastated," he said. "All of these projects I had been working on were gone. It was a dark time for me. I was burned out and needed to take some time off. I knew I would go back to Hollywood, but I needed a break." He decided to finally begin working on the movie idea that had been tumbling around in his mind for years. "I think I started writing *Hoosiers* as a stalling mechanism so I didn't have to go back to work [immediately]," Pizzo admitted. "I don't think I ever really thought I could do it or finish it. It was just a way of not facing the rest of my career at that moment."

Earlier in his career, Pizzo had tried to find someone in Hollywood who could help him translate his concept of a movie based on Hoosier Hysteria into screenplay form. "I wanted the writer to know how [Hoosiers] walk, how they talk, how they breathe basketball," he said. "I saw Indiana as a character in the movie, and it had to be accurate." One factor that influenced his viewpoint was *Breaking Away*. Although Pizzo liked the film, he insisted "it was Bloomington, Indiana, as seen through the eyes of two outsiders"—British director Peter Yates and writer/producer Steve Tesich, born in Yugoslavia. Pizzo contended that Bloomington ended up looking like a generic college town. "I saw my hometown being depicted, and I didn't recognize any of the people in it," he said.

"I put the search out to all agents: 'Wanted: writer from Indiana,'" Pizzo said. "I read a lot of stuff, but nothing quite worked for me." He had eventually concluded that, if the screenplay were ever to be written, he was probably the best person to do so. "For some projects, it's just not enough to do research," he explained. "You've got to have an understanding of the place you're writing about. You've got to know it in your bones."

Because Pizzo felt that the story of Milan's state championship had achieved folktale status, that's what he gravitated toward.

* * *

When Coach Marvin Wood, just 24 years old, arrived at Milan (pronounced *My*-lun) to lead the Indians in 1952, he found himself in a less-than-ideal situation. The previous, well-liked coach, Herman "Snort" Grinstead, had been fired for ordering new uniforms without permission. His dismissal led to a firestorm of protest from the squad's fans—who also weren't thrilled about the prospect of turning over their talented team to a youthful, relatively unproven leader. And Wood didn't gain many fans by closing practices to the townspeople. He also didn't hang out at the local restaurant with the fans on Saturday mornings to rehash the previous night's game.

Wood was quite different from Grinstead, a tall, demanding man in his mid-50s who was prone to fits of anger. Wood was a churchgoing married man with two young children. He spoke softly and rarely got mad. Although initially Milan residents didn't embrace their new coach, they began to accept him after seeing his emphasis on demonstrating techniques and running offensive patterns pay off. At the end of that season, in the state tournament the Indians won at the sectional, regional, and semifinal (later renamed semistate) levels, making it all the way to the state finals. There, in the first matchup of the day, they lost to South Bend Central, 56–37. Milan had never before made it further than the first game of the regional in the tournament. They finished the season with 25 wins and five losses.

The following year the Indians did even better, ending the regular season with only two losses. They entered a state tournament field of 751 teams. Tiny Milan, with an enrollment of only 161, secured its place in Indiana sports history by defeating Muncie Central, 10 times larger than Milan, 32–30 in the final game. They won on a last-second shot by starting guard Bobby Plump.

* * *

Pizzo began his research for the script by heading to Versailles, the county seat of Ripley County, home of Milan. There he read local newspapers from 1952 and 1953. "I looked at more than the sports pages," he said. "I wanted details of how people lived their lives, what was important to them. Those little details ended up in the script." Pizzo talked to people about the farming and social practices of that era as well. He also interviewed Gene White, a member of the 1954 Milan team. Pizzo asked him if Marvin Wood had any difficulty being the new coach. White replied, "Nope. Everybody liked him." Pizzo continued, "Were there any problems, any adversities?" White answered, "Nope. Everybody got along real good." Pizzo pressed on. "You didn't have even one troublemaker?" Mused White, "Well, Bobby Plump used to show up late. Coach made him run laps."

"I knew I didn't have a movie," Pizzo said. He concluded that the coach and players' lives "were not dramatic enough. The guys were too nice; the team had no real conflict." And Pizzo felt that conflict is the essence of drama.

So he chose to take a detour from the real-life Milan Miracle, retaining only a few elements of the original story. He created the town of Hickory and its team, the Huskers. He felt he was remaining true to the spirit of the Milan story while giving himself the freedom to invent. Pizzo believed that in any good story, "in the course of the journey of the characters, there are things in the way that they have to work out and get through. They have to solve problems. They have to overcome emotional roadblocks." Because the story would not actually be based on the Milan Miracle, Pizzo decided not to use Coach Wood as a consultant. "I didn't want to hurt his feelings by [taking the Milan] story and, basically, doing it my way," he said. "I didn't know if he would take umbrage at what we were doing."

For additional inspiration, Pizzo said, he recalled "the atmosphere of the sectional games I saw up at Martinsville, where they had 14 or 16 teams playing at times. Kids from small towns such as Smithville, Stinesville, and Unionville grew up knowing each other and playing together. I never personally experienced what it was like for a small school like Milan to go up to the state finals. But I drew on my personal experience of watching great, dramatic sectional games. Those made such a huge impression on me. To me, that was the essence of Indiana high school basketball."

Although the intense love of basketball known as Hoosier Hysteria was a strong influence on the plot, Pizzo chose to put human relationships rather than basketball at the heart of the story. His intention, he said, "was to really capture the essence and the soul of what Indiana was about, and that is the people—the community structure and how they interacted." To remind himself of this tactic as he was writing, he made a sign and hung it above his desk. It said "This is not a sports movie."

As he retreated to his family's summer home to begin working on the script, Pizzo fought feelings of inadequacy; he didn't consider himself a creative person. "I started thinking about all the great writers, and I knew I wasn't even close to them," he said. "I always had it in the back of my mind that if [the screenplay] wasn't any good, I could just throw it away." He said that due to a lack of confidence, "I only told my girlfriend and my family what I was doing. It would have been too embarrassing to tell my industry friends in California." He explained that, in Los Angeles, "if you said you are working on a spec script, everybody would interpret that as you're out of work."

Because he enjoyed the social aspects of production and development work, Pizzo said, "the idea of going into a room all by myself for any length of time to just write seemed both boring and terrifying to me." In the cold, quiet isolation of the cabin along the Lake Michigan shore, Pizzo found it hard to get started on the script. He procrastinated by spending time on unproductive tasks such as cutting vines off trees in the woods. Writing proved tedious. In fact, "it was a terrible experience," Pizzo said. "I hated every minute of writing that script. I didn't know what I was doing." Even though he had evaluated many scripts and worked with numerous writers during his years in TV, "everything I thought I knew about screenwriting went out the window," he said.

After struggling to write at the cabin for two and a half weeks, Pizzo returned to Los Angeles and kept working on the script. He was starting to believe that "the rational, linear, objective part of your brain is your enemy" when you're writing. He made little progress, doing frequent revisions and continually second-guessing himself. "There was always a critic on my shoulder," he said. "I would write a scene and read it and then tear it up." Eventually TV writer, producer, and novelist John Sacret Young, whom Pizzo had met while working on *The Fitzpatricks*, suggested a helpful writing strategy: After finishing a page, Pizzo should turn it over and not look back at it until he was done with the entire screenplay.

The rookie writer determined that although he needed a general idea of where the story was headed, he would give himself room for discovery along the way. He also knew he must be "specifically clear about my destination—the end." Pizzo remembered hearing that research done with test audiences revealed that how they feel about what happens in a movie's final minutes strongly influences how they feel about the movie as a whole. He wanted to fashion an ending that would stay with the viewers and not evaporate from their minds as they left the theater.

A necessary element for the story, Pizzo asserted, was "a protagonist that has a compelling and emotional character arc and can elicit from a possible audience a strong rooting interest." Originally he patterned Norman Dale after Milan's young coach, Marvin Wood. Pizzo also wanted to make redemption a major plot point, because it was "a theme that's been around a lot longer than any sport," he said. "It's in the folklore and literature of every culture." However, that theme seemed as if it wouldn't work well with a coach in his 20s, because such a character would have decades to correct his mistakes. So Pizzo changed the coach to an older man in need of a second chance.

Because Pizzo was a longtime fan of IU basketball, it was unsurprising that Coach Dale's personality was somewhat reminiscent of notoriously volatile IU coach Bob Knight. Coach Dale's requirement that the Huskers pass the ball at least four times before shooting also came from Knight. For further inspiration, Pizzo recalled the story of Ohio State University football coach Woody Hayes, who was fired for punching an opposing player during the 1978 Gator Bowl.

Pizzo believed that, when you write, your characters have to be a part of you. But he also knew they needed their own voices, as well as room to grow. He found that characters "take on a life of their own, and they start doing things you never expected them to do. Their presence becomes so dynamic and powerful that you have to deal with them." This belief was most evident in the evolution of the character of Shooter, who was inspired by a similar man Pizzo had encountered during junior high football. Originally the alcoholic Shooter was conceived as a minor character with little or no dialog; he was just a distraction and embarrassment to his son, Everett. The emphasis was more on how Everett's problems with his father were negatively affecting his basketball playing. But after Pizzo wrote a scene in which Shooter shows up drunk at a game and Coach Dale pulls him off the court, "I felt a recognition," the writer said. "I felt that [Shooter and the coach] saw something in each other that connected them. As an experiment, I decided to write another scene, to see if that would carry over when [Shooter] was sober, and that was the coffee shop scene. And his voice really came alive for me. And I couldn't keep him out of the movie after that. He wanted to be in every scene." Shooter's relationship with Norman "suggested a whole different avenue, emotion, and path for that character," Pizzo said. "Shooter became richer and more interesting. He became an essential part of the *Hoosiers* troupe instead of a fleeting backdrop."

Rounding out the trio of main characters was teacher Myra Fleener. Although she had grown up in Hickory, her failure to comprehend and join in on the town's obsession with its high school basketball team made her somewhat of a pariah. Pizzo described Myra's purpose in the story as asking the questions an audience member from outside a basketball-loving culture might pose; she challenged the community's accepted traditions. And as she and Norman took some tentative steps toward a relationship, she would help him open up emotionally.

Pizzo envisioned each of the three main characters as being stuck in their current situation. Each one would unconsciously perceive in the others something that could help them become unstuck.

To generate ideas of what the different Huskers' personalities should be like, Pizzo recalled his school friends. "The guys on the team are based on guys I knew when we were growing up," he said. "In some cases, I kept their own names."

The first draft was over 200 pages long. (As a general rule, one page equals about one minute of screen time.) Pizzo was hesitant to show the completed screenplay to anyone. He finally decided to give it to his mentor, Philip Mandelker, and he waited for his friend's comments with trepidation. To Pizzo's dismay, Mandelker stated it was one of the worst scripts he had ever read. Recalled Pizzo, "[He said] there was not one redeeming factor; there was not one interesting character; it was a badly told story. [He thought] I was great in development, excellent working with writers, but that I was not a writer. His exact words were, 'Angelo, you simply are not a writer. Let it go!' Devastating was not even the word for it. It was humiliation. It was a shame. There was a guilt, a self-loathing, a feeling of waste. The sense of failure was so profound." A depressed Pizzo took the script and hurled it into his closet.

Eight months later, at a dinner party, Pizzo struck up a conversation with award-winning biographer A. Scott Berg. The author figured Pizzo had the sensibility of a writer and asked him if he had ever written anything. Pizzo told him the story of the failed script, and Berg asked if he could read it. Pizzo declined, not wanting to invite more harsh criticism, but Berg persisted over the next two months, and finally Pizzo reluctantly gave in. After reviewing the script, Berg said, "There's a great movie in here, and I have some ideas for cuts." Pizzo came to realize that "your first draft in some ways is a big concrete stone you've created, and then you go back and start carving and chipping until you get the sculpture you want." Berg helped him understand that he needed to choose a particular thematic approach. Pizzo decided to focus on telling the story from the coach's perspective only, omitting side stories he had written for the supporting characters. Berg's feedback and encouragement enabled him to transition from regarding his screenplay as merely a writing experiment and made him believe a movie existed in all those pages. After completing the revisions, Pizzo showed the reworked script to his friend Anspaugh, whom he wanted to direct the film if its production ever became a reality.

After graduating from IU in 1970, Anspaugh had landed in Aspen, Colorado, where he worked as a ski instructor, substitute teacher, and waiter. One day a friend invited him to go to Spain and watch some of the filming of the movie *The Passenger*, starring Jack Nicholson. There Anspaugh struck up a friendship with the actor.

Anspaugh wished that, like Pizzo, he could attend the USC film school. During his days at IU, Anspaugh had imagined that he might teach film one day, figuring that was as close as he would ever get to Hollywood. However, he feared that the grades he'd earned as an undergraduate would preclude his admission to grad school. But after Nicholson wrote a letter of recommendation, Anspaugh was accepted into USC to work toward a master's degree in film history, theory, and criticism. As he began his studies, he hoped he could compete at that level. Regardless, he said, "I knew I was in the right place." At first, he didn't plan to ever become a filmmaker. But then he took a class in film production that altered his assumption. Legend had it that *Star Wars* creator George Lucas had been the last person to get an A in that course, in the late '60s. When Anspaugh also earned an A, "suddenly," he said, "people start coming to me and asking, 'Could you look at my film?' and 'Could you edit my film?' I started to believe that maybe there is something going on here, so I took my first directing class, and it changed my life." As Pizzo had done, when Anspaugh got a chance to begin working in the industry, he left school—eight credits shy of his degree.

Anspaugh's first Hollywood jobs were as a production assistant and then a location manager for MTM Productions. During this time he also took acting classes. "I didn't know that I would be a director," he said, "but I figured I better know something about this process. That's where I learned how to communicate with actors." In 1979 he produced a couple of TV movies and became an associate producer on Steven Bochco's short-lived TV series *Paris*. The next year Anspaugh began work on Bochco's *Hill Street Blues*, serving at various times as associate producer, coproducer, and director. For *Hill Street Blues* he won two Emmys as a producer and a Directors Guild of America Award. He also directed episodes of *St. Elsewhere* and *Miami Vice*. Anspaugh appreciated the unlikelihood that both he and Pizzo had ended up working in Hollywood. "The odds that one of us would make it in this industry were astronomical. That both of us did was amazing," he said. Anspaugh was eager to make the transition from directing TV to helming motion pictures. "The more work you do in television, the harder it is to get into movies," he said. Although in the past he had received offers to direct films, he turned them down because of the nature of the material. "They were teenage *Flashdance*-type love stories," Anspaugh said. He wanted to be passionate about the first movie he directed. Collaborating with longtime friend Pizzo on a movie would be "a really incredible thing to imagine," he said.

Pizzo wanted to team with Anspaugh to make *Hoosiers* because he knew they shared similar sensibilities and values and because Anspaugh's ego wouldn't get in the way. Pizzo couldn't think of another director who would be as respectful to his script as Anspaugh. He also felt his friend knew and understood the characters at a deep level. Furthermore, Pizzo said, "David is not the kind of director that will call attention to himself. He uses the camera very sparingly and lets the characters tell the story."

Anspaugh reacted enthusiastically to Pizzo's screenplay. He thought it was a brilliant piece of writing whose simplicity emphasized profound truths. He was convinced it had a universal quality that would interest a wide spectrum of the moviegoing public. His favorite kind of movie was one in which he cared about the characters at the end of the story. "By the time [*Hoosiers*] is over," he predicted, "you'll be absolutely in love with the coach and the kids." With the script ready to go and themselves in mind as director and producer, Anspaugh and Pizzo began looking for a production company.

Selling Hoosier Hysteria in Hollywood: The Search for Financing

"Be patient. Work for the good shot." —Coach Dale

After completing the script, Pizzo showed it to an agent he had worked with before, who told him, "We don't do this kind of movie. It's an independent regional film. Go raise the money for it in Indiana." Pizzo and Anspaugh then approached Mel Simon, an Indianapolis-based retail property magnate and co-owner of the NBA franchise Indiana Pacers. Simon also owned a movie production company, whose most recent release was raunchy teen sex comedy *Porky's*. But he passed on the chance to finance *Hoosiers*. Pizzo said, "We worked very hard, but all we could raise was about $700,000. To do the film, we felt we needed at least $4.5 million." Pizzo was disappointed that he and Anspaugh were unable to generate much excitement about the script in their home state. "We got comments like 'Oh, this guy doesn't know Indiana.' 'This guy doesn't know basketball,'" he said. "All of the [basketball] experts, the aficionados, were the first people who turned us down."

What's a Hoosier?

As he was writing, Pizzo hadn't yet chosen a name for his first movie. But after he and Anspaugh decided to seek financing in Indiana, he settled on the appellation *Hoosiers*. He believed this title would grab the attention of potential investors who lived in the state. He also hoped it would generate early excitement about and support for the film throughout the state.

A Hoosier is simply a person who was born in Indiana or who currently lives there. The origins of the word are murky and have been much debated.

In Pizzo's view, a Hoosier is "someone who lives in the state and is a member of the tribe. It is a sense of belonging to the place that is Indiana. Living in Indiana for a few years doesn't make you a Hoosier. You have to claim the place."

The aspiring filmmakers returned to Hollywood to continue shopping the script around. Even though they knew many agents, actors, and studios, initially they were unsuccessful. "Everywhere we went, people thought it was nice, sweet, called it a small film at best, and wished us luck," Anspaugh said. "[They said] it really didn't have any commercial potential they were looking for. There was no sex, no violence, no chases, no special effects, so it was hard for them to find a way to market it." But Anspaugh asserted that the moviegoing public was "in great need of a product without sex and violence. There is plenty of room for the *Rambo*s, and also the *On Golden Pond*s and *Terms of Endearment*."

Another difficulty was that sports films in general could be a hard sell. Many major studios were not thrilled about the prospect of taking on a motion picture centered around a sport—for several reasons. For one thing, Americans attended a lot of real-life sporting events, whose outcome often was exciting, suspenseful, and unpredictable, unlike the athletic contests in most movies. Furthermore, some studio executives conjectured that women wouldn't attend sports films. Finally, commercially successful sports movies such as *Rocky*, *Chariots of Fire*, and *The Natural* were not that common. Most motion pictures in this genre were box office flops—sometimes even with the presence of major stars. Even the critically acclaimed *Raging Bull* earned back only a few million dollars over its budget. "[Studios] all told us the same thing," Pizzo said. "Sports movies are box office poison." But Anspaugh and Pizzo argued that such films offered many positive traits. They had natural, built-in drama; the characters often overcame great odds to reach their goals; and sport could be used as a framework or metaphor for greater themes, such as relationships and redemption.

An additional issue Pizzo and Anspaugh struggled with was how to effectively convey their vision for the movie to studio executives. "How do you make a pitch and reduce it to one sentence," Pizzo pondered, "and not make it sound banal: 'A coach goes to a small town to coach a basketball team'? If you cannot communicate the essence in one sentence, you're in trouble."

Many prospective executive producers and financiers who did show interest proposed major changes. One of them wanted to set the story in the present day and work dope smokers and alienated students into the plot. Another producer suggested scaling back the project by making *Hoosiers* as a TV movie. Still another wanted to drop Anspaugh as the director—but Pizzo had no intention of doing that. "I knew what would happen," he said. "Some Brit would end up directing it, with no clue about what basketball means to Indiana." When you're a screenwriter, he said, "the only way to truly protect your property is to direct it yourself or get someone you trust."

One production company recommended filming in Canada to save money. "They claimed there was a certain terrain and that all the things [in Indiana] could be duplicated up there," Pizzo said. "Because of the favorable wages for the crew and the [tax] breaks the Canadian government gives to film companies, it would cost about $2 million less. We said forget it; it was out of the question. At every step of the way, David and I said we will not make this movie unless it's in Indiana. It's not worth it to us." As Pizzo saw it, "the environment is as important a character in a movie as the leading protagonist." Pizzo and Anspaugh also were certain that if they filmed in Indiana, they would have no trouble attracting enough extras to fill the gyms for the multitude of game scenes. Their determination to shoot in their home state was the first step in the strategy to make the movie as authentic as possible. "Having grown up here, we wanted to get it right for the people of Indiana," said Pizzo. He hoped people wouldn't think *Hoosiers* was "too Hollywood."

Another condition was crucial to Pizzo as well. "In Hollywood, writers are disregarded completely in almost every circumstance," he said. "They're the lowest man on the totem pole." Therefore, "From the start I wanted to produce the script," he said. "As a writer, having control was important to me. I would never have [let the film be] made unless I had control." So he rejected offers to sell his screenplay and thus relinquish further input into the project.

After being turned down by numerous possible financiers, Pizzo said, "I got to the point where I thought that this was a movie I'd get to make after I made the big-money movie. I'd do a successful film and then be allowed to do this personal project that didn't have commerciality." He realized that "any film by its nature is a long shot." But he didn't give up on *Hoosiers* because "all it takes is one person with a checkbook to believe in your project."

Eventually the script made its way to Carter DeHaven, a movie producer with almost 20 years of experience. "A lot of passion, a lot of caring [went] into this story. I loved it," he said. "It works on so many levels." DeHaven showed the script to Englishmen John Daly and Derek Gibson of Hemdale Film Corporation, an independent production company and distributor with whom he had made four films previously. Hemdale's most recent and most profitable production was sci-fi thriller *The Terminator*, from second-time feature-film writer/director James Cameron. Daly regarded his production company as an alternative to the traditional Hollywood system. Daly was willing to entertain scripts from innovative filmmakers, many of whom had been turned down by the major studios. He recently had made a two-film deal with writer/director Oliver Stone, who for years had attempted to interest mainstream producers in a gritty screenplay based on his experiences as an infantryman in Vietnam. DeHaven called Daly a champion of the underdog and a bit of a renegade who had a gift for sifting out good material.

Daly was moved by the *Hoosiers* script because his father had been an alcoholic who embarrassed his son by sometimes showing up drunk at his soccer games. Daly wept while reading the screenplay and said, "I have to make this movie." Unlike most of the other producers who had seen the script, he didn't insist that Pizzo make changes or do rewrites, because he believed in letting moviemakers do their work without interference. Daly offered Pizzo and Anspaugh a modest $6 million to make *Hoosiers*. They were fine with this amount. Even if they had a $12 million budget, Pizzo said, they would shoot the same movie; they would just take more time. Although Anspaugh was relieved to have made the deal with Hemdale, he remarked that signing over production rights felt like giving away his child.

Because Daly had a contract with the seven-year-old Orion Pictures, Orion would be the distributor and thus would handle the marketing (including newspaper and TV advertising), create the movie poster and trailer, and decide how many prints of the film to produce.

With the financial arrangements completed, it was time to let Indiana know about plans for the movie. When Anspaugh returned to his hometown of Decatur for Christmas in 1984, he shared details of his upcoming film with a couple local newspaper reporters. The first story about the motion picture tentatively titled *Hoosiers* appeared in the *Fort Wayne Journal-Gazette* on December 23.

2

Setting the Scene: Location Scouting and Extras Casting

"This place doesn't even appear on most state maps." —Myra

In late March of 1985, a one-column last-page newspaper article in the *Indianapolis Star* announced that locations were being sought in which to film *Hoosiers*. The filmmakers needed a town that contained a high school and gymnasium built in the 1940s or earlier, as well as an appealing downtown. The ideal town would have only a few hundred residents. Also needed were gyms for the tournament games and away games, and a couple houses for the home scenes. The crew wanted sites that were authentic to the early '50s and that would require little modification, because they didn't have enough time or money to make extensive changes or to build sets from scratch. Also required for the production were a nearby airport, caterers, and quality motel space of 150 rooms.

Aiding in the location search was the Indiana Film Commission. The IFC also would be able to help the producers with such tasks as finding equipment and special items such as classic cars. The organization had been established by the 1982 session of the Indiana General Assembly to help sell the state as a site for filming movies, TV shows, and commercials. It was estimated that a production company could spend as much as $55,000 a day while on location. The producers of *Breaking Away* had spent about $1.5 million in Bloomington in 1978. So far the IFC had worked with people filming documentaries, commercials, and industrial and promotional films. *Hoosiers* was the first feature film the group would assist. "We've tried so hard, and this is our big break," said IFC member Ann Harrison as production got under way. The movie was expected to bring about $3 million into the state through expenditures and salaries. "We've been waiting for something like this to happen and working toward it," said Karen Galvin, head of the IFC. "Once you get a major film production company in here and they like you, then the word spreads. We want other production companies to consider us."

Anspaugh and Pizzo began their site quest in the rolling hills of southeastern Indiana near Milan, the town and school that served as inspiration for *Hoosiers*. (Ironically, Milan, with a population of about 1,600, was too large to be used as the town in the movie.) They toured Rising Sun, Vevay, and Madison, all on the Ohio River, as well as Versailles, Butlerville, Osgood, Vernon, and North Vernon. According to Anspaugh, many of the towns were too big, or their high school and gymnasium looked too new. Not finding what they were seeking, the filmmakers moved their search north.

In April they found a suitable town—Waveland, in southwestern Montgomery County in west-central Indiana. Its 1912 school building and 50-year-old gym, along with the town's main street, were "95 percent of what we want," said Pizzo. "It is just about perfect … that dignified Middle America look." But then they were dismayed to discover that construction on a new school, right in front of the old one, was imminent. The townspeople called a meeting and voted on whether to delay the project to accommodate the filming. They decided to proceed with the construction because financing arrangements were in place and contracts had been signed. So the filmmakers' search began anew.

Pizzo, Anspaugh, and production designer David Nichols traversed the state, touring over 80 sites. Bloomington business executive Bill Cook lent them his helicopter for a day so that they could conduct their search by air. Location manager Rick Schmidlin hit the road and drove about 50 miles in each direction from Indianapolis, carrying a shopping list of locations he was seeking. He said the search for filming sites was like putting together a puzzle and that it was a great adventure.

The crew tried to carry out their expeditions in a quiet, low-key way. "You have to be careful when you tell people in those small towns that you're scouting a movie location," explained Galvin.

"Sometimes they get the wrong idea. They think you're telling them that their town *is* the location, and they go crazy."

Some Hoosiers took the initiative to contact the IFC and ask that their town be visited. The retired athletic director at Richmond, Charles Hilton, created a video for the filmmakers that showcased his city and one of its best high school basketball players, Kyle Clark. And after reading about the location search in the newspaper one morning, longtime Knightstown resident Peg Mayhill drove to Indianapolis that afternoon to visit the IFC in person. She took with her a yearbook to show Commission members pictures of her town's charming 1921 gymnasium. In the following weeks she called the IFC a couple times to make sure they wouldn't forget about her community. Her wish was granted when the filmmakers arrived in late spring to take a look. As they toured the 675-seat gym with the elementary school principal, superintendent, and school board president, Mayhill waited in the schoolyard on pins and needles. But the visitors didn't share their impressions that day. Mayhill and the rest of Knightstown, along with all the other towns that were in the running, wouldn't know for several more months if they had been chosen.

During a late-summer press conference held at Butler University's Hinkle Fieldhouse in Indianapolis, which Mayhill attended, Pizzo and Anspaugh announced that the list of possible locations had been narrowed to five. Because they had been unable to find a single town that had all three of the needed locales—a school, gym, and downtown—they would have to film in more than one community. Under consideration were Nineveh in Johnson County (about 23 miles south of Indianapolis), Wanamaker (just southeast of Indianapolis), New Palestine (about 8 miles southeast of Indianapolis), Knightstown in Henry County (about 22 miles east of Indianapolis), and Linden and New Richmond, both in northern Montgomery

Pizzo speaks at the press conference.

County, about 45 miles northwest of Indianapolis. The final selections would be made shortly.

Officials in Nineveh had already figured out that their 78-year-old high-school-turned-primary-school was a finalist, because the filmmakers had made multiple trips to their town. Nichols had appeared on August 21 to photograph the premises. A week later he was back, accompanied by director Anspaugh. Three days later the two men returned, this time joined by producers Pizzo and Carter DeHaven. "They really liked our building," said the school's principal, Nancy Thompson. "It's funny—you never think of this building as attractive to Hollywood."

Upon learning that Nineveh Elementary had indeed been chosen to portray Hickory High, Nineveh-Hensley-Jackson school superintendent Norman L. Stockton hoped the filming wouldn't be too distracting for the students. "I have to think in terms of education and how much disruption that it will cause," he said. "I do want to work with the state and the film people, so we'll be glad to sit down and see what we can work out." Thompson also had some concerns that the filming "will mean a certain amount of disruption," but she added that "it is certainly something the children will never forget." Also, the building would be shutting its doors forever at the close of the school year and might someday be torn down. So the people of Nineveh were hopeful that being in *Hoosiers* would help the structure live on—if only on film.

School representatives in Linden concluded that they were out of the running when they didn't hear back from the movie people after an initial visit. The film crew thought Linden's 1910 school and gym had possibilities. But they eventually ruled out the gym because its original hardwood floor had been replaced with linoleum after suffering water damage.

Mayhill saw her efforts with the IFC pay off as her town's elementary school gym was selected as the Huskers' home court. After touring countless gymnasiums, Anspaugh said, "We walked into this gym in Knightstown, and there was no mistake. We were home; this was it." The moviemakers were impressed by the former high school gym's interior. Windows on three sides brightened the space and gave it an ambience of openness. The rafters formed a latticework. Green-gray paneling separated the playing floor from seven rows of wooden bleachers, which the filmmakers planned to pack with spectators during the filming of the home games. Fans also could crowd onto the stage at the east end of the gym, below which sat the narrow gray locker room. Pizzo said it was evident that the facility had received a tremendous amount of care over its lifetime. The building reminded him of the glory days of Indiana basketball, before school consolidation, when every town, no matter how small, had its own school and team. Nichols declared that the gym's design reflected "a simple, native, communal style of architecture which is pure Americana—and vanishing rapidly."

The producers pledged to donate $1,000 to the schools in Nineveh and Knightstown in return for being allowed to film there. They also would pick up the tab for custodial overtime and increased utility bills caused by the bright movie lights.

Other gyms were chosen for the filming of the away game and tournament matchups. The 1926 St. Philip Neri School gym in Indianapolis would become Cedar Knob. The Brownsburg Elementary School gym was selected for the sectional tournament game, and Memory Hall in Lebanon would be the site of the regional.

Anspaugh explained that he and the location-scouting crew members had discovered the village of New Richmond "quite by accident. We were in a car for days, driving all over. We started 30 miles north of Indianapolis, and then we'd go from east to west, and then 30 miles south of Indianapolis." New Richmond "was a town that we had not even considered. It was barely on the map. We had had lunch somewhere, and we were driving through town, and I was sitting in the back half-asleep, and I just kind of opened my eyes, and I said, 'Whoa, whoa, stop! Go back.' Most of the storefronts were vacant. It was a production designer's dream. Basically, we could create whatever we wanted."

Nichols and art director David Lubin soon toured New Richmond, population 400, taking pictures, asking questions, jotting down notes, and meeting the citizens. Postmaster Wilma Lewellyn was worried because the townspeople knew very little about the movie's plot—only that it concerned a high school basketball coach and his team. No one in town had read the script, so no one knew how the community and its inhabitants would be represented on the big screen. Before the town board voted on whether to allow the production to shoot there, Lewellyn wanted reassurance from the filmmakers that *Hoosiers* would not show their town in an unfavorable light—that it would, in fact, make residents proud.

After location manager Schmidlin met with the town board, it was official: New Richmond would become downtown Hickory. "It is very pretty and isolated, and it just has this wonderful feeling," said casting director Ken Carlson. Set designer Jo-Ann Chorney believed the town would be easy to work with because it had few overhead wires, and the empty storefronts could be decorated easily. Nichols liked the openness of the downtown area, which showed plenty of sky. "We like this town because it is uncluttered. It is a beautiful little town and can be restored to the look we want," opined Schmidlin. He noted that because the brick buildings had not been painted, they still appeared much like they did in the '50s. Striving for authenticity was crucial, because, for example, "if a house in the neighborhood was built in the '60s, someone [in the audience] will spot it for sure," Schmidlin said. As a bonus, New Richmond's relative isolation meant that traffic would be easier to control, because no major highway ran through town.

A Town Transformed

The movie crew got to work on New Richmond, turning back the clock to the early 1950s. Filming would begin there in mid-October, and preparations were already three weeks behind schedule, according to Nichols. Painters, carpenters, and set decorators swarmed the town, dressing up storefronts and buildings. Most store owners were paid less than a hundred bucks for the use of their shops. Those who gave permission for their name to be used on an establishment's sign received up to $200. The crew created a barbershop, hardware store, furniture store, drugstore, grocery store, diner, bar and grill, dress shop, feed and seed, auto repair shop, plumbing and heating repair shop, doctor's office, and volunteer fire department. The words "New Richmond" and the zip code were removed from the post office window, and "Hickory, Ind." was put in their place. A barbershop in nearby Linden that had changed little over the years supplied 1940s-era items used to decorate the Hickory barbershop. The existing furniture store would remain relatively unchanged, as would the restaurant, except for a new sign renaming it Linda's Hickory Tree. Although caterers would be brought in to provide meals for the cast and crew, restaurant employees would help by furnishing coffee and soft drinks.

Electric signs, TV antennas, and unleaded gas pumps were taken down, and the Coke machine outside the tavern was rolled away. Every newspaper delivery box in town was pulled out of the ground and piled behind the hardware store because such boxes didn't exist in 1951. Commented Pizzo, "You have no idea the amount of effort it takes to get every single detail right. If someone sees one television antenna, one Coke can, one Reebok tennis shoe, it throws people out of the movie."

In the town's museum, run by Al Boone, the crew found an old traffic light that used to stand on a cement pedestal in the middle of the intersection. They considered placing it there again for the filming. The set decorators were quite pleased to have the museum at their disposal. They hoped it would turn out to be a treasure trove of items they could use to dress the sets.

New Richmond resident Byron Alexander was somewhat concerned about the changes he saw the crew making to the town. "They dirtied things a bit, made us look a little hicky," said the 73-year-old. One of the altered storefronts belonged to his furniture store. "They tore it up—antiqued the front of it," he remarked. "Of course, they say they'll come back and do it over the way it was. That's fine, but I figure it will be winter by the time they get back here." Karen Galvin of the IFC acknowledged to the citizens that the filming would "mean two or three weeks of inconvenience for you probably. But it should be sort of a fun interruption in your normal routine." Said resident Ralph Kunkel, "For a town of 400 people, it creates a lot of problems, but the positives outweigh the negatives."

Two meetings were held to answer people's questions about the movie's production and to address any issues. Topics raised included town security, children's safety, the film company's liability insurance, traffic control, parking sufficiency, business accessibility, restroom availability, street cleaning, and trash collection. Farmers wanted to ensure that the main roads wouldn't be blocked off when they needed to move their large grain trucks through town. People also brought up the fact that the filming could serve as an incentive for New Richmond to develop short- and long-term plans to jump-start tourism and economic development.

The townspeople were warned to expect more traffic, as well as tourists who were curious about the filming. Contemplating the number of strangers who would soon invade their space unsettled some denizens. The production would "draw a lot of people here to watch," predicted Harold Widmer. "Who's going to watch *them?*" Roger Kunkel was more blunt: "We're going to get a lot of kooks." Added Janet Brown, "We're concerned we're going to have to lock our back doors [and] not leave our keys in the car." Sheriff Dennis Rice said his department would work with the Indiana State Police on these issues. He was willing to increase the number of patrols, but he warned that he didn't have the manpower to provide around-the-clock security. Byron Alexander had already spotted one visitor to New Richmond. He could tell because he saw the man lock his car doors.

Extra, Extra! Casting the Townspeople

"We got ten games to play. ... You come along for the ride." —Coach Dale

An open casting call was held in New Richmond to find individuals who could serve as permanent extras or continuity people. They would play townsfolk in some of the scenes. They also would help fill the Hickory gym by portraying the Huskers' loyal fans, so they needed to be willing to travel to Knightstown for the filming of the home games. "When we're panning the crowd, we want to see familiar faces," said casting director Ken Carlson. Local people also would play roles such as reporters, referees, and coaches. Permanent extras would be paid minimum wage—$3.50 an hour. Those who were lucky enough to be chosen to speak some dialog would be considered day players and would earn $361 a day. "I can't promise you you'll be day players," said Carlson. But, he added, "if David likes a face he sees, he works you in." Scores of people lined up outside the tiny, dark-wood-paneled town hall, where the interviews took place. Applicants had their picture taken and filled out a size chart for the costuming department. About one-tenth of the roughly 300 people who showed up at the call were selected as permanent extras. They were informed that, when they would be needed for the filming, a casting assistant would call them the night before and tell them where and when to show up.

A woman from Lafayette (about 13 miles north of New Richmond) at the casting call expressed doubts about the moviemakers' intentions. She said she'd heard that men trying out as extras were being asked to show up looking dirty and unshaven. This request made her fear that the extras would be portrayed as hicks in the film. Extras casting assistant and Henry County native Debby Shively rushed to correct this misimpression: "We told people [not to dress up] so they wouldn't show up in their Sunday finest. This is supposed to be a farm town—that's why we're asking people to wear work shirts and jeans. We need people to look like they live in a very small farm town, not like they're city slickers."

Pizzo caught wind of these concerns. "One of the people being interviewed for extras made the comment, 'Well, it sounds like they're making Indiana like *Tobacco Road* or real hicks,'" he said. "We want to be authentic, but we're certainly not doing *Tobacco Road*. People are not poor here; they're farmers that make a good living." Pizzo insisted that he and Anspaugh were "very sensitive to local people's fear that they will be portrayed as rubes, hicks, living a very disparaging life. We don't want to do that." Pizzo also addressed the complaint that the name Hickory was reminiscent of the word hick. "I happen to love hickory, like the hickory tree," he explained. "It seemed rural to me. I don't know why I chose certain names. It just popped into my head, and it seemed right."

Casting sessions for day players, continuity people, and extras were held in Knightstown as well. Shively suggested that her father, Ralph "Whitey" Shively, try out for a part. Said the elder Shively, "They liked my voice. So they were going to cast me as a preacher." But if he accepted that role, he would have to be away from his auction business for several days. So instead he became team physician Doc Buggins, a role that would require only two days' work. Insurance agency owner Dick Leakey tried to become a day player as well. He commented that Debby Shively "said my voice had a perfect Indiana twang. [She] asked me to audition for the part of the minister." Leakey said that when he arrived at the tryouts, "they asked me to sit in a room. And three or four other people were sitting there, and they had Bibles. They were [real] preachers!" When it was his turn, Leakey said, "I was terrible." However, he said, "so were the preachers. [She] ended up hiring a professional actor." Debby Shively caught the acting bug too, casting herself as a nurse in one of the hospital scenes.

Hopeful extras were encouraged to provide their own costumes, although the movie's wardrobe assistants could offer some items where necessary. To show people examples of period dress, librarians set out an old *Ladies' Home Journal* clothing book and copies of the high school yearbook from the '50s. The movie's costumers also held a meeting for interested residents to discuss appropriate styles of clothing to wear at the game filming.

The requirements for being an extra were not stringent. Said one crew member, "Just about everybody from Knightstown will make it unless he is a big guy wearing a ponytail." Those who were chosen as gym-filling fans were divided into seven groups, each of which was assigned to a different day of filming. Everyone was issued an admission ticket that said "Your presence here is your agreement that your likeness and voice may be used in a motion picture for exploitation in all media and in the advertising and promotion thereof."

Because a large number of extras would be needed to fill the gyms in Brownsburg and Lebanon for the shooting of the sectional and regional games, casting calls were held in those towns too. People were urged to bring their entire family and, again, to dress in 1950s attire. "About 60 percent made an attempt at period dress," said casting coordinator Stephen Meyers. Kathy Flannery wore a long skirt and a sweater trimmed in fur. "I've saved this thing for years," she said. A group of middle school students showed up in letter sweaters, saddle shoes, bobby socks, rolled-up jeans, and oxford cloth shirts.

Approximately 2,200 people would be required for the filming at Memory Hall. When about half that many extras showed up at the Lebanon casting call, the production staff decided to canvass the community to publicize the movie. "We will be going to civic organizations, fraternities, and schools to talk about group participation in the film," said key second assistant director Harvey Waldman. "We have to count on enthusiasm from people around here. We need people who are excited about being in the movie."

Calling All Cars

Old vehicles also were "auditioned" at the extras casting sessions. Owners of cars and trucks from 1951 or earlier could earn $50 per day for the use of their vehicles, which were required to be in working condition. Transportation coordinator William "Fleet" Eakland was looking for "cars, tractors, and pickup, flatbed, or panel trucks, because 60 percent of the film will look like a working farming community," he said.

Mike Hendrickson of Indianapolis helped the crew acquire vehicles by attending auto shows, perusing classified ads, and talking to people until he had a list of about 200 prospects. Cars didn't need to be pristine; they just needed to be authentic to the time period.

After conducting a wide but fruitless search for a team bus that would be shown transporting the Huskers to away games, the crew was referred to mechanic Jesse "Jack" Baker of New Ross. He owned a 1939 Chevy bus that had been used as a school bus in Indianapolis and Lebanon for 10 years. After it was retired from service, Baker purchased it and installed a new Wayne bus body. He removed the seats and added couches, beds, an icebox, a gas stove, storage areas, and curtains to transform the bus into a vehicle suitable to take on cross-country vacations. For the movie, the crew restored the bus by painting it and adding five bench seats on each side.

Outfitting and Styling the Extras and Actors

Costumers Mary Weir and Jeanne Mascia advised women who wanted to be extras to dress in earth tones for the filming. Styles could include cotton housedresses or four-gore, pleated, circle, or straight skirts that fell at least three inches below the knee. They also could wear round-necked sweaters with little buttons, and blouses that had Peter Pan collars. Pants were forbidden. Women's shoes needed flat heels and round toes, and girls could wear saddle shoes or penny loafers with bobby socks. Men were asked to dress in plaid or dark solid-colored collared shirts of cotton, wool, flannel, or gabardine, with a white T-shirt underneath. Their pants needed belt loops, pleats, and cuffs. Their footwear could be work shoes, or dark oxfords or wing tips with argyle socks.

The female extras were told to wear little or no makeup, because women in the '50s were natural looking, said hair and cosmetics director Daniel Marc—except, perhaps, for a dab of red on their lips. As for the men's faces, mustaches and beards were not allowed. Women and girls who had modern hairstyles would have trouble imitating early '50s styles. Marc said women's hair back then usually was flat on top, with a part, and permed around the ends; their hair wasn't "poufy," as was typical in 1985. The boys' and men's hairstyles were easier. Their hair could simply be cut or slicked back with Brylcreem. The hair issue helped Debby Shively "find out real fast who's really interested and who's not," she said. "Some of the boys have to get crew cuts. The ones that do will be in the classroom. The ones that didn't want to will be in the crowd with everyone else and have their hair slicked back."

As the extras pulled together their outfits, costumer Jane Anderson and her assistants visited vintage clothing store Off The Avenue in Greenwood. There they purchased dozens of men's shirts and pants, as well as skirts and women's blouses, to create a collection of basic apparel to loan to extras who were unable to find appropriate clothing. They checked thrift shops and Goodwill stores as well. Anderson researched clothing trends from 1948 to 1951 by studying farm publications, newspapers, yearbooks, family photos, and Sears fall and winter catalogs.

The Huskers' home and away basketball uniforms and warm-ups, as well as outfits for 18 other teams, would be custom-made by Kajee Inc., an athletic clothing manufacturer housed in the Varynit Garment Factory in Franklin. Anderson had acquired two uniforms from the 1948 and 1950 Indiana-Kentucky All-Star games for the company to use as a guide. The jerseys would be a 50/50 cotton/polyester blend, and the shorts, pants, and jackets would be created from the same kind of satin used 35 years earlier. After much searching, Anderson had managed to locate satin authentic to the time period in an old warehouse in upstate New York. After school colors had been assigned to each team, "We had to film the colors and fabrics to determine how they would actually look," Anderson said. "Color records differently on camera." As soon as the players on all the opposing teams were chosen and their measurements taken, sewing could begin. Anderson noted that because 1950s basketball shorts used buckles at the waist instead of elastic, proper fit was crucial.

The screenplay mentioned that Hickory's school colors were blue and gold, but Anderson decided to change the blue to red. She thought a cardinal shade for the home-game jerseys would be rich and wonderful, she said; it reminded her of royalty. The design of the Huskers' uniforms was simple because Hickory was a small school of modest means. The warm-ups and uniforms for Hickory's regional and state opponents, which were larger schools, had more elaborate designs than those of the other rival teams. All the rival-team uniforms were assigned different color combinations and had slight variations in appearance.

Another company made the letter jackets. Converse provided dozens of pairs of canvas high-tops. The uniforms for the home-team and opposing cheerleaders also were custom-made. A company in Los Angeles loomed the sweaters and manufactured the skirts. Costumes for the main actors were rented from the Paramount and Burbank studios in Los Angeles.

* * *

Having chosen their locations and extras (or background artists, as Anspaugh called them), the filmmakers were on their way toward creating a movie in which, according to Pizzo, "place is as powerful as a leading character." The writer/producer maintained that "the details in any film really accumulate to build something that's bigger than even the story itself, or the characters. The details create kind of the backdrop and the texture that make [the film] feel like it has dimension."

3
The Starting Lineup: Casting the Main Roles

"I'm very excited to be a part of Indiana basketball." —Coach Dale

As well as being a seasoned actor, Jack Nicholson loved basketball and knew independent film, having been involved with several indie features early in his career. Anspaugh had stayed in touch with Nicholson ever since meeting him a decade before *Hoosiers* got under way. So after Pizzo finished the script, Anspaugh decided to give it to Nicholson to get some feedback; Pizzo hoped the actor also could help advise them on fund-raising. To their surprise, Nicholson told them he wanted to play Coach Norman Dale. They knew they wouldn't be able to offer him the kind of salary he was accustomed to. But this became a moot point when problems with Nicholson's work schedule prevented him from taking the part.

Nicholson's temporary involvement with *Hoosiers* helped generate buzz about the script in Hollywood. "When he expressed interest, suddenly we were on everybody's radar," Anspaugh said. Burt Reynolds was considered for the role of the coach. So was Robert Duvall after Pizzo and Anspaugh saw him play a washed-up country singer in need of redemption in *Tender Mercies*. But Pizzo said that, while writing the script, when he envisioned the coach, Gene Hackman's face sprang to mind. So they sent him the script, and he accepted the part. "One of the most exciting things about this project was getting him," Pizzo commented. The writer/producer was pleased to have a Method actor in the role. The 55-year-old Hackman was a performer of remarkable range and versatility. He had starred in such films as *Bonnie and Clyde*, *The French Connection* (for which he won an Oscar), *The Poseidon Adventure*, *The Conversation*, and *Superman*. The filmmakers could afford to hire him because he agreed to a salary of $400,000, lower than his normal rate, in exchange for receiving 10 percent of the film's gross profits, including videocassette sales. Although he usually acted in big-budget productions, Hackman argued that "sometimes it can be more satisfying as an actor to be in a small film. You've got more to do, and they're really more interesting."

Hackman had been acting steadily on TV and in movies for 25 years, but he followed a circuitous route to fame. He grew up in Danville, Illinois, near the Indiana border. "From the moment I saw my first movie," he said, "I knew that's what I wanted to do." As a high school basketball player, Hackman didn't get along with his coach. "I was walking home from school one day," he said, "and I saw this sign by the post office with this Marine in dress blues. I liked that uniform better than the one I was wearing in school." So he dropped out at 16 to join the Marines. He left the service four and a half years later and moved to New York, where he worked a succession of jobs—truck driver, shoe salesman, soda jerk. He briefly studied journalism and TV production at the University of Illinois before being accepted into the acting program at the Pasadena Playhouse in California in 1956. However, Hackman's instructors considered him an unpromising student, so he returned to New York. He became a restaurant doorman, joined an improvisational theater troupe, and began landing guest spots on TV shows. His career got a boost when he started appearing in off-Broadway plays, and soon he transitioned to film.

Hackman said that, when considering whether to accept an acting role, he based his decision "almost purely on story as opposed to character, because I feel I can find something to make a character interesting if the story is strong enough." *Hoosiers* appealed to him because "it tells an interesting story and as an actor it stretches you, because the character goes through a lot of changes in the course of events and [through] the people he meets. I guess overall it's a sports film, but I wish it were more of a relationship film. Whenever I can put in my two cents in terms of a scene, I try to make it with as much human behavior as possible, as opposed to what one might think of as a sports-oriented film. I think if we can do both then it becomes more attractive for the audience. But this really is a sports film first and a relationship film second." Hackman viewed his character as "a very competitive man, and he does what he feels is the right thing to do rather than play the political game."

When creating the character of Shooter, Pizzo had imagined Harry Dean Stanton in the role. The filmmakers gave the script to Stanton's agent, who declined the project on his client's behalf. (Pizzo and Anspaugh learned years later that Stanton never even saw the script and regretted missing out on the chance to play Shooter.) After that, Anspaugh recalled, "We interviewed, read character actors all over the country, and we couldn't find anybody we thought could pull it off." Then one night Anspaugh caught Dennis Hopper's performance in a TV movie called *King of the Mountain*. He starred as an "old hippie guy who lived in L.A. and raced cars on Mulholland Drive," Anspaugh said. "There was something about seeing him again and something about the quality of the character he was playing." Coincidentally, a few nights later Anspaugh spotted Hopper in a restaurant. He introduced himself and told the actor about the *Hoosiers* script. "About 48 hours later he showed up in our office, and we sat and talked for 3 hours, and he had such an understanding of the character," Anspaugh said. "He was newly sober. He talked about his sobriety and his troubled days as an alcoholic and drug addict, and it was clear he knew this character inside and out." Pizzo said he and Anspaugh were confident that Hopper understood Shooter's dark side, and they knew from some of his past work that he also could show a poignant, tender side.

Hopper was drawn to the part because he felt Shooter would be a role that meant something; he believed the screenplay took a good look at an alcoholic. "Shooter is bottoming out. He's losing his son and his family," Hopper said. "And he's begging in the streets." Hopper doubted that Shooter's efforts to become sober would spur real-life alcoholics to do the same. "I know about how to be a drunk real well," he said. "I don't think it probably helps anyone that Shooter ends up in treatment, because unfortunately most drunks are charming, devious people. So I don't know that it helps anyone to see what happens to him, except that he's a terrible embarrassment to his son, and he's hurting people around him, and he's hurting himself."

Hopper was glad that his character had "his own story, with a beginning, a middle, and an end. Most supporting roles simply drift in and out." He also was excited about appearing in a movie with Hackman.

Hopper was born in Dodge City, Kansas, and spent much of his childhood on his grandparents' farm. When he was 13, his family moved to San Diego, where he enrolled in acting classes and performed in youth productions at the Old Globe Theatre. He also acted at the La Jolla Playhouse and Pasadena Playhouse. After high school he moved to Hollywood and began landing minor roles in TV shows and movies. He appeared in such classic films as *Rebel Without a Cause* and *Giant* with James Dean, *Cool Hand Luke*, *Easy Rider* (which he also directed), and *Apocalypse Now*. Although he was a promising actor in his younger days, Hopper's descent into serious substance abuse began negatively affecting his work and professional reputation as he became increasingly volatile and unpredictable. He was mostly absent from American films during the 1970s but embarked on a comeback in the early '80s, aided by his efforts to finally overcome his addictions. In 1985 he had been sober for two years.

Christine Lahti originally was cast as schoolteacher Myra Fleener. But when she had to drop out of the project shortly before filming began, Barbara Hershey took over the role. Like Hopper, Hershey had been acting steadily since she was a teen. She had recently appeared in *The Right Stuff* and *The Natural* and was fresh off a starring role in Woody Allen's *Hannah and Her Sisters*. In Hershey's view, Myra "never fulfills her destiny, because she's too frightened to leave. She becomes bitter and uptight and pushes other people to do things she herself couldn't." She believed Myra was "fiercely proud of Hickory, but determined to help its brightest youngsters get away to a better life." In short, she thought Myra had "quite a few problems in her life." In fact, Hershey said, "I have never played a character with as many levels of inner conflict. [It's] a chance to stretch myself as an actress." Like Hopper, she was looking forward to working with Hackman.

Oklahoma native Sheb Wooley, chosen to play school principal Cletus Summers, had enjoyed a long and varied career as a singer, songwriter, and actor. His novelty song "The Purple People Eater" debuted at number seven on the *Billboard* Hot 100 in 1958 and then jumped to number one, where it stayed for six weeks. He also made comedy recordings and wrote the theme song for *Hee Haw*. As an actor he appeared on the TV show *Rawhide* and in the movies *High Noon* and *Giant*.

Fern Persons (Myra's mother, Opal, the oldest cast member at age 75) and Chelcie Ross (troublesome townsman George) were cast out of Chicago. After accepting his part, Ross learned that, following his audition, Anspaugh had turned to Pizzo and exclaimed, "That's the jerk we're looking for!" Other supporting actors were from Indiana. Gloria Dorson, who played Cletus's wife, Millie, was from Bloomington. Sam Smiley, an IU theater professor, was cast in two roles: a referee who throws Hackman out of the Cedar Knob game, and a reporter. Michael O'Guinne, chosen to play Rooster the barber, grew up in Bloomington with Pizzo and appeared in an episode of *Hill Street Blues* directed by Anspaugh.

Some of the supporting roles were cast through the Act 1 Model and Talent Agency in Indianapolis. John Robert Thompson auditioned for the parts of Cletus and one of the ministers before landing the part of the sheriff. Stockbroker and occasional local-theater actor Mike Dalzell was cast as the mayor, Wil Dewitt became Reverend Doty, and Skip Welker was chosen as the Terhune coach. Most of the referees and some coaches of opposing teams would be played by real-life referees and coaches. Jack Schult, former basketball coach and assistant athletic director at Lafayette Jefferson High School, was cast as the coach of Oolitic, Hickory's first home-game opponent. Selected as one of the referees for the regional game was Ken Gorrell, a middle school health teacher from Franklin who had been officiating high school games since the late 1960s. He planned to do some research to learn about the signals used and uniforms worn by referees of the early '50s.

Rich Komenich auditioned for a speaking role but instead was chosen as Hackman's stand-in. "I've got 18 years' acting experience, and I got the part because we have the same coat size," he said with a laugh. In this role Komenich would stand in Hackman's place while the lighting and camera angles were set, thus giving Hackman more time for tasks such as learning rewritten lines of dialog. The other main actors and the team members would have stand-ins as well.

Handpicking the Huskers

As part of the goal to give the movie an authentic feel, Pizzo and Anspaugh made a bold but possibly risky decision: They would hold an open casting call in Indianapolis to find the Hickory Huskers. From the start of the project, they had been "very opposed to the idea [of] bringing a whole corps of actors out from Los Angeles or New York who really couldn't compete on the same level, in terms of basketball and having a regional dialect," said Anspaugh. The filmmaking team believed it would be easier to teach real basketball players to act than to instruct actors to play basketball. "You can't fake playing basketball," Pizzo asserted. "There are so many kinds of skills. It is a second sense that you only get by playing basketball for years and years." Furthermore, he said, "There is no question that there are differences between someone who grew up in the San Fernando Valley and someone who grew up in Brownsburg, Indiana. It shows in the way they walk, the way they look, the way they talk."

When Anspaugh and Pizzo had sought potential financiers for *Hoosiers*, some movie studios were leery about the filmmakers' determination to cast non-actors as the Hickory Huskers. "There was resistance to casting non-pros," Anspaugh said. "One of the studios told us to go out and get some name actors to play the team members. Somehow we couldn't see Matt Dillon and Matthew Broderick as our starting guards."

Those who landed roles as Hickory team members had the potential for fame, but maybe not fortune. They would earn union scale, between $10,000 and $15,000.

In late summer, the open casting call was announced. Those trying out had to be no taller than 6-foot-2 and between the ages of 18 and 22. They needed to look young enough to be in high school and couldn't be too muscular, because boys in the 1950s didn't lift weights. "The primary requirement is basketball ability. I'm looking for excellent shooters, excellent forwards, guys who can handle the ball," explained casting director Ken Carlson. "This state loves basketball. We don't want people saying, 'This guy can't shoot. Why'd you hire him?'"

Accordingly, round one of the auditions, held on August 26 and 27 at the Natatorium gymnasium at Indiana University–Purdue University Indianapolis (IUPUI), involved only basketball. The young men were asked to shoot outside jumpers and layups. They also played one-on-one and scrimmaged in groups of 10 for 5 to 8 minutes. In the first half of the first day of casting, about 20 percent of those auditioning were invited back for the second round. Hundreds of *Hoosiers* hopefuls from all over the state showed up over the two days, among them some very promising prospects.

Maris Valainis never played basketball for his Catholic high school, Bishop Chatard in Indianapolis. He tried out for the team his freshman, sophomore, and junior years but didn't make the cut. As a college student at IUPUI he played pickup basketball every Monday night at the St. Luke school gym—and that's where the *Hoosiers* casting director discovered him. One of the young men who showed up for the open casting call mentioned that some talented hoopsters could be found at St. Luke's open-gym night. So Carlson and Spyridon "Strats" Stratigos, who was helping audition the players, went there on a scouting expedition at the conclusion of the first day of open casting. Stratigos, a former player for South Bend Central, spotted Valainis repeatedly making shots from all over the court and told Carlson, "There's the guy you want." The casting director, said Stratigos, "thought Maris had sex appeal. I had no clue about that, but I saw the guy was hitting jump shots." At the end of the evening, they approached Valainis and asked him if he would like to be in a movie. The following morning Valainis arrived at the auditions and encountered a line of 400 people. After standing around for a short while, he decided to leave. But just then Carlson emerged from the gym, saw Valainis, and took him right in. "I was really nervous for the audition," he said. "A local TV news crew was there filming some of the auditions, and thank God they filmed the guy before me instead of me. I would have been so nervous, I wouldn't have made it."

Ball State University junior Todd Schenck read about the tryouts in his campus newspaper and decided to go. He told his brother, high school senior Wade, because he figured Wade might want to try out too. When Todd arrived early at the auditions and saw that scores of people were already in line, he called his brother and told him not to bother making the 75-mile trip from their hometown of Lyons. But Wade was not deterred and showed up anyway. He had averaged 12 points a game in the previous basketball season at Lyons and Marco (L&M) High School. It had been the best year ever for this 132-student school, which received national attention after being written about in *Sports Illustrated*. Some people predicted that L&M would be the next Milan Miracle. But that hope ended just short of the state finals, as L&M lost in the last game of the semistate.

Kent Poole's high school, Western Boone in Thorntown, also made it as far as the semistate in 1982, Poole's senior year. A top scorer and forward on his team, Poole could relate to the movie, he said, because "I had a strict coach like that. I come from a small rural school. For us to go to Sweet 16 was a big, big deal in these parts." He attended Ball State for a year but returned home because he missed farming. "I like being outside. I like working the land," he said. His fiancée, Judi Johnson, and several family friends encouraged him to go to the tryouts.

The dream of high school basketball glory had ended well for Steve Hollar. In the final game of the 1984 state championship, with only 3 seconds left and his team up by 1 point, he calmly sank two free throws to ensure victory for his Warsaw Tigers. "He's a highly skilled ball handler and passer," commented Hollar's high school coach, Al Rhodes. "It makes sense to choose him. Having someone who has lived through a championship season and has a good understanding of the emotions you go through, that should help everyone." Hollar read about the *Hoosiers* casting call in the newspaper as he prepared to leave for his freshman year at DePauw University, but he didn't give it much thought. Soon after he arrived on campus, the sports information director slid a flyer under his door telling about the tryouts, but Hollar threw it away. However, the basketball team's senior starting guard Phil Wendel *was* interested in going, and he asked teammate Hollar to drive him to Indianapolis. "I thought to myself, this is a once-in-a-lifetime thing. I have to try out," Hollar said. Fellow students Griff Mills, Brad Cofield, Mick Lewis, and Bill Chestnut also auditioned.

One of the hopeful actors was from Decatur, director David Anspaugh's hometown. Ball State University sophomore Brad Boyle had been a starting forward on his Bellmont High School team. In the summer of 1985 he completed basic training with the National Guard. He went to the casting call with his brother, Dan, and four friends from high school. "Some of the guys around here got involved [in the auditions], and they had room for him, and he went along," said Boyle's father, Bob. "He had a crew cut and was in real good shape."

Recent college graduate Brad Long had just begun a job with Jostens, a supplier of class rings, yearbooks, and graduation-related items. He had played basketball at Center Grove High School in Greenwood and had been a guard on the team at Southwestern College in Winfield, Kansas. At 23, he suspected he might be too old to play a high school student, but he also believed he looked young for his age.

Scott Summers, an engineering student at IUPUI, had played basketball for four years at Bethesda Christian School near Brownsburg. His friend and high school classmate Eric Baker accompanied him to the tryouts.

On Wednesday, August 28, those who had survived the first round were called back for a second round of casting, this time to read from the script. "I tried to get a sense of who they were as human beings and just wanted them to be themselves," Anspaugh said. A third round of casting tested the prospects' improvisational skills.

The callbacks continued through September as the filmmakers kept narrowing down the field of possible Huskers. As they got closer to making their final selections, Anspaugh advised the candidates that, if he and Pizzo ended up making as good of a film as they hoped to, the lives of those chosen to be the Huskers would change forever.

Hollar's many trips between Greencastle and the state capital caused him to fall behind in his studies. He failed his first chemistry test because he had never attended that class. However, the further he progressed at the auditions, the more he realized he really wanted to get a part. Finally, after six rounds of callbacks, the filmmakers had decided whom they wanted as the Huskers.

"This is your team." —Coach Dale

One day in early October, Hollar found a phone message in his dormitory mailbox. It read, in its entirety, "You got the part. Report next Monday." Two days later he withdrew from school. When he was contacted by a reporter who had heard he landed a role, Hollar responded, "I'm really excited, and I'd love to talk to you, but right now I'm not supposed to, and I want to do what they say." The filmmakers didn't want the Huskers speaking to the media before the press conference that would take place in a few days. On October 14, after Hershey and Hackman had arrived in Indianapolis, the entire cast was officially announced. Hollar had been chosen for the character of Rade Butcher, an impulsive player who can't control his mouth.

Valainis was selected for the pivotal role of the elusive Jimmy Chitwood, who joins the team in midseason, resulting in a string of wins and the retention of Coach Dale. It was ironic that the guy chosen to play the character who makes the shot that wins Hickory the state title had never played on a high school team. "I immediately felt that Maris was Jimmy when I saw him," Pizzo said. "He had the face, the innocence, the kind of opaque quality I had imagined in the character. And he had the shot. He had it all." Anspaugh agreed: "So much of who he is is emitted from his eyes and his face and his presence and the way he carries himself. He sort of physically embodies everything Angelo had written and implied in the character. If you watch his body language, there's just something that sets him apart from everyone else."

Long landed the part of Buddy Walker, the disrespectful Husker who is thrown out of the first practice but later comes back to the team and becomes its unofficial leader. "They told me when I tried out they were looking for somebody with a lot of confidence," Long said. Boyle was cast as Whit Butcher, Rade's brother, who walks out of the first practice at Buddy's urging but later returns to apologize. Poole was chosen as the beneficent Merle Webb. At the state finals he would utter one of the movie's best lines: "Let's win this one for all the small schools that never had a chance to get here." Summers was cast as preacher's son Strap Purl, who prays before games. "As far as I'm concerned, I pretty much believe that," he remarked. "I really don't know if I could have condoned [being in the movie] otherwise." Said Summers' father of his son's participation in *Hoosiers*, "I think it's fine as long as the movie is wholesome in the subject matter it deals with." Pizzo said he created the character of Strap because, as he did research before writing the screenplay, he "read about one kid who was really religious, and it affected the way he played. I found that interesting." Wade Schenck, the smallest and youngest team member, was perfect for the part of Ollie McPike, the team manager and reluctant player who becomes a game-winning hero. "I think what they like about me is my shortness," said the 5-foot-8 Schenck. He noted that almost everyone at the auditions had hoped to land the Jimmy Chitwood role. This was unsurprising, considering that casting director Carlson had predicted that whoever was awarded that part would become a star. "Nobody wanted to be Ollie," Schenck said.

The team's final member was David Neidorf, the only Hickory Husker who wasn't from Indiana. After conducting auditions in

Chicago and Los Angeles, the filmmakers had cast the 22-year-old aspiring actor from L.A. as Everett Flatch, Shooter's estranged son. In that role, he would have more lines than the other team members in key scenes with Hopper. Like the other Huskers, he'd had to demonstrate his athletic abilities at a basketball audition, held at the Beverly Hills YMCA.

Mills, Cofield, Lewis, Chestnut, and Baker didn't make it through to the final rounds of tryouts. Like some of the others who auditioned but didn't become Huskers, they were offered roles as members of the rival teams Hickory would face.

Cast as the Hickory cheerleaders were Schenck's sister Libbey and Indiana Central University cheerleaders Nancy Harris of Wanamaker and Laura Robling of Indianapolis. Robling's character was named Loetta, and she was principal Cletus's daughter. Along with the cheerleaders for the opposing teams, Robling, Schenck, and Harris began attending Sunday practice sessions. They were given typewritten pages that listed cheers specific to the 1950s. Linton Wildcat cheerleader Teresa Trout described these yells as "real dorky"—of the "rah-rah-rah" variety and without detailed movements.

The Name Game

Pizzo borrowed the character surnames Chitwood, Webb, and Fleener from some of his fellow alumni of University High School in Bloomington. Ollie McPike was the name of one of Pizzo's junior high school friends. (Coincidentally, the team manager of the 1954 Milan state champions was named Oliver Jones.) And Pizzo's IU friend Jade Butcher had a name that was just one letter different from Husker Rade Butcher.

After accepting roles in the movie, the Huskers quickly made plans to leave their regular lives behind for the next two and a half months. Schenck dropped out of his senior year of high school. Along with Hollar, Boyle and Summers temporarily left college. Hollar said his parents told him, "Steve, you can make 25 movies, but sometime finish college one way or the other." Although

Summers struggled with the decision to quit school, he ended up leaving IUPUI even before he knew he had secured a role as a Husker. "I was pretty much going on a hunch that I'd make it," he said. "If I didn't, I'd go ahead and finish out the movie as an extra." Schenck and Poole left their farming families during the fall harvest, one of the busiest times of the year. This fact caused Poole a bit of guilt. "The call [confirming his role] came during harvest time, and I had to leave four days later. I just basically laid everything on my parents." Long was forced to postpone his November 30 wedding to high school sweetheart Lisa Boling.

The cast and crew settled into their Indianapolis digs that would serve as home base during the filming. Hackman, Hopper, and Hershey stayed at the plush Canterbury Hotel downtown. The crew and the Hickory team members were housed at the Ramada Inn Northwest, two to a room. Poole and Long, two of the oldest team members, decided to room together, because they hit it off right away. They had a lot in common, and each faced an upcoming wedding. The moviemakers wanted the team members to get to know each other and develop a closeness and team unity that would seem natural on-screen. To help them get into the spirit of their roles, they were instructed to always call each other by their characters' names.

The soon-to-be stars began adjusting to life in the spotlight. Summers called the experience mind-boggling, adding, "I consider [being in the movie] an honor, not only to be with the players but with the actors involved." He continued, "If you stop and think about it, it's overwhelming—especially being with Gene. I have to work on it and get it in my mind that they're just people like anyone else." Despite often being sought out for interviews, Poole didn't yet feel famous. "To me, [I'm] still just Kent Poole from Advance, Indiana, who grew up on a farm," he said unassumingly. Said Long, "I'm just kind of stunned by the things that happen each day. It's really exciting. I always wondered what kind of things went into Hollywood movies, and I'm actually beginning to see it firsthand. Just little things, everything's taken care of. We're whisked here; we're whisked there." He concluded, "Everything's really happening so fast. I'll be honest with you—I'm not real sure it's hit me that I'm in this movie."

The Huskers, pre-haircuts, in the courtyard of the Ramada Inn Northwest. Front: Steve Hollar (Rade), Wade Schenck (Ollie), Brad Boyle (Whit). Back: Brad Long (Buddy), Maris Valainis (Jimmy), Scott Summers (Strap), David Neidorf (Everett), Kent Poole (Merle).

4
Tip-off: Filming Gets Under Way

"There's a lot of talent there; it's just raw and undisciplined." —Coach Dale

The newly formed Hickory Huskers began basketball practice sessions at Tri-West High School in Lizton, west of Indianapolis. They needed to learn some basic plays they could run during the basketball scenes. Technical advisor Strats Stratigos wanted to create an offense and defense, as if the Huskers were a real team. Hired to instruct the squad in 1950s style of play was Tom McConnell, who had coached at Orleans, Batesville, and Mitchell in the '40s and '50s. South Bend native Tom Abernethy, a member of IU's unbeaten 1976 NCAA Division I championship team, also worked with the Huskers. He emphasized that the team members "shouldn't do fancy moves or give each other high fives, which is more a contemporary move." The boys found the 1950s style difficult to get used to. Scott Summers had to resist the urge to dunk the ball. "I've worked hard to develop the skill, and I love to dunk," he commented. "It's hard to constrain myself; I have to think about it." Said Steve Hollar, "You have to continually remind yourself that you're in the '50s. I'm supposed to be a 1950s basketball player, not a 1985 basketball player. That means I can't dribble behind my back or between my legs—which is a big part of my ball handling, normally." And because the jump shot didn't exist back then, the guys had to do a set shot with a hop at the end. Hollar hoped the finished film would convey that the Huskers were truly skilled cagers by showing, in unbroken shots, the ball leaving their hands and sailing through the rim. He feared the games wouldn't look authentic if they were edited with many cuts during the action.

Along with being schooled in and watching films of old-style hoops, the Hickory team members received acting tips from Anspaugh. He told them the art of acting is *not* acting, but mainly being yourself. According to Brad Long, the director was adamant about not teaching them how to act for fear they would become too self-conscious and analytical. Anspaugh also had decided not to invite the Huskers to watch the dailies (the results of the previous days' shooting) for the same reason—they might stop being natural and start trying to become actors. Brad Boyle said Anspaugh put the Huskers through exercises that were similar to playing charades; the boys simulated situations and learned voice control and how to project feeling.

In the screenplay, Pizzo had written a few lines of dialog for each team member to differentiate the boys from each other and to give the audience a sense of their personalities. But he also was careful not to make their roles too hard acting-wise. For the most part the young men weren't that different from their characters. "That's how they get by having non-actors," Hollar said. "We're just playing ourselves." About his character he noted, "Rade and I have a lot in common. He's the class talker, and I was kind of that way. We're both confident and sassy. But [our demeanor] on the court [is] very opposite." Kent Poole believed his role truly fit his personality: "When I played [high school] ball, I always played with the attitude of trying to help the team." And Long was looking forward to being team captain. "I did play college basketball, and I am a little bit older," he said. On the other hand, he said, "I don't feel I'm cocky" like Buddy. He felt confident about his role, "except for the brash troublemaker part of it."

Two of the Huskers were cast against type and had to portray characters who were unlike themselves. Brad Boyle had to figure out how to play team member Whit, whom the script merely described as "in a word, dumb." Said Boyle, "The producers told us they tried to pick people that already seemed to fit the character's personality. Then they stopped for a moment and said, 'Well, not necessarily everyone' to make me feel better." Because the filmmakers gave the Huskers some input into creating their characters, Boyle decided to act "dumbfounded, not quite with it." And Wade Schenck, a talented guard on his high school team, had to work at becoming a poor player—the hapless Ollie.

David Neidorf remarked that *Hoosiers* was "set in a rural place, and I didn't grow up like that." So he tried to absorb the feelings and lifestyles of the native Hoosiers around him in developing his character. He saw Everett as "someone who has been abandoned by his father and is lonely and embarrassed in a very small community where everyone knows that about you, and that's the first thing they think about you."

"I'm gonna be learning from you, just like you learn from me." —Coach Dale

Hackman decided to help the Huskers by giving them acting tips. "You're somewhat limited when you're working with people who haven't had any professional experience," he explained, "because you have to come to their level. They can't rise to your level." Hackman put the Huskers through acting exercises such as having them compose and deliver a monologue, envision something so sad it made them cry, and sing a song of their choice. In return, the Huskers assisted Hackman by schooling him in basketball lingo. They helped him so that it would be natural for him to yell something like "Cover the weak side" or "Get back on defense."

Hackman didn't just teach the Huskers about acting; he also offered them advice. Maris Valainis said Hackman told them, "Just remember, this is going to be on film forever, and you're not going to be able to change it 10 years from now. So give it your best all the time." When they asked him if they should pursue acting careers, he warned them that "there are only so many Michael Jordans." He also "talked about going to restaurants in L.A. and having starving actors waiting on him and asked if that's really our goal in life," said Hollar. Boyle said Hackman also advised them, "If [acting isn't] something you wanted to do your whole life more than anything, it's not worth doing."

"The boys and I are getting to know each other, to see who we are and what we can be." —Coach Dale

Reflecting on the filming many years later, Hollar described practiced performer Hackman as "a no-bull guy. He knew his lines, and he expected you to know yours. He wouldn't get mad if you messed up. He'd just give you that stare." Eventually Hollar figured out something about Hackman's methodology. "From day 1, he was in character, and we never knew it. He was acting as our coach. He was forming the relationship of coach to player, not of Gene Hackman to Steve Hollar, giving him acting lessons." David Neidorf commented, "Gene was pretty intense. Maybe he was trying to keep some distance because he was playing the coach and didn't want us to be too friendly." Anspaugh noticed the same thing. "Sometimes [Hackman] was really helpful, and sometimes he was a bit standoffish," the director said. "But that helped the character, because in the movie [the townspeople] never really embrace Coach Dale until the end. It sort of worked." Neidorf also noticed that Hackman sometimes would get frustrated and lose his temper. He may have had good reason to be gruff and impatient. Said Long of the Huskers, "You can imagine getting eight boys together. There were a lot of shenanigans." Pizzo agreed: "When you get guys of that age together, it's like *Animal House*." Anspaugh speculated that although "Gene knew what he was getting into [with the amateur actors] ... I don't think it really hit him until he got there."

Although team member Neidorf wasn't a Midwesterner, he had no trouble blending in. "You have a perception of what people from L.A. must be like," said Poole, "but David fits right in, just as Hoosier as you and me." Added Pizzo, "He has a rural quality about him. You can't tell he grew up in California, and he plays a good game of basketball."

Hershey was another of the few actors not from the Midwest, having been born and raised in Hollywood. Anspaugh noticed that although she had limited time to prepare for her role, she immersed herself in picking up the local dialect. She got some help with her accent from cheerleader Laura Robling. "The directors and everybody wanted me to get together [with Hershey] and have her just listen to me. They thought I had a good Hoosier accent," Robling said. "I went out to her hotel and read through some of her lines so she could hear how I talked. She recorded me."

Anspaugh didn't work extensively with the three lead actors in developing their characters. After his initial 3-hour interview with

Hopper about the role of Shooter, Anspaugh felt Hopper had a thorough grasp of his character. The director also thought Hershey totally understood Myra. And as he reviewed each page of the script with Hackman in order to solicit his opinions and feedback, Anspaugh could see that Hackman was a smart actor with good instincts. "With somebody like Gene," Anspaugh said, "you kind of sit back and let him go. If I thought he was not getting the character or was heading down the wrong path, I would have tried to get him to change course. But when we did the first read-through, Angelo and I looked at each other and knew we had stumbled into the best choice we could have made."

"We're way past big speech time." —Coach Dale

During rehearsals, Hackman admitted that he disliked it when his character stated what he was thinking and feeling, rather than showing it. One example was an early scene in which Norman tells Cletus that coaching college basketball "brought me great pleasure and great pain." Hackman wanted Norman to express himself more through behavior than dialog. He pointed out several places in the script where, he said, "I don't need to say that; I can act it."

Pizzo recognized the wisdom of this approach and agreed to the trimming and even deletion of many lines. In the script, when Myra asks Norman why he hit one of his college players, he starts out by saying, "I guess my need to win and win my way were the only two things that mattered in my life then." But in the filmed scene, he begins his answer with "I can't really explain that." And in the screenplay Norman gives a longer speech before kissing Myra: "First time I saw you, unfriendly as could be, there in the school hallway, all I thought about later was kissing you...." This sentence got shortened to "I've imagined kissing you ever since I first saw you." Pizzo had never dealt with an actor who wanted fewer lines instead of more.

Another area that required adjustments, Pizzo soon found out, was the dialog for the supporting characters. Confessed Steve Hollar, "The first time I read the script, I thought it was hick city." Pizzo had written their lines in what he considered Southern Indiana dialect. This included pronunciations such as "cain't" instead of "can't" and "yer" instead of "your," consistent omission of the "g" from words ending in "ing," and liberal use of ungrammatical terms such as "ain't." A snippet of Buddy's dialog offered a typical example. In the locker room before the regional game, as Norman advised the team to forget about winning and losing, Buddy interrupts:

> *Coach, we're gonna forget about losin' but ain't forgettin' about winnin'. You always talkin' about playin' to potential. That don't matter now. We ain't got this far to go out and lose.*

When Pizzo heard the Hoosier actors practicing their lines, he realized they sounded like hillbillies, so he made some adjustments. "I try to work out lines so they flow more smoothly for the actors," he said, "as long as it doesn't change the concept of the script."

* * *

As the first shooting day drew near, Pizzo grew apprehensive about all the unknowns he and Anspaugh were facing. He believed they would be "taking a leap of faith—in ourselves, in each other." The constraints of the minimal budget also were on his mind.

Because of his background in television, the 39-year-old Anspaugh felt he possessed the skills and experience he needed to direct his first motion picture. When he'd had the opportunity to progress from producing to directing TV episodes, he said, "I felt I was ready, although I don't know how one ever really knows that. It's the only art form that there is really no way to prepare for. A cast of 20 and a crew of 60 all turn to you and say, 'What would you like us to do?'" Anspaugh felt prepared to take the helm of *Hoosiers* because the shows he had worked on were challenging. "I've done [*Hill Street* episodes]—like the one with a basketball game in it, a hostage situation, a big gang summit meeting—[with] 30 characters in the scene," he said. "I'm not a newcomer or novice to this complexity of big scenes and having to do it fast." In the episodes he directed, "the long scenes and overlapping dialog [were] like Chinese puzzles," he said. "I spent so many nights trying to find the key to the next day's scenes, how to do them and do them in the time allowed." Anspaugh described *Hill Street Blues* as being like boot camp; it was great training. To direct that show, he had needed to move fast, think on his feet, and trust his instincts. So, for those reasons, directing *Hoosiers* wouldn't be too different.

Nevertheless, before production got under way, Anspaugh found himself in a state of semi-panic. His anxiety stemmed, he said, from the pressure of having to film 121 scenes on the "ridiculously ambitious schedule" of only eight weeks, which was all the budget would allow. Anspaugh told Pizzo to delete some of the scenes he had written, because there simply wouldn't be enough time to shoot them all. But this necessity became a source of friction between the director and the screenwriter as Pizzo dug in his heels and refused to give up any of his material, Anspaugh said. Eventually Pizzo relented and began cutting some scenes he decided were nonessential. These deletions and revisions would continue through the first weeks of filming.

The night before principal photography was to begin, Anspaugh stayed awake, walking the floor. "What was I thinking?" he asked himself. "Who is gonna care about a bunch of high school kids in the '50s running around in black high-tops in Indiana? I'm nuts. Why did they say yes?"

Cameras Roll in New Richmond

> *"The only thing that ever comes into Hickory from the outside is a train, and it's here for about 5 minutes." —Myra*

As New Richmond residents anticipated the arrival of cast and crew, Byron Alexander recalled that "a tornado came through here one time, but it didn't bring us as much excitement as this." Noted Janice Kunkel, "There are a lot more people coming in now, people you don't recognize. I'd come home at 5:30 and there used to be no one downtown, and now there are people all over, kids riding their bikes down to see what's going on. It's fun." Said postmaster Wilma Lewellyn, "It's not uncommon to see strangers in town with cameras. We've learned to be ready to have our pictures taken and be ready for an interview." Al Boone remarked, "The film's helped wake up the town. It's brought people together."

Deputy town marshal Mark Clapp was hired as a movie-set security officer. "To actually see what it takes to make a movie [has] intrigued everybody," he said. He noticed that out-of-town visitors were coming in from everywhere because of all the publicity about the filming. On two different Sundays, more than 100 people toured the town's museum. The movie's security staff had to rope off some areas to keep the tourists out of the way. "The movie is probably New Richmond's 20th century claim to fame," Clapp said. He reflected that the town hadn't experienced an event of this magnitude since the bank robbery of 1982.

To the souvenir shirts Alexander sold in his store, which said "Beautiful Downtown New Richmond, Ind.," he had a printer add "Home of the movie 'Hoosiers.'" The apparel began flying off the racks after someone had the idea of buying a shirt and having Hackman autograph it. Other items for sale included bags of hickory nuts, plastic miniature basketballs, bumper stickers, commemorative plates, caps proclaiming "Hickory: Indiana's Hollywood," and buttons that said "I watched the filming of the movie *Hoosiers*."

Pizzo and Hackman autograph Beautiful Downtown New Richmond T-shirts for young fans.

About 6 a.m. on Friday, October 18, a caravan rolled into town, consisting of equipment trucks, cargo vans, wardrobe trucks, RVs, the catering wagon, and the honey wagon—a semi containing the makeup and dressing rooms and restrooms. Before filming began, transportation manager Fleet Eakland reminded onlookers to avoid the equipment trucks, which carried heavy gear, and the high-voltage cable lines used with the lights. The Indiana State Police blocked off all four of the arteries leading into New Richmond but noted that the town would never be closed down completely during production.

The first scene to be shot that morning was of Hackman driving his 1951 Chevrolet Styleline Deluxe coupe into town from North County Road 400 West. As he was filmed from far down the street, dozens of townspeople looked on from south of the intersection, along with newspaper and TV reporters. Crawfordsville resident and crowd member Joe Boswell recorded the proceedings on his video camera. After cruising through the intersection several times for different takes, Hackman decided to relieve the monotony by improvising. When he stopped at the blinking red light, he rolled down the window, stuck out his head, and surprised the two female extras crossing the street by asking them how to get to the school. To create a different perspective of the same scene, next the Chevy was towed by an El Camino topped with a metal framework holding crew members. The camera was mounted between the two cars and photographed Hackman through the windshield.

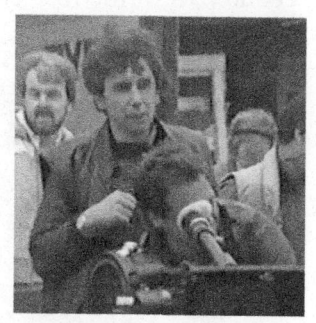

Director David Anspaugh and cinematographer Fred Murphy discuss the setup of the first scene in New Richmond.

Then it began raining, which delayed the shooting for an hour and a half. Anspaugh waited impatiently for the storm to pass, confessing, "I'm just wound up like a spring." Eventually they picked up where they left off, and things wrapped up around 4 p.m.

The cast and crew returned the following Wednesday. The first order of business was a meeting in the town hall for the approximately 30 local people who would fill the background in the street scenes.

On hand that day was Husker David Neidorf. He wasn't needed for the filming; he was simply curious about the moviemaking process. Also present was supporting actor Sheb Wooley, whom a casting assistant initially mistook for one of the background extras.

In the morning everyone rehearsed the scene in which Norman drives into town, walks past some guys sitting outside the barbershop, and encounters Opal and Myra outside the feed store. Anspaugh checked out the setup using a viewfinder, which looked like a little handheld telescope. As the actors rehearsed the part where Norman helps Myra and her mom load bags of seed into their truck, Anspaugh occupied the same space as the actors, observing them up close. "I'm not the kind of director who sits in a chair," he explained. "I'm rarely off my feet." After the first part of this scene was committed to film, everyone broke for lunch. The cast, crew, and extras got food from the catering truck and then sat at two rows of long tables with metal folding chairs that had been set up in a vacant lot. In the afternoon, as gray skies gave way to sunshine, the second part of the feed store scene was committed to celluloid.

Norman (Gene Hackman), Opal (Fern Persons), and Myra (Barbara Hershey) load the pickup truck.

At the end of each filming day, the permanent extras were handed an envelope containing their pay. Because none of them had seen the script, and because the scenes were being filmed out of order, they didn't know the details of the plot or how the scene they were shooting that day fit into the overall story.

> *"Now, folks, let's make him feel welcome. Your new coach, Norman Dale."*
> —Cletus

New Richmond grocery store owner Carolyn Fiddler was impressed with Gene Hackman, calling him very congenial and nice. Added Mark Clapp, "It was interesting to see Gene walking down the street and interacting with all the people. If you didn't recognize Gene for who he was, you would just think he lived here." Fannie Stephens, 82, made sure to seek out Hackman and introduce herself during a break in filming. She told the actor that she and his mother, Lyda Gray, were neighbors and best friends while growing up in Danville, Illinois. She gave Hackman two pictures of his mother. During subsequent breaks that day, Hackman resumed his reminiscing with Stephens and her husband. "What really got to me was how they kept calling me Gene Allen," he laughed about the use of his middle name. "No one has called me that for years."

The townspeople also got good vibes from the crew members. Remarked Al Boone, whose museum had been turned into a hardware store for the movie, "They are so absolutely fabulous, you'd think they were from New Richmond."

> *"Real friendly town you got here."* —Coach Dale

Likewise, the crew enjoyed working in the town. Casting director Ken Carlson described the residents as very cooperative. Said set designer Jo-Ann Chorney, "The people are so great; they come up and offer us things—cars, everything." Location manager Rick Schmidlin commented that the residents responded "like people did in the old heyday of Hollywood. That's important to the crew. It makes them want to do the best job they know how, and that makes for a better movie." Enthused Pizzo, "I love shooting on location in the Midwest. People here don't view productions as an intrusion, but an honor, an opportunity. There's so much more energy here than on the jaded West Coast."

> ### Where Is Hickory, Anyway?
>
> If the movie's hamlet were a real town, where in the Hoosier State would it be? The landscape might offer a hint. It's not hilly, but relatively flat, like most of central and northern Indiana. Another indication appears on the side of the school bus parked outside Hickory High. It says "Wabash County," which is in the northeast part of the state. A final clue is to look at the neighboring schools the Huskers play during the regular season and in the sectional. Lyons, Dugger, Holland, and Birdseye are southwestern towns, and Bloomington and Oolitic are in the south-central part of the state. Franklin and Terhune are close to the middle, and Decatur is in the northeast. Considered together, these clues indicate that Hickory must be located—well, nowhere.

Most screenwriters don't get to watch their scripts come to life, but because Pizzo also was a producer, he planned to be present for each day of filming. Anspaugh found that helpful. "I like to have the writer on set at all times so that I can have that constant communication to make sure that I totally understand their intent," he said. "They also have to understand, then, that I will give [the movie] my spin, as will the talent." Anspaugh appreciated Pizzo's script because "he gives you a solid skeletal framework from which to work" with "so much room as a director to expand." The duo agreed to work as a team and make all key decisions together.

> *"I'm trying hard to believe that you know what you're doing."* —Cletus
> *"I know what I'm doing!"* —Coach Dale

However, the production got off to a rough start. During the first week, Pizzo stuck close by Anspaugh's side, often questioning his decisions. And Anspaugh usually deferred to his friend's wishes in an attempt to show respect for Pizzo's script and vision and to preserve their almost-20-year friendship. Hackman soon stepped in and advised the two men that the film needed only one director. Anspaugh realized he was being too cautious and was trying to please everyone. Nevertheless, the director wouldn't let Hackman's misimpression of him as being irresolute change his determination to embrace a collaborative working style. He remained willing to entertain suggestions from anyone in the cast or crew.

Hackman didn't go easy on the first-time moviemakers, testing them every step of the way. Hackman seemed to wonder, Pizzo said, if he and Anspaugh knew what they were doing. At the beginning of one of the early days of filming, Hackman, unhappy with his dialog, refused to come out of his trailer until his lines were rewritten. A little later that day, after the completion of what Anspaugh viewed as a scene that should have made for a relatively easy shoot, Hackman demanded, "You're satisfied with that? You really thought that was good?" Pizzo and Anspaugh perceived a similar negative vibe from Hershey. Pizzo believed she lacked respect for what they were doing, for them as filmmakers, and for the script. He was offended that Hershey wanted to rewrite much of her dialog herself. And sometimes, after wrapping a scene, she would turn to Hackman, not Anspaugh, and ask, "How was that?" Anspaugh theorized that perhaps Hershey felt she needed to side with Hackman in the ongoing strife between Hackman and the filmmakers.

Anspaugh briefs Michael O'Guinne (Rooster the barber), John Robert Thompson (the sheriff), and Mike Dalzell (the mayor) outside the barbershop.

School Days in Nineveh

In late October the crew descended upon Nineveh—tripling the town's population in the process. "At any given time there are seldom more than 50 people in town," noted Yvette Casucci. Her husband, Mike Casucci, owner of the Nineveh General Store and

Princes Lakes Deli, was convinced that the filming would be a positive event. "Anything like this is always good for a community," he said. "It brings good recognition and business."

Although location manager Rick Schmidlin opined that "the Nineveh school is probably the best-kept intact of that era," the State Board of Health disagreed. It had ordered that the building be shuttered at the close of the school year due to issues such as a leaky roof, cracks in the walls, and other structural problems. Principal Nancy Thompson appreciated the irony that "some of these things that are fitting [the filmmakers'] needs precisely are no longer meeting ours." She added, "I'm glad they will have part of this school on film. It will be a historical reminder of what we have here."

The building had been a high school until 1967, when Nineveh High and two other schools were rolled into Indian Creek High. Some townspeople could remember the glory days of Hoosier Hysteria, before school consolidation. Darlene Dugan saw similarities between the Hickory Huskers and her old high school team, the Bluebirds. "The gym was packed for any Nineveh game," she said. "It was standing room only." Former team member Bruce Lucas lamented that, in the present day, "with the larger schools you don't have the closeness that you did back in the '50s." He concluded, "It's a different paced game. You don't have the old set shot. But the ball still bounces the same, I guess."

The crew prepared the school's interior by repainting two classrooms from blue and yellow to shades of brown and by replacing fluorescent lights with incandescent ones.

Some outdoor scenes were scheduled for the first day of Nineveh filming, Saturday the 26th, but Anspaugh postponed them because the sun was too bright. Instead, the crew shot interior scenes, such as the one where Norman enters the school for the first time and meets Myra. Members of the drama club at Indian Creek High School in nearby Trafalgar, as well as kids from Knightstown and Triton Central in Fairland, showed up for the scenes that required students. "We spent hours just walking up and down the stairs for hallway shots," said Triton senior Kristine Klever. "They even made sure we stayed in the same order." Commented Triton student Jim Bowman, "It was fun even though we spent a lot of time waiting." The extras reported to the set at 8 a.m. and were in costume by 9, but some of them were not needed until late afternoon, if at all.

Because school was in session the following Monday during the remainder of the interior filming, the crew worried about possible noise from the classrooms. But the teachers successfully contained any commotion. At the conclusion of the day's shooting, Hackman addressed the elementary students: "Thank you for being so quiet today. I didn't realize there were so many of you here. You were like little mice."

> ### Floatin'
>
> When Norman enters Cletus's office, he finds the principal sitting cross-legged on the floor, facing the window. "Cletus? What are you doing down there?" Norman asks. "Floatin'," he replies. Pizzo explained that this term is a colloquialism for "meditating."

One disadvantage of the Nineveh location was that it sat just west of Camp Atterbury, a training base for the Indiana National Guard. This meant fighter jets often roared by overhead, interfering with the outdoor scenes. The filmmakers ended up shooting between takeoffs.

The crew made a few changes to the school's exterior for the outdoor scenes. The steel basketball post and backboard were replaced with a wooden unit, and the court was covered with dirt. The paved parking lot also was covered with dirt and was filled with bicycles, old cars, and a 1946 Ford school bus.

The scene outside the school in which Myra and Norman discuss Jimmy while walking toward the entrance was populated with extras from the other filming locations. Retired teachers and sisters Alma Rogers and Louise Grantham of New Richmond entered the building just ahead of Hershey. Hackman said "Good morning" to Knightstown student Ross Wells in the same shot.

The outdoor scene in which Jimmy shoots a series of baskets while Norman talks to him was done in just one take. This was a good thing, because they were losing the light, and rain was moving in. "I was nervous because I felt the pressure to get it done," said Maris Valainis. He didn't listen to Hackman's speech; he just focused on making his shots. Missing the thirteenth and final basket "was purely accidental," he said. "I just stopped concentrating because the speech was done."

> ### Men Like Norman
>
> When Myra confronts Norman in the school hallway and asks him to leave Jimmy alone, a look at the original script solves the mystery of what she means by "I know men like you." Her discussion with Norman about whether Jimmy should join the team initially was longer. "There's no way anyone who is a basketball hero in these parts can be somebody 'they' don't want him to be," she says in an early version of the screenplay. "I saw it happen to my brother. People around here treated him like a god and acted as if they owned him. They pushed their own frustrated fantasies and dreams into his head until there was no room for his own." She fears Norman will do the same thing with Jimmy.

Pizzo described the moviemakers' time in Nineveh as the most difficult days they had experienced so far, because the tension between Anspaugh and Hackman was growing. The problems between the director and lead actor were evident after the outdoor basket-shooting scene wrapped at the culmination of another long, slightly rainy filming day, as Hackman lost his temper and exploded at Anspaugh. According to the director, such a display of emotion was not uncommon for the actor, who seemed more comfortable with conflict rather than calm on the set. "I depend on energy to make characters work," Hackman explained. Anspaugh didn't take these disagreements personally; he learned to tolerate Hackman's attitude. Supporting actor Chelcie Ross theorized that because Hackman was an Oscar-winning actor working with a fledgling director, he must have been thinking, "I know what I'm doing here. Thanks for your direction, but no thanks."

In a 1988 interview, Hackman commented on the movie's production: "I had never worked as an actor in the Midwest, so I was looking forward to it. But when we got there it was difficult. Everything was in disarray because there were so many nonprofessionals in the cast and so many unpaid extras. It was chaotic."

Hackman's mood improved somewhat about three and a half weeks into the filming, coinciding with Dennis Hopper's arrival in Indiana to assume his role as Shooter. Hopper brought a confluence of energy that changed the relationships between the actors, Pizzo said, and altered the tone, tenor, and atmosphere on the set. He helped decrease the friction generated by the other two lead actors. Hopper made Hackman and the Huskers laugh. And, unlike Hershey and Hackman, he was supportive of the freshman filmmakers' efforts. Voicing confidence in Anspaugh, Hopper remarked, "I don't need a lot of help as an actor, and Gene doesn't need a lot of help as an actor, and I appreciate it when we're just sort of left alone. I don't find that nondirecting; I find it just appreciation. I find David is doing well. He's doing fine."

And Rain Fell Upon the Earth 40 Days and 40 Nights

"The sun don't shine on the same dog's ass every day, but mister, you ain't seen a ray of light since you got here." —Opal Fleener

The autumn of 1985 was unusually rainy. Cinematographer Fred Murphy developed a fondness for the often-overcast skies. The abundance of rain, he said, caused the movie to take on a "wonderful sort of gray, misty, foggy, slightly damp atmosphere" that felt like "fall into winter." Said Pizzo, "That kind of gloomy, dark look serves the film well. It indicates the kinds of lives people lived in Indiana during the winter." Anspaugh agreed, going so far as to say the filmmakers got lucky with the overcast, gray, powerful weather, because the filming of the game scenes would seem "bright and dreamy" by comparison.

5
The Second Half: Filming Continues

"Remember what got you here. Focus on the fundamentals.... Most important, don't get caught up thinking about winning or losing this game." —Coach Dale

The pressure of the time constraints did not abate as November approached. Hopper felt Anspaugh was undertaking "a really difficult movie to do as a first film because of basketball itself, the nature of the game. You read a couple of paragraphs and you're talking ten days of work." Hickory Husker Steve Hollar noted that they might "film all day and finish maybe one page of script." Assistant directors Herb Adelman and Harvey Waldman estimated that shooting the basketball games alone would end up consuming half the production time.

One result of the lack of time was that Anspaugh didn't have the luxury of doing lots of takes of every scene; he had to settle for a handful of takes of each setup. Planning and thinking things through ahead of time also were crucial, he said.

Pizzo conceded that he and Anspaugh sometimes clashed during the shoot, engaging in "spirited debate." On one occasion the director went so far as to ban the screenwriter from the set for the day. Anspaugh clarified that even when they "banged heads," their disputes were never personal. "We have our squabbles," Pizzo admitted, "but we fight like brothers in the same family; we're both just trying to get the best movie out there." Supporting actor Chelcie Ross opined that Pizzo and Anspaugh kept each other sane. As fatigue set in over the weeks of production, the number of arguments between the two men diminished as they began to exist in survival mode, Pizzo said.

> **And They Rested on the Seventh Day from All Their Work**
>
> On Sundays, their only day off during the week, the crew members caught up on sleep and did laundry. Reflecting on this fact made Adelman laugh when he considered how most people view filmmaking as a glamorous profession.
>
> Location manager Rick Schmidlin sometimes went antique hunting in his free time; Barbara Hershey accompanied him on one such trip. One of his best finds was the little Philco radio on which Shooter listens to the regional and state-finals games in his hospital room.

Courting Fame in Knightstown

For the next phase of filming, the crew moved their base of operations into the elementary school next to the Huskers' home court in Knightstown. Schmidlin had considered using the 109-year-old building for the filming of the school scenes, but he concluded doing so would require too much preparation. Instead, one classroom served as the costume shop, the top floor was transformed into the hair salon, and the makeup artists occupied yet another room. No classes were forced to move, but the teachers and students had to adjust to the increased noise and activity. "There have been some inconveniences," said superintendent William Freel, "but they're outweighed by the positive things done for the community." One such bonus was Hackman's taking the time to visit some of the classrooms and speak with teachers and students.

> *"I'd like to thank those of you who have made me feel so welcome here."*
> —*Coach Dale*

As had happened in New Richmond, the townspeople embraced Hackman. They found him to be personable, friendly, and willing to sign autographs. Proclaimed Henry County resident Ralph "Whitey" Shively, "Gene Hackman is probably one of the nicest people I've ever met. I gave him a Shively Auction hat, and he wore it that one day. He's as common as an old shoe." Said Knightstown High

School senior Eddie Hager, who served as a stand-in for Steve Hollar, "You meet him once, and he remembers who you are." One woman baked Hackman a pie, and another gave him a plaque. The actor commented, "The people are very nice here. It has been really pleasant in all these small towns." The citizens liked Hopper as well. But they noticed that Hershey spent much of her free time in her RV, usually preferring not to sign autographs, have her picture taken, or hang out with the locals. New Richmond permanent extra Wilma Lewellyn theorized that perhaps Hershey was aloof with the townsfolk because she was staying in character the whole time.

The narrow street next to the gym was filled with the RVs, in which the actors could rest and learn their lines between scenes. The eight Huskers sometimes used their two shared RVs to catch a nap. The meals for the cast and crew were provided by caterers. They whipped up delicious selections such as Italian sausage marinara, ocean perch, red snapper, beef stroganoff, buttered noodles, scalloped potatoes, corn on the cob, tomato Florentine soup, chocolate Bavarian pie, and chocolate layer cake.

The gym was changed a bit for the filming. The glass backboards were replaced with wooden ones. The floor's free-throw lanes were narrowed, and the panther-head design in the center was replaced with a gold letter H inside a red circle. Because the home games in the movie took place at night but would be filmed during the day, the windows would be covered during the games. Much brighter overhead lights were installed using a hydraulic scissor lift. Parts of the interior were painted, banners were hung, and the all-digital scoreboard was switched with one that had an analog clock in the middle.

What's the Score?

The film crew managed to locate five scoreboards from the 1950s, to be used in the different gyms, but none of them were in working order. As luck would have it, though, an expert on old scoreboards lived not far from New Richmond. Seventy-six-year-old Roy Meharry had worked on many of these older devices for decades. The former electrical contractor had even helped invent what he believed was the state's first electronic scoreboard. Although parts and schematics were no longer available for the boards the crew had collected, Meharry was confident he could fix all of them in time for the filming.

As a bonus, he was chosen to play the role of the Huskers' scorekeeper.

In the first scene to be filmed in the gym, reporters crowded into the south entrance to interview Coach Dale about the upcoming state finals. Scott Miley, who wrote many articles on the making of *Hoosiers* for the *Indianapolis Star*, became a part of the story when he was cast as one of the reporters. After getting a haircut and putting on a suit he described as "three sizes too big," Miley joined a group of about 25 extras, including Fort Wayne Realtor Robert Sutton, who asked Coach Dale about a scouting report, and Crawfordsville radio reporter Jay Farlow. Representing Knightstown were Dick Leakey and Ed Dunsmore, an attorney. Dunsmore wasn't thrilled with his mandatory haircut. "I haven't had my hair this short since 1965," he grumbled. Miley got to shout a line—"Coach, how'd you do it?"—as Hackman and a couple Huskers made their way through the mob of newsmen.

The extras were surprised to see crew members walking around with what resembled smoker pots used by beekeepers. The puffs of smoke generated by the pots created a haze in the gym that would soften the background and accent the shafts of artificial sunlight streaming in through the windows.

After half a dozen takes of the scene with the reporters, Anspaugh was ready to move on to the next scene—the pep session introducing that year's team. The large group of extras who would make up the crowd had been waiting at the high school half a mile away since 10 that morning. They had been encouraged to participate by posters put up around town that said "Be an EXTRA in the Motion Picture HOOSIERS! Be a part of Indiana's Movie!" About 3 p.m. they arrived at the gym, having been shuttled there in vans. Although a few lucky people from Knightstown had been allowed to watch the filming earlier in the day, this time the bystanders were ordered out. "Everybody [on the crew] was running around trying to get things done," said one spectator. "I can see why some of us may have been in the way." Outside the gym, the Indiana State Police helped with crowd and traffic control.

On the second day in Knightstown, the actors filmed the first basketball practice. Said Chelcie Ross, who played self-appointed assistant coach George, "I was all nerves, the new guy jumping right in with the screen legend. I had no need to be nervous. Gene was generous and complimentary and treated me as if we were equals, peers." When the Huskers struggled with the part where Coach Dale kicks out Buddy, Hackman suggested that Brad Long transition his reaction from surprise to anger. Long improvised by slapping the door in frustration on his way out of the gym.

Buddy's Bad Attitude

When Buddy mouths off and gets thrown out of practice, no reason is evident for his blatant disrespect for the new coach, whom he has just met. The screenplay offers a clue about his actions: George is Buddy's father. Therefore, when Norman makes it clear at the first practice that he doesn't want any help, and George storms out, Buddy is understandably upset with the man who just disrespected and embarrassed his dad.

Son and father: Brad Long (Buddy) and Chelcie Ross (George).

Also captured on the second day was the movie's final scene, staged on the Huskers' home court. "I wanted an image that's evocative of past and future, that the legacy of the team will live on," explained screenwriter Pizzo. The script described the camera zooming in on the large team photo hanging on the wall, but it was Anspaugh's idea to include a little boy shooting baskets. After rehearsing the shot in the empty gym, the director sensed that the scene could be improved. As a painter or composer might put it, he said, a color or stroke was missing. So he decided to head to the elementary school next door and find the best young basketball player in Knightstown.

Recalled Roger Hamilton, Jr., years later, "We were lined up at the door getting ready to go home for the afternoon when [Anspaugh] walked in, just looked at me, and said, 'Come with me.' I didn't know who he was." The director told the third-grader he wanted him to be in the movie. When Roger arrived at the gym, he saw the Huskers leaning against the stage, waiting to observe the filming. The costumers had no clothes for someone Roger's age, so they were forced to improvise. They found a white T-shirt he could wear and cut the Levi's tag off his jeans. They had no footwear for him either, so Hackman helped by pulling black socks over Roger's shoes. Hamilton commented, "I'd seen him in *Superman*. It amazed me that he was actually right there, putting socks on me." Roger had never played organized basketball, just playground pickup games. Nevertheless, he made all his shots during the filming, even as the socks over his shoes caused him to slip around on the floor. Because he was a nonspeaking extra, Roger didn't receive any pay for his role. But when the scene was complete, Hackman took a $20 bill out of his wallet, autographed it, and handed it to the boy.

Lieutenant Governor John Mutz visited the set on the third day of Knightstown action. He was the director of the Indiana Department of Commerce, of which the Indiana Film Commission was a part. He was one of the movie's early supporters, having attended the press conference at which the location finalists were announced. The cast and crew threw a surprise party to celebrate Mutz's 50th birthday. The team members presented him with a cake decorated with a basketball flying toward a hoop. After that the lieutenant governor watched the filming of the scene in which the barber, the sheriff, and five townspeople played by New Richmond residents interrupt afternoon basketball practice.

Husker David Neidorf didn't enjoy the filming of the basketball drills. Because he was "not in basketball shape," he said, running all those exercises left him exhausted and breathing hard—all while the acrid haze created by the smoker pots hung in the air and burned his lungs.

The home-gym locker room scenes were captured the next day. The room's compact size limited possible filming angles. "It had kind of a claustrophobic feel," said cinematographer Fred Murphy. In addition, "There was one [ceiling] pipe that kept getting into shot that we couldn't get out." But overall he liked the locker room because its simplicity conveyed that "this isn't a well-to-do high school."

As the evening wound down, Anspaugh prepared for the scene in which Norman lectures the Huskers after their frustrating first home-game loss. Anspaugh had planned to have the actors run through the scene seven or eight times as they were shot from different angles. But with the day almost over, he had time to shoot only one of the setups. (He hoped he would have some time left at the end of production to go back and film more coverage and pick-ups of certain scenes if necessary.) The director settled on what he described as "a simple, low-angle, static shot that showed the entire team, with Hackman sitting by the door. Time deadlines force you to distill things." When Anspaugh viewed rushes of the scene a few days later, he was satisfied with it. It seemed to him that shooting from just one point of view, instead of cutting away for close-up reaction shots, sharpened the focus and would make the audience feel as if they were present in the locker room.

By the middle of November, the moviemakers were ready to begin filming the home games. Every morning, the cast and crew attended a briefing to discuss that day's shooting schedule. After that the Huskers and the visiting team would practice their plays, which were choreographed by basketball advisor Strats Stratigos.

Aside from the core group of permanent extras, the people who played the fans in the stands were mostly students from area high schools. Over a dozen kids from Connersville were present at the filming of the Dugger game, accompanied by teacher Joe Glowacki. Senior Chris Hushour received permission from Anspaugh to videotape the action from the area in the bleachers where the crew was sitting. Dale Basham, a teacher at Muncie Southside, and his 32 drama club students attended a day of game filming, along with 15 members of the drama club from Randolph Southern in Lynn. The extras had to undergo preparations before they were ready to be seated in the gym. Their first stop was the makeshift hair salon in the old school next door. While the boys got their hair cut and slicked back, the stylists used curling irons, hair spray, spritz, and bobby pins on the girls' hair. It wasn't easy turning their permed, fluffy, layered '80s hairdos into a rough approximation of midcentury styles. When their hairstyles were complete, students who had not come dressed in their own '50s-type costumes were sent to the wardrobe room.

From there the kids were ushered into a large tent set up on the lawn, where they sat on metal folding chairs, talking and listening to a boom box. Eventually extras casting assistant Debby Shively arrived to give them their marching orders. She told them that, in the gym, assistant directors Herb Adelman and Harvey Waldman would shout instructions to them over a bullhorn. If they said, "Back to number one," that meant the entire scene would be done over again. During close-up shots of time-out huddles, the extras were to mime cheering motions so that the actors' dialog wouldn't be drowned out by their yelling. They also were reminded never to look into the camera. Finally, Shively recited the Hickory High fight song line by line, with the kids echoing each line, in case they would need to sing it during shooting:

Fight on, Hickory
We're here to say
We'll back our Husker team
And we'll back them all the way
Fight! Fight! Fight!

Our colors we will fly
And we'll proudly do or die
We'll fight for you
We'll see you through
Our Hickory High

The melody was borrowed from the fight song of Manchester High School in North Manchester.

The students were seated on one side of the gym and on the stage, while the cameras and crew occupied the other side. Key second assistant director Waldman, who was in charge of the extras, paced the sidelines with his walkie-talkie and bullhorn. Before a scene was rehearsed, he informed them what the action would entail and how they should react. He kicked off each scene by shouting, "Quiet! Roll cameras! Background, cheering! Action!" Or, when the extras were to do their silent cheering or emoting, he yelled, "Background, pantomime! Action!"

Waldman (with bullhorn) observes the action from the upper corner of the bleachers.

Anspaugh fires up the fans.

The crowd was taught cheers that were specific to the 1950s. When at one point they broke into an impromptu chant of "*De*-fense, *de*-fense!", Pizzo quickly intervened. "I didn't want any specific chants that they spontaneously came up with that we had not authenticated through research," he said. The fans also were reminded not to make contemporary gestures such as high fives and pointing "We're number one" fingers while rooting on their team.

One special group of extras was the Hickory High pep band, made up of members of the Knightstown High School band. The band and a handful of other students, including some from the high school's drama club, would participate in several days of filming—not just in Knightstown, but in other locations as well. Knowing that most of the shooting would occur on weekdays when school was in session, school officials wanted to ensure that the kids wouldn't miss too many classes. "We can understand it is a once-in-a-lifetime kind of thing," said superintendent William Freel. "But we will have to control it." Added school board president Kemper Rice, "There has to be a limit on the number of days students can be out." He explained, "You have to remember, we're in the education business, not the movie business."

Other local students helped the production crew by acting as gofers and aiding the production assistants. They worked with the art department, the costumers—wherever they were needed.

The novice actors in the cast found out just how time-consuming shooting a movie is and how much downtime occurs during an average day. Before filming, Anspaugh and cinematographer Fred Murphy, a native New Yorker who was relatively unknowledgeable about basketball, would discuss, sometimes for hours, camera placement, shooting angles, and the positioning of the lights. The basketball plays were staged using stand-ins as Murphy and Anspaugh walked around the court with a viewfinder to decide where to place the camera. As Murphy described it, their approach was to break the basketball action "into almost scenes, as opposed to just sort of covering it, watching people run around and make shots." A typical sports film, he said, "might have one important play, but often it's photographed from a distance, and there'll be some close-ups. But it's not like a continuous scene where something is evolving and happening that's emotional."

The Huskers spent a fair amount of time standing around waiting for the cameras and lights to be set up. To amuse themselves during the many periods of inactivity, they played cards (sometimes with Hopper), ran up and down the court to stay loose, practiced free throws, and challenged each other in games of H-O-R-S-E. Maris Valainis noted that the Huskers also tended to get into trouble, accidentally "knocking over lights or something" when not shooting a scene. Kent Poole and Brad Long helped corral their younger teammates. Wade Schenck described the two as "like the older brothers of the group" who watched over them and made sure they stayed in line. Pizzo said Poole took the filming more seriously than anybody else, saying things like, "All right, guys, let's get back to work."

The fans in the bleachers also had to find ways to fill the downtime. Commented Adelman, "Being an extra can be very, very boring, because it can be an hour or two between takes." Long opined that only in Indiana could you find people willing to sit around for 8 hours to see a basketball game. Extras casting assistant Debby Shively suggested that the extras bring knitting or books. The New Richmond permanent extras exchanged recipes. IUPUI senior Marcia Wright, a cheerleader for Hickory opponent Oolitic, worked on her studies at the scorer's bench during breaks in the filming. The high school students left their seats and ventured onto the playing floor to obtain autographs from both the home and visiting teams. Said Hackman after one of the games, "We had anywhere from 200 to 300 extras. And they were all volunteers. So, since they weren't being paid, they pretty much did what they wanted to. When we'd finish with a take, they'd immediately be down on the court, shooting baskets and getting autographs. It was really tough trying to get them back up in the stands."

When basketball scenes were rehearsed, cheering was replaced by murmurs from the crowd, making the pounding of the basketball audible. During one rehearsal, Husker Steve Hollar, on defense, collided with an opposing player, and instantly two others joined the pileup. Anspaugh called out, "Clean that up! Whoa! Start again." He strode onto the court, accompanied by technical advisor Strats Stratigos, to remind the boys how the play should be carried out.

Rade (Steve Hollar) and other players bump into each other.

The competitors were filmed half a dozen times from one angle and then again from other angles, often at only one end of the court. Said Dale Basham, "They had choreographed those basketball plays so they did them the same way for each take. It was almost like a dance." Noted Hickory Husker Brad Boyle, "We were all dying to play a game of basketball—a real game, not just individual plays." During breaks in the action, the makeup artist sprayed the players with a mixture of water, baby oil, and glycerin to make them look sweaty.

A Steadicam was one of the cameras used in the basketball sequences. Explained Fred Murphy, "With the Steadicam, you're moving inside the court, with the players, as opposed to being on the sidelines, watching them."

The Huskers became acquainted with Hackman's style of working. David Neidorf said the Oscar winner didn't memorize his lines until 15 minutes before shooting. He theorized that the actor, working from "a highly agitated place," was attempting to generate "some sense of excitement that he would screw up. But being a pro, he never screws up." Steve Hollar noticed that Hackman occasionally liked to extemporize during the multiple takes of each scene, perhaps to keep his team on their toes. Hackman would change a line or throw in a wrinkle, Hollar said, probably to keep the reactions of the Huskers and the other actors fresh.

Hackman also could be a prankster. During one game he surprised the fans with an action that was reminiscent of notoriously temperamental IU coach Bob Knight. After being ejected from the game, Hackman walked off the court, headed for the locker room, and disappeared. He emerged moments later with a folding chair and hurled it across the gym floor, just as Knight had done during an IU/Purdue game earlier that year. The crowd sat in stunned silence. Waldman always prepared them before every scene by telling them how to react, and no one was expecting this. But then Hackman put his hands on his hips and grinned, and the gym exploded with hooting and hollering.

The Season Opener: Oolitic

The first home game to be filmed was Hickory's initial game of the season, against Oolitic. All 324 students from Union City Community High School, along with their teachers and principal Tom Goldsberry, traveled to Knightstown by chartered buses paid for by private citizens and led by a police escort. They took with them sack lunches prepared by the school's cafeteria workers. Upon their arrival, Waldman welcomed them. "Thank you very much, Union City, for being here today," he shouted over his bullhorn. "Give yourselves a round of applause!" In the days before the filming, the kids had scrounged their own costumes from Goodwill stores, the Muncie Mission thrift shop, and their parents and grandparents. They also consulted old yearbooks and their teachers.

For the scene in which the Huskers find themselves with only four players in the game, the hometown fans were supposed to react with loud disapproval when Coach Dale refused to put Rade back in. But when cameras rolled, Hackman's line "My team's on the floor" was met with cheers and clapping instead of anger. Anspaugh halted the filming and corrected the crowd. "No one should applaud—unless you're all sadists," he joked. Certain fans, including a group of men near the top of the bleachers, were assigned to stand and shout at the coach. "That's most of my teachers up there," said Goldsberry.

Sheb Wooley entertains the extras.

The shooting of the Oolitic game stretched over three days. The last scene planned for the third day would become one of the film's best images: The Huskers rush up from their downstairs locker room as Coach Dale follows, pausing for a moment before entering the noisy, packed gym. After lunch that day, Anspaugh and the crew began discussing and planning the setup for this Steadicam shot. All the equipment and crew that normally resided in the gym away from the cameras' gaze would need to be hidden. The shot would begin on the locker room stairs and proceed into the hall and through the door into the gym, where Coach Dale would cross the floor diagonally. By 3 p.m., filming still was not ready to begin. With the crowd growing bored and restless, Sheb Wooley pulled out his guitar and serenaded the fans with "(Back Home Again in) Indiana," prodding them to sing along.

This scene was one of Anspaugh's favorite moments in the movie, and one that held personal meaning for him. He hoped to express in that one shot, he said, "the feeling that I used to get when, as a kid, I would walk into our high school gymnasium on a cold winter night and just get smacked in the face with all of that color and sound and excitement." For all the basketball games, the filmmakers hoped to convey "that sense of being closed in by the sound, being closed in by energy," Pizzo commented. "In many of these farming communities, the only time [the townspeople] could come together and kind of release was in church and in the basketball gymnasium. It was a very slow, contemplative, kind of gray-and-brown life until they came into those gyms."

Because she had been chosen as a permanent extra, New Richmond postmaster Wilma Lewellyn found herself seated in a prime spot for the home games—in the first row of bleachers, behind the Huskers' bench. During breaks in the filming, fans sitting farther away would pass down pieces of paper for the stars to autograph, which Lewellyn would hand to the actors. Serving as a permanent extra allowed her to witness much of the filming and to get to know the moviemakers. It also eased her concerns about whether *Hoosiers* would be a quality production that would make Indiana proud. She mused, "I don't see how I could not like it. It's got basketball in it. And it's got us."

Norman's Last Chance: Lyons

Offered a role as a referee was Strats Stratigos, the film's basketball advisor and a longtime friend of Pizzo and Anspaugh. They let him choose which game he wanted to be in. He picked the Lyons game because one of its referees had a speaking role. His character slapped Coach Dale with a technical foul and threatened to put him on file with the state commission. "I had trouble hitting my mark; I kept going too far," Stratigos said of his performance. "Dennis Hopper was sitting there, and he kept teasing me. But Hackman was not happy. Because one thing about Mr. Hackman, he's a pro. And he never misses his mark. After about two or three takes, he was getting agitated. After the scene was finished, he shook my hand and said, 'Very good job.'"

Running the Picket Fence: Dugger

One of the film's most memorable snippets of dialog was Shooter's mention of the picket fence play during the Dugger game. Screenwriter Pizzo invented the term "picket fence," which he intended to sound colloquial. "I knew the kind of play," he said. "I knew they were double-stacked triple screens." He described the strategy as follows: "Three players go down to set a wall of screens, so when a defender comes around the outside, he runs into three guys. If you're guarding a man one-on-one, the defender has to fight through three picks to get to his man."

Kent Poole and Maris Valainis chat before the filming of the picket fence play, in which Merle was the swingman and Jimmy was solo right.

The "fence" was a four-man screen that would cut off Husker Kent Poole's defender. "All the other guys converged down there for me to roll off of them," Poole explained. "The very first time we did it, I made the shot. But it wasn't pure net. We ran it the second time through, and I drained it—I hit it just the way they wanted it."

Before the play, temporary head coach Hopper added a personal touch by ad-libbing his final instruction to the Huskers: "Now, boys, don't get caught watchin' the paint dry!" Said Pizzo, "We liked it so much—even though we weren't sure what it meant—that we left it in."

Scott Summers (Strap), Wade Schenck (Ollie), Brad Boyle (Whit), Robert Swan (Rollin), and Dennis Hopper (Shooter) at the Dugger game.

Overall Objection

While watching the filming of the Hickory home games, longtime Knightstown resident Peg Mayhill had one gripe about the extras' costuming: "I've been going to ball games since I was 6 years old, and I don't remember ever seeing anybody at a ball game in overalls. Maybe since a lot of the crew was from the city, they assumed that all country folks wore overalls."

Amateurs Become Actors

As production proceeded, the greenhorn performers who made up the Hickory team grew into their roles. Eventually they even were comfortable enough to improvise. In the locker room scene after their first game, when Hackman made his speech and then left, Anspaugh kept the camera rolling to let the players react to being chewed out. Later, during the regional game, Kent Poole (Merle) ad-libbed his words of encouragement to Ollie just before Ollie's victory-ensuring free throws. Anspaugh was pleased with the novice actors' efforts. "These people aren't just acting," he insisted. "They're responding to something that is part of their lives. That's passion, and it's worth a great deal." The young men were turning out to be "much, much better actors than we ever expected," the director said.

Anspaugh noted that the Huskers' foray into acting had "happened so quickly that they haven't had time to think about it and analyze it. They don't have agents and managers and other friends who are actors giving them advice. This hasn't been their livelihood. For them, there is nothing to lose." Pizzo added, "They are not adulterated by a lot of the neuroses that attract people to acting in the first place. Another thing is the feeling of comfort that they have in themselves because they are athletes." He concluded, "We all knew they could play basketball, and that they had interesting looks and qualities about

> them, but the kind of fearlessness that they have shown as actors has been exciting."

* * *

Just as New Richmond had done, Knightstown altered its souvenir T-shirts and sweatshirts. To the slogan "A good place to visit, a better place to live," they added a line about *Hoosiers*. Despite the general air of excitement, town board president Jack Shore wasn't convinced the filming would have a positive economic impact on the town. "I haven't heard of anybody having any extra business," he said. "[The filming] is confined to that one particular spot [the gym]. If it was being shot on the street, it would probably have more of an effect." The Chamber of Commerce might have disagreed. They sold thousands of dollars' worth of souvenir shirts, as well as numerous fish sandwiches from the Chamber's "fish wagon" that fed the extras. Shore believed the community might benefit most from increased tourist traffic after the movie's release: "Then, people might say, 'Well, we're out for a Sunday drive. Let's drive to Knightstown. That movie was filmed there.'"

After the majority of the home-gym scenes were complete, a problem arose with some of the over 20 student permanent extras who had missed several days of school for the filming. A few members of the Hickory pep band complained to the school board that their teachers had penalized them for racking up unexcused absences, assessing them a 3 percent grade reduction for each unexcused day. The superintendent had issued a memo on November 7 stating that five days of absenteeism would be allowed, and any missed days after that would be considered unexcused. But as one student pointed out, by the time the memo came out, filming had already occurred on three weekdays in Knightstown. At that point, said student Brian Hulse, he was committed to his role as a permanent extra and didn't want to back out. He said, "[I was] ecstatic I got to participate, and I will continue to participate." He vowed that the grade reductions would not wipe the smile off his face.

School board members were displeased about the demands that the movie had placed on the kids' time. Ron Westerfeld said the filmmakers had led them to believe the students would miss very few days of school. Richard Armstrong said he felt the movie production was taking advantage of the students. Another board member, Sarah Ward, mulled over the kids' complaints: "I wonder in 20 years what they will think about the board. Were we a bunch of sticks in the mud?"

Cedar Knob Game

The St. Philip Neri School gym on the near eastside of Indianapolis played the part of the yellow and green Cedar Knob court, site of the Huskers' first away game. This one scene, which wouldn't last that long in the movie, required 15 hours of work. Veteran stage actor Sam Smiley, who played one of the referees, noted that in the theater you must maintain your performance for 2 hours, but appearing in a movie could be considered "'minute-and-a-half acting.' You are on the set for hours before they lay down any footage, so your sense of attack has to be wonderful." In the Cedar Knob game, Hackman argued with Smiley, who then ejected him and Rade after the fight. During rehearsals, Anspaugh advised the two actors to "take it easy, be cool and laid back," Smiley said. "When we began filming, though, Hackman grew very angry in the scene. Both [Anspaugh] and Hackman pushed me to lose my temper. I really flew off the handle, and it became a real shouting match." The men got along better in real life. Smiley found Hackman "enormously friendly and helpful" and "not at all pretentious."

The Cedar Knob coach, whom Hackman also yells at, was portrayed by former high school coach Tom McConnell, who had helped teach the Huskers 1950s-style basketball before production began. Greg Eckstein of Anderson Highland High School was the Cedar Knob Knight who collides with Whit and knocks him to the floor at the beginning of the scene. Eckstein observed that the players enjoyed filming the fight scene, because for most of the day they had done "all these setup shots and hadn't really gotten a chance to run up and down the floor a lot." Eckstein's father, David, who had driven his son to the filming and had intended to watch from behind the scenes, was recruited to be the second referee.

Appearing as a benchwarmer for the Knights was IU junior Todd Baxter. He had learned about the movie's need for extras from a flyer he saw posted in his school's theater department. He and his teammates were not given specific instructions for the fight scene, other than to engage in pushing and shoving. Baxter decided to stand next to their coach so that he would be easier to spot on-screen.

After the fight, as Steve Hollar and Hackman exited the gym, the fans in the balcony pelted them with popcorn boxes and other debris. "They hit me right in the head!" Hollar exclaimed about the filming of that scene. "Somebody had good aim, because they nailed me."

Town Names: Real and Fictional

Pizzo's screenplay incorporates both actual and made-up town names. His lawyer advised him not to use the names of any schools Milan had played during the period of time depicted in the movie. Pizzo made sure to include his hometown, Bloomington, and Anspaugh's birthplace, Decatur, as Hickory opponents. In the regional game, where Ollie becomes a hero in the final seconds, Hickory plays Linton, which is near where Wade Schenck (Ollie) grew up. Terhune and Jasper are real towns. The unusual-sounding Oolitic also is genuine; it got its name from an adjective that basically means "limestone." Indiana has no Cedar Knob, but it does have a Floyds Knobs. The movie's fictional town of Deer Lick was inspired by the real town of French Lick, birthplace of NBA legend and Indiana Pacers president Larry Bird. The movie has some fun with the made-up Verdi when Norman pronounces it "*Ver*-dee" and Shooter corrects him by saying "*Vair*-dye."

Sectional Game

During the location scouting phase of production, Brownsburg real estate agent and former Chamber of Commerce president Mary

Miller had contacted the Indiana Film Commission to see if her town's former high school gym could be considered. It hadn't been used much after a new gym was built in 1957. The moviemakers agreed to tour the College Avenue gym only if their visit would be kept quiet, because they said they had been subjected to pressure in other communities. Miller asked Brownsburg's police chief, fire chief, town board president, and school superintendent to write letters to the filmmakers, expressing their interest in the movie and promising full cooperation and secrecy if their gym was chosen. Unfortunately, being selected as a *Hoosiers* location wouldn't change the building's fate. School officials had already decided to either sell the 56-year-old structure or allow it to be demolished.

The shooting of the sectional game commenced on October 21. The crew had retained the gym's purple-and-white color scheme and left the bulldog design at center court. These were the movie's first basketball scenes to be captured. The long day of running, jumping, shooting, and defending wore out the Huskers. Kent Poole told a reporter, "I was never as tired in my life as I was after Monday's filming."

The movie crew wanted to ensure that they could fill all 800 seats in the gym for the two remaining days of sectional shooting, scheduled for November 8 and 9. So on those dates they hired a bus to take New Richmond residents on the 45-mile trip to and from the filming location, about 7 miles west of Indianapolis. Those who wanted to go could expect at least a 12-hour filming day. As usual, extras were asked to wear appropriate '50s clothing and hairstyles, and they were advised to bring their own lunch and snacks. Soft drinks would be provided. They would not be paid, but prizes would be given away.

November 8 was Dennis Hopper's first day on the set. He arrived in time for the scene in which Shooter stumbles into the sectional game drunk. Because the Huskers had not been introduced to him, before cameras rolled, David Neidorf took the initiative to approach Hopper and tell him, "I'm your son."

Neidorf described the fight scene as expertly choreographed. It took half a day to complete. "I think it was fun for all of us," he said. "Boys getting to crash and break things—what could be more fun?" Neidorf noted that being shoved into the breakaway glass of the trophy case stung a bit, because even though it didn't shatter, it still got into little bits. "I had to hit that thing in the right way," he said, "so that my head wouldn't smash into the frame of it, which was real wood." He admitted to ruining one of the takes by cursing as he crashed into the case.

Sixth-grader Shane Headlee of Brownsburg, who showed up to be an extra, was acquainted with Huskers Wade Schenck, Scott Summers, and Kent Poole, as well as cheerleader Libbey Schenck. After arriving at the gym, he was given a crew cut, received a light brown sweater to wear, and was seated on the stage. This prime location made it easy for him to quickly run to the middle of the court at the game's finale, when the crowd rushed the floor. He ended up standing right in front of Hackman in the final shot as the coach held up the game ball. For a split second Shane turned and looked into the camera, even though the extras had been warned not to.

All in the Family

Terhune Tiger number 5 at the sectional was James D. "Jimbo" Rayl, son of James R. "Jimmy" Rayl, who led Kokomo to the state runner-up title in 1959. The elder Rayl, who received the Trester Award and was named Mr. Basketball, went on to play for IU, graduating in 1963. Pizzo may have had him in mind while writing the script, which mentions "Billy Rayl," the best player on Jasper's team at the regional.

Regional Game

Hickory Husker Kent Poole was eagerly anticipating returning to his home county to film the regional game shortly before Thanksgiving. The site of this matchup, the 54-year-old Memory Hall, originally the Lebanon Senior High School gym, was located about 16 miles northwest of Indianapolis. As the Huskers were progressing in their fictional tournament, the gyms were getting bigger, and assistant director Harvey Waldman was uneasy about the prospect of finding enough fans to occupy all 2,200 seats in Memory Hall. So he contacted area high schools to see if they could help provide a sufficient number of extras. But three of the filming days were weekdays, and school officials found themselves facing the same issue that arose in Knightstown—whether students should be given permission to miss class. "We [at] first turned [the filmmakers] down simply because we didn't have the right to call off school," said Western Boone High School principal Dan McClain. The State Department of Education mandated that kids could be excused from school only for an educational experience. But after consulting with an aide to Lieutenant Governor John Mutz, McClain relented—although he allowed his students to attend the filming for only part of the school day. On the first day of regional filming, about 750 high school and junior high students from Western Boone, Lebanon, and Hamilton Heights in Arcadia, along with some teachers, filled the stands. "It is really exciting for me to be able to act in front of kids from my school. I am really looking forward to this," Poole commented.

"It has really been work," Poole said of being in the movie. "Not as much physically, but mentally. We get up real early and usually work late. And that doesn't count the time it takes to learn lines and basketball plays for the next day's shoot. It's a hurry-up-and-wait situation," he continued. "We sit for hours and then all of a sudden they call us, and we have to look and act our best." He added, "Although we keep busy, I think I will have time to get away and talk with some of the students."

The spectators got to see another hometown favorite as well—Lebanon High School graduate and IU freshman Jeff Moster, number 52 on the Linton team. Moster had learned about the *Hoosiers* production from his mom, a freelance journalist who wrote about the movie for *Indianapolis Magazine*. When she found out the filmmakers were looking for some taller young men to serve as menacing opponents for Hickory in the tournament games, she helped her son secure an interview with basketball advisor Strats

Stratigos. The 6-foot-3 Moster was cast as a Linton Wildcat without having to prove his skills on the court.

As filming of the regional game neared completion, director Anspaugh had yet to choose which well-built Wildcat would try to intimidate the frightened Ollie by sneering, "Didn't know they grew 'em so small down on the farm." Moster decided to assert himself by walking up to Anspaugh and reciting the line. "They probably didn't put much thought into [who would say the line]," Moster said. "When you speak up, you get yourself the opportunity to get the nod."

All in all, Moster found the shooting sessions at Lebanon to be "long, methodical, tedious. It's not backbreaking work, but the days drag on." At the same time, he said, he was humbled to have had the opportunity to be in the movie.

In portraying the inept Ollie, Schenck needed several tries to lose the ball while dribbling. When he was shooting too well in the game-winning free-throw scene, one of the technical advisors suggested he try an awkward underhand shooting style. Schenck was "a terrific basketball player—one of the leading scorers on his high school team and arguably the best shooter among all the Huskers," Pizzo said. "It was really tough on his pride to get out there and dribble off his foot and all the things we wanted him to do."

Sitting behind the basket and taunting Ollie as he attempted his charity tosses was the opposing pep band, portrayed by kids from Southport High School in Indianapolis. Southport's fight song was used as Linton's song; it can be heard faintly in the background as the Huskers sit in the locker room before the game and also during the final time-out.

All in the Family, Part 2

Jim Rayl wasn't the only cast member with IU family connections. Husker Brad Long (Buddy) was the son of Gary Long, who played for Shelbyville before attending IU, graduating in 1961. Gary Long served as the Linton coach in the regional game. Originally he was assigned three words of dialog—"Foul the runt!" (referring to Ollie). But Long, immersed in his coaching role and excitedly running back and forth on the sidelines, didn't realize he was supposed to sit still on the bench and be filmed in close-up in order to say his line. "They just told me to act like a coach," he said. "They didn't tell me to stay on the bench." Therefore, Long unintentionally missed his big moment.

Another Husker's dad also was in the film. Bob Boyle, father of Brad Boyle (Whit), played a referee in Hickory's home opener against Oolitic.

Senior Cords

Many Indiana high schoolers in the 1950s and '60s observed the tradition of decorating and wearing senior cords. These were light yellow or cream-colored corduroy skirts and pants that seniors wore to school and games on Fridays. Students painted them with such things as images of cartoon characters and pictures representing the students' school activities and interests. Cords also could include the wearer's graduation year and nickname, friends' signatures, and a slogan or humorous saying. In *Hoosiers*, during the regional, right before Ollie enters the game, a girl in the first row of fans can be seen wearing a senior cords skirt.

While they were still in Lebanon, the filmmakers decided to shoot some nighttime footage in the downtown square to be used in the montage before the state-finals game. Rain threatened to spoil the crew's plans; the weather forecast called for an 80 percent chance of showers. They ended up filming the marquee of the 61-year-old Avon Theater, which said "Closed for big game."

Other Filming Locations

Downtown New Richmond, the Nineveh school, and the gyms weren't the only shooting sites. Several other central Indiana locations were used as well.

Opening Credits

The establishing shots during the opening credits were staged in a few different areas. Coach Dale's journey to Hickory began on U.S. 40 near Stilesville and on Montgomery County roads. A stand-in driver was used when the car was filmed from a distance. Two other opening-credits images were captured in the northeast corner of Boone County. The white barn where a couple boys were shooting hoops was located just west of Sheridan. The shot where Norman pulls over to get gas was filmed in Terhune, population 65. The crew placed two old gas pumps in front of the John & Calverts grocery store.

Probably the most striking image of the opening credits is the tiny white church amidst the cornfields, where Norman briefly stops at a rural crossroads. This 96-year-old clapboard structure was located in southern Boone County at the northeast corner of the intersection of County Roads West 600 South and South 25 West (Pittsboro Road). Built in 1889 for $640, it contained eight pews and had no plumbing. The original landowner had set aside a corner of his farmland and constructed the church for whomever wished to worship there. A 30-member Baptist congregation occupied and cared for the building but did not own it.

The Town Meeting

The 91-year-old Elizaville Baptist Church in Boone County, not far from Terhune, was the site of the referendum at which the townspeople would decide Coach Dale's future. The film crew prepared the church by painting the interior, installing sconces, and spraying the pulpit with a matte finish. The blue-green carpeting in the front was covered with red carpet, and the glass front doors were replaced with wooden doors that had glass panels. Although most members of the congregation were excited about the filming, others were concerned; they wanted to be sure their church would be returned to its original condition after the production.

The Elizaville Christian Church, just south of the Baptist Church and around the corner, served as the staging area for costuming and hairstyling and for the serving of box lunches. The approximately 40 active church members were invited to attend the two days of filming. Permanent extras from New Richmond and Knightstown, as well as nursing home residents from nearby Sheridan, were brought in to fill all of the approximately 150 seats. Senior citizen Faye Wolf said that if she weren't serving as an extra, she would be at home knitting or watching *The Guiding Light*. When asked if she liked being part of the movie, Wolf replied, "Well, I don't know. I enjoy *The Guiding Light*." For another older woman, witnessing the behind-the-scenes action spoiled for her the magic and mystery of moviemaking. "They took all the glamour out of it," she complained. A crew member replied, "It never had any, ma'am. Believe me." Others found the process more interesting. Ten-year-old Daniel Louks and a handful of other spectators hung out with the crew in the balcony and watched the filming from above.

Chelcie Ross (George), Mike Dalzell (the mayor), and Wil Dewitt (Rev. Doty) at the referendum.

The extras and actors were told where to sit. Hackman's place in the next-to-last center pew was marked with a piece of masking tape that had "Gene" written on it. Before breaks, crew members took Polaroids of the congregation to help remember where everyone was situated and how they looked to ensure continuity.

The town meeting scene, which came at the midpoint of the movie, was the first of only two scenes in which Jimmy Chitwood spoke.

This scene helped Maris Valainis discover that acting was "almost easier than being yourself." He explained, "I'm always at a loss for words, but when you have something you're supposed to say, it's easy." Teammate David Neidorf complimented Valainis's acting ability, observing that the Huskers' star hoopster conveyed a "quiet, sturdy Midwestern presence"—qualities that Neidorf himself was trying to project.

In the midst of the second long shooting day, discord arose during the rehearsal of the call for a revote. Much time passed as the filmmakers tried many different configurations of which extras should vote aye and which ones nay. Hackman became impatient and annoyed with the drawn-out deliberations and eventually attempted to wrest control of the direction from Anspaugh by dictating who should vote which way. First assistant director Herb Adelman noticed over the course of production that Anspaugh didn't let such incidents rattle him: "David kept his cool the entire time because he knew he had a terrific film on his hands."

Home Scenes

One day in September, Bob and Debbie Burns returned to their rural Hendricks County home and found a note on the door from production designer David Nichols: "We're interested in using your house in a movie. Please call...." At first they assumed it was a joke. But they ended up allowing their house to be used for the interior shots of principal Cletus Summers' house. The crew got to work undoing some of the restoration work the Burnses had completed on their 105-year-old Italianate residence. New wallpaper was put up and sprayed with dirt to make it appear old, causing the rooms to look "like when we first bought the house," Debbie Burns said. During the filming the family lived in two upstairs rooms of their 12-room house and ate out a lot. Most of their furniture was stored on a semi outside because the crew brought in different furnishings. Added Debbie Burns, "There were 135 people traipsing through my house on the rainiest, muddiest day of the year. There was trash piled up in the yard, and there were trailers outside leaving big ruts. But they made everything OK."

Debbie Burns told Nichols about a property south of Danville that would be perfect as the Fleener residence. Said homeowner Jody Whicker, "If [she] hadn't called to say David was coming, I would never have let him in the door with his story about putting my house in the movies." The home, which dated from 1847, had been in her family for four generations. Nichols called this location "a lucky find. The house is overstuffed with history, full of materials others have touched and used." He added, "I could never create out of my imagination what the Whickers have created out of living." Said Whicker, "I've always loved this house, but this production crew has left me with a genuine pride in what we have."

Two scenes were filmed in the house's kitchen. And the home's interior appeared in two additional shots as well. In the montage of images before the state-finals game, two different families are shown listening to the game on the radio. The shot with the large radio (with the Burns family as the extras) was staged in the Whickers' living room, and the shot with the smaller radio on a table (with the Whicker kids as some of the extras) was set up at the top of the stairs.

The home actually did double duty: Part of it was used as the interior of Norman's house. The rear enclosed porch was transformed into his kitchen, and the adjoining parlor became his living room.

In the scene where Shooter makes an unannounced visit to Norman's house to discuss the upcoming Cedar Knob game, initially Anspaugh disapproved of Hopper's choice of headgear. During the actor's first day on set, he had investigated the wardrobe selections and picked out a top hat. When Anspaugh saw the chapeau, an argument ensued. "I thought it was a ridiculous choice," the director said. "I felt I needed to draw the line and put my foot down. And he goes, 'No, man, this is great. This is what this guy would wear.' He was so sincere, and he said, 'David, just trust me with this.' And he talked me into trusting him."

Two more scenes were filmed outside the house. The sorghum grinding, for which the Whickers' neighbor provided the stalks that were crushed to make syrup, was shot on an unseasonably cold day.

The man who brought the horse was asked to stay and be in the scene; he fed the stalks into the mill. Norman and Myra's walking scene was to be shot on a nearby hill with a tree, but that location was too muddy. Hackman suggested that they stroll along the fencerow on the Whicker property instead. The crew had to cut away some branches and undergrowth to make room for the camera to roll on its track. Right before Hackman kissed Hershey, she stepped on a little platform to become somewhat taller.

Whicker chose not to be an extra in the home scenes; she preferred to assist the production staff by lending them, or helping them locate, whatever they needed. She donated such items as tablecloths, antiques to decorate the sets, and articles of clothing for Hershey and Fern Persons to wear in their outdoor scenes. She also helped the crew find pumpkins to pile against the pigpen on Cletus's farm. Whicker witnessed almost all of the filming. She and the Burns family also were invited to watch the dailies with the filmmakers.

The exterior shots of the Summers' property, including the principal's red-brick house, the coach's white house (which actually was a garage), and the barn, were filmed about 6 miles south of New Richmond. In the scene where Cletus and Norman discuss Jimmy Chitwood on Cletus's farm at sunset, the Liberty Chapel Church is visible in the distance as they walk toward the hog pen. The pig being fed, Arnold, belonged to David and Joan Oppy of New Richmond, who laughed at the irony that Arnold would achieve movie stardom but his owners wouldn't.

Location manager Rick Schmidlin said Shooter's house was the hardest home filming site for him to acquire, because "it was supposed to be a quirky kind of place." In fact, the script said Shooter lived in a cave in the woods. Instead of looking for a cave, Schmidlin chose an abandoned cabin on the site of the former Camp Short, located in a patch of woods in southeastern Hendricks County, off South County Road 101 East. The scene where Shooter is found unconscious in the woods was filmed in the same area.

THE SECOND HALF: FILMING CONTINUES 97

Gloria Dorson, Sheb Wooley, and Gene Hackman await the sunset scene on Cletus's farm.

Hackman and the crew prepare for the scene along the fencerow.

Hospital Scenes

One of Schmidlin's most fortuitous finds was the Wishard Nursing Museum in Indianapolis; it was the perfect location for Shooter's rehabilitation stay. The museum was set up in the lounge of the former nurses' residence at the Marion County General Hospital (later renamed Wishard Memorial) School of Nursing. When the school closed in 1980, alumni and others associated with it decided to preserve hospital artifacts, old nursing equipment, records, and documents. As a result of their efforts, the museum opened the following year.

To prepare for the scene in which Everett visits Shooter in the hospital, David Neidorf isolated himself to focus on generating the necessary emotion. On the first take, he cried a lot.

Additional Scenes

In the montage of game scenes before the Huskers play in the sectional, the caravan drives past a red barn on which two men are painting GO HUSKERS in white. This barn was south of New Richmond, on West County Road 750 North. In the series of shots of different towns the night of the state-finals game, the rain-soaked street was in Amo, in southwestern Hendricks County. The image of the sun breaking through clouds over a cornfield, shown after the state-finals game, was captured in Elizaville, scene of the town meeting. A day-long corn-harvesting scene that was omitted from the movie was filmed at the Dinsmore farm, south of Danville at West County Road 200 South and South 75 West.

Nightly Dailies

Filming in so many far-flung locations led to an exhausting production schedule. Each day the cast and crew had to get up early and drive to the filming location, shoot all day, and then drive back; but the workday wasn't over yet. After returning to Indianapolis, the filmmakers retreated to the screening room at the Ramada and reviewed the scenes that had been shot about a week before. There they watched footage until midnight or later.

The time pressure, along with director Anspaugh's tendency to internalize his anxiety, eventually took a toll. One night, while viewing the dailies, Anspaugh became so discouraged that he got up and walked out. Pizzo went to find him. Anspaugh told his friend, "We've [dreamed about] this movie for 18 years, and I think I'm screwing it up. If you want to replace me, it's OK."

> Pizzo replied, "Go to bed, and I'll see you on the set in the morning." Pizzo had faith in Anspaugh because he felt that "no one can translate to the screen what I put on paper better than David." After that night, Anspaugh said, he decided to take things just one hour at a time and one day at a time.

Returning to New Richmond

When the cast and crew came back to New Richmond at the beginning of December to wrap up a few final scenes, the weather had taken a turn for the worse. The pleasant autumn days and colorful leaves were gone as winter quickly approached. As temperatures lingered in the low double digits, those who ventured outside were buffeted by flurries and gusty winds. Luckily, the filming that took place inside Rooster's barbershop was unaffected by the weather. First up was Norman's contentious meet-and-greet with the townspeople, in a smoky scene populated by men from New Richmond. Crew members and a few onlookers crowded into the adjoining feed-and-seed store, which shared an interior doorway with the barbershop. Taped to the doorframe was a handwritten sign that said "LIVE SET." As the actors rehearsed, cinematographer Fred Murphy walked through the shop, holding up his hands in a rectangle shape to picture how the scene would be framed.

The extreme cold caused Anspaugh to change the location of the scene in which Coach Dale meets Shooter for the first time. Originally they were supposed to encounter each other on the streets of downtown Hickory, but the director decided to move the scene inside, to the diner. The painters and carpenters scrambled to have the restaurant ready for filming the next day.

Meanwhile, preparations began for the caravan scene, which could not be relocated or postponed; it had already been rescheduled from the week before due to rain. Huge banners were hung over the street. The set decorators attached gold and red crepe paper streamers to the vehicles. They also painted the vehicles and the store windows with slogans encouraging the Huskers.

The following day dawned sunny and no longer windy, but still very cold, as minor accumulations of snow lingered on the streets and sidewalks. The entire cast was needed for the scene in which the Huskers would hit the road to the state finals, followed by their loyal fans. Many extras also were present, including students from North Montgomery High School and Coal Creek Middle School. The cast and extras ducked into the downtown buildings between takes to warm up. Some of the girls wore sweatpants under their skirts until it was time for cameras to roll. One of the costumers made sure all the Huskers had long johns to wear. The catering crew offered piping-hot soup and chili. Hackman, a vegetarian, refused them because they contained beef.

Escorted by the state police and the sheriff, the caravan was composed of the Huskers' bus, the school bus, a 1935 Diamond T fire truck carrying the pep band, and vintage cars including Chevys, Fords, Packards, Hudson Hornets, DeSotos, and LaSalles. The caravan scene was filmed until dusk, and then the production moved into the diner, which was now ready for the scene with Norman, Cletus, Shooter, and Everett. Lights set up outside in front of the windows created the illusion of daytime. After they finished the scene, Hackman complimented David Neidorf by saying, "That was good; it was really simple." One more setup shot in the barbershop, showing the Huskers getting free haircuts, concluded the tiring, and final, day of filming in New Richmond.

Night is turned into day at the diner.

Wade Schenck (Ollie) sits in the barber chair as the crew are reflected in the mirror.

Byron Alexander's store carried a variety of souvenir T-shirt that said "Wherethehellis New Richmond, Ind." But the filming of *Hoosiers* had rendered these shirts obsolete. The town would never return to its state of relative anonymity.

The Reality of Living Your Dream

Years after *Hoosiers* was filmed, Pizzo reflected on how difficult it had been for him and Anspaugh to enjoy the movie-creation process. "Part of it was our lack of experience," he said. "We had not made a feature film before. There was so much we didn't know." But they were fortunate to have seasoned producer Carter DeHaven on their side. He served as a buffer between Anspaugh and Pizzo and the chaos and hid the ugly stuff from them, Anspaugh said. Pizzo described DeHaven as a suave diplomat who made it easy for them to do their jobs.

Pizzo confessed that "during this entire movie, I never had any confidence. It never, in my mind, was coming together." In fact, "every day I thought we were making a terrible movie." He wondered if anyone would care about the project that meant so much to him. Anspaugh said that during production he lost all objectivity about the movie's quality and felt like he was in a daze. And he found it increasingly hard to look ahead. However, Anspaugh wasn't completely downbeat about the film's chances of success, because, he said, "even in my numbed state I had a feeling I was seeing something I had never seen before in film."

During production, when asked whether he thought *Hoosiers* would be a hit, Hackman had stayed positive when being interviewed. "It's not just an Indiana story," he told a reporter in 1985. "Basketball is popular all over the United States. If Indiana was the only place they played it, I might be a little concerned." But privately, he had expressed doubts to his costars. Maris Valainis overheard Hackman compare *Hoosiers* to the notorious big-budget flop *Heaven's Gate*. According to Pizzo, Hackman called *Hoosiers* a career-killer. Recalling the production, Hopper commented, "I remember sitting down with [Hackman], and Gene remarked, 'What are we doing here?' No movie about basketball had ever made money." The two lead actors also had been perplexed at the amount of time being devoted to "all those damned basketball games," Hopper said. "We were saying, 'Here's the big money. Why aren't you shooting *us*?'" But Hopper said he could see that *Hoosiers* was a work of love because of Anspaugh and Pizzo's obvious commitment to making a really good movie about their home state and its residents. The filmmakers appreciated the actor's moral support. "Hopper was our champion, our defender," Pizzo said. Commented Anspaugh, "A lot of actors don't realize how stressful and ridiculously difficult it is to direct." But because Hopper had worked as a director, Anspaugh said, "Dennis had that respect for me and Angelo."

* * *

Although navigating the production of their first feature film wasn't easy, Pizzo and Anspaugh were grateful for the kindness, cooperation, and dedication shown by the townspeople in all the filming locations. "The local community and state support have been extraordinary," Pizzo enthused. "We would never have been able to pull the film off if it weren't for fellow Hoosiers believing in what we were doing." With weeks of shooting behind them in early December, the moviemakers now faced the filming of the most complex scenes—those of the state-finals game. Again they would call upon regular Hoosiers for assistance. But this time, they would need the help of thousands.

6
The Last Shot: Filming Winds Down

"I think you'll find it's the exact same measurements as our gym in Hickory." —Coach Dale

In *Hoosiers* and for decades in real life, state-finals games were played at Hinkle Fieldhouse on the campus of Butler University in Indianapolis. The Fieldhouse could be considered Indiana's roundball palace. When it was built in 1928, it was the second-largest basketball arena in the U.S. (behind Madison Square Garden), and it retained that distinction for more than 20 years. Originally named Butler Fieldhouse, the facility hosted the state boys' basketball finals from 1928 to 1971. It was renamed in 1966 to honor Tony Hinkle, who coached at Butler for 41 seasons, ending in 1970.

Construction of the Fieldhouse was financed by 41 prominent Indianapolis businessmen. Its completion was guaranteed when Butler signed a lease agreement with the Indiana High School Athletic Association (IHSAA) stating that the basketball finals would be played in the massive new gymnasium.

In 1928, Butler University had 2,800 students. "To have a 15,000-seat arena, it's certainly making a statement about what the game means to the people of Indiana, what Tony Hinkle's position was, and where the university wanted to position itself on the national map," said Todd Gould, who filmed a documentary about the building.

The Fieldhouse was designed to give Butler one of the finest athletic facilities in the nation. The arched steel truss system supporting the roof eliminated posts or pillars that might block spectators' views. It also was the first arena to use a ramp system leading to the upper-level seats.

Playing at Butler Fieldhouse "was the ultimate," said Indiana basketball legend Oscar Robertson. "I mean, man! Just to be able to play at

Butler Fieldhouse, get on the court. You heard so much about it, and you know, I thought it was mystical. It's like going to heaven to get on [that] court and play a basketball game." Anspaugh symbolized the reverence with which the Huskers regarded the Fieldhouse by having them and their coach remove their shoes before stepping onto the playing floor for the first time.

Also in this scene, Coach Dale produces a tape measure and has the team members take a couple measurements to remind them that the Fieldhouse court has the same dimensions as their home gym. The actions depicted in this scene, a favorite of fans, didn't happen in real life to the Milan Indians; they were Anspaugh's idea. Years before the filming of *Hoosiers*, during a visit back to Indiana from California, Anspaugh had sneaked into the empty Fieldhouse, made his way to the top far corner of bleachers, sat down, and surveyed the cavernous space. He imagined what it would be like for a small-town team to walk in and feel dwarfed by the gigantic gymnasium.

In the Fieldhouse's practice gym, the crew built a replica of a small portion of the Brownsburg gym, site of the sectional game. It consisted of seven rows of purple-and-white bleachers, the Huskers' bench, and the scorers' table. The camera rolled from side to side on a track, capturing close-ups of Coach Dale pacing the sidelines as the fans clapped and cheered. Anspaugh and key second assistant director Harvey Waldman ran back and forth behind the camera, acting as stand-ins for the basketball players and indicating where the fans should be looking.

In the Locker Room

Before the Huskers take the floor for the championship game, Coach Dale reviews with them the game plan in the locker room. The blackboard displays the last names of the South Bend Central Bears—which are actually the Huskers' real-life names. From top to bottom are written Boyle, Schenck, Hollar, Long, Poole, and Valainis. To the left of this list, the name Scott (as in Summers) also is visible, as is part of a name that looks like "Nydorf." This spontaneous tribute to the young actors was Hackman's idea; the opposing players had different names in the script.

Another change from the original screenplay involved Shooter and had personal importance to Dennis Hopper. Pizzo had written what he envisioned as a happy ending for the character. Instead of forcing Shooter to miss the state-finals game, one of the most meaningful moments of his life, Pizzo had him escape from the hospital rehabilitation ward and unexpectedly walk into the locker room at the end of the pregame huddle. But Hopper, a recovered addict in real life, was convinced that this plot point sent the wrong message. The actor told Pizzo and Anspaugh "if we wanted to believe Shooter is committed to sobriety, then we had to keep him in the hospital," Anspaugh said. Hopper explained, "Being an alcoholic, I felt that it was really destructive to have Shooter leave [rehab]. Maybe he'll never get sober, but he ain't going to get sober if he goes to that game." The filmmakers ultimately agreed. "Angelo and I fought it pretty hard at first," Anspaugh said, "but he was dead-on right."

The Fieldhouse had changed so little since the 1950s that the crew didn't have to make many modifications. The free-throw lanes were narrowed from 12 feet to 6. The space for a third digit was removed from the scoreboards. The uppermost bleachers were obscured with black cloth on a frame, and the large four-sided electronic scoreboard hanging from the ceiling was covered also. Fortuitously, the university generously declined to charge for use of the Fieldhouse, instead settling for a mention in the movie's closing credits.

Hinkle Hassles

Anspaugh and Pizzo allocated four nights, December 4 through 7, Wednesday through Saturday, to film Hickory's triumphant state-finals victory. They hoped to pack the Fieldhouse to the rafters with fans each night. But they figured they could make the gym look completely full even with only half the seats occupied. The group of

New Richmond permanent extras would help by being present all four nights, earning $113 for their efforts.

A press conference was held on Monday, December 2 to publicize the shooting of the final game and the need for extras. Casting assistant Debby Shively spent Wednesday morning on a radio show, talking about the upcoming filming at Hinkle, and that afternoon she called every school in central Indiana. Flyers and newspaper articles before and on the first day of filming urged people to turn out to be extras. They were encouraged to wear 1950s clothing, although some costumes would be provided. Those who wore team colors—either red and gold for Hickory or royal blue and white for South Bend Central—would have a better chance of sitting close to the floor, in camera range. Filming would take place from 5 p.m. to midnight each of the four nights. Celebrity guests would appear, and entertainment would be offered during breaks in the filming. Prizes including stereos, VCRs, TVs, cash, and tickets to a John Cougar Mellencamp concert would be awarded. And a drawing would be held to give away the grand prize—Coach Dale's 1951 Chevy coupe. Producer Carter DeHaven said the production crew assumed that so many extras would show up that some would actually have to be turned away. But to the filmmakers' dismay, only a couple hundred people materialized the first two nights.

"One second, everything I'd worked for was all finished." —*Coach Dale*

Anspaugh recalled the first evening of Hinkle filming: "Angelo came into my trailer and said, 'I don't think you want to go in the gym.' There were, like, 250 people, tops. And we literally sat on the floor. It was like, well, there goes the movie." Pizzo remarked, "We thought our careers were over, that the movie was done, all that work for nothing." Crowd member Jody Whicker attempted to boost Pizzo and Anspaugh's spirits by holding up a large sign that said "Andy, David, keep the faith." Filming went on as planned, but with some adjustments. The few extras were crammed into a small space for tight shots; even those who were supposed to be playing reporters instead became fans for those setups. The sparse crowd had to be moved around to accommodate the different tight camera angles. Close-ups of the newspapermen and broadcasters sitting on press row, and photographers snapping pictures, also were captured.

> ### Star-Spangled Singers
>
> Performing the national anthem were the Travel-Aires, a country-music quartet from Kirklin who sang mainly at fairs and festivals. Twins Darrin and Dennis Lafferty, Kenny Jobe, and Kent Kercheval had been invited to the state-finals filming to provide vocal entertainment during breaks. They also had done so at the regional game. The script didn't mention a performance of "The Star-Spangled Banner," but, said Dennis Lafferty, "We kept putting [the idea] in a lot of people's heads. Pizzo said it sounded like a good idea, but he didn't know if they had time to work it in." The group was surprised and excited when, without warning, they were summoned from the stands to sing the anthem. After being costumed in white shirts, black bow ties, and black pants, the four young men took to the floor and nailed their rendition on the first try. Said Darrin Lafferty, "[The filmmakers] had never heard us sing 'The Star-Spangled Banner' until that time." The moviemakers were so impressed that during postproduction they asked the Travel-Aires to record the spiritual "Do Lord" as background music for the movie. This song was heard on the team bus radio as the Huskers traveled to the Cedar Knob game.

The filmmakers tried to come up with ways to attract more extras to the remaining two nights of filming. Newspapers helped by printing articles on Thursday and Friday that again asked people to show up. A driver hopped into Coach Dale's 1951 Chevy and took to the streets. The car had "Be an EXTRA!" posters taped to its sides, and it was equipped with a public address system so that information about the Hinkle filming could be broadcast. But a crane operator working on the film came up with an even better idea. He suggested that, to draw a large crowd, they get two local high school teams to play a game at the Fieldhouse on Friday. Filming could take place at halftime and after the game. An assistant to Lieutenant Governor

John Mutz called the coaches of Broad Ripple and Chatard, Maris Valainis's alma mater, and persuaded them to move their game scheduled for that night to Hinkle. The producers pledged to donate $1 to each fan's favorite charity, club, organization, or school, which the fans would designate by writing the group's name on the back of their tickets. These strategies worked, as more than 5,000 people came to the Fieldhouse on Friday.

They waited in long lines for wardrobe and for haircuts courtesy of students from the National Barber College of Indianapolis. Extras who had arrived dressed appropriately were checked over by the costuming assistants to make sure they weren't wearing modern jewelry, watches, or glasses. Women were asked to remove any makeup.

Cletus (Sheb Wooley), Millie (Gloria Dorson), Rev. Doty (Wil Dewitt), and Preacher Purl (Michael Sassone), along with cheerleader Nancy Harris, root for the Huskers at state.

The filming didn't cease during the real high school basketball game. The crew used that time to gather reaction shots from the crowd. During the game's extended halftime, the Huskers and Bears were run ragged, filming without a break and without following a game plan or choreographed plays. Assistant director Herb Adelman said they did a day's work within a half hour. At the conclusion of the real game, the moviemakers implored the fans to stay for the rest of the night's shooting. With so many more extras the third and fourth nights, the camera angles could finally be wider. However, a planned panorama shot of a full Fieldhouse had to be scrapped. A camera placed on a platform and raised by a crane was used to photograph the fans sitting higher up. Assistant director Harvey Waldman exhorted the 32 rows of extras to cheer by jumping, pumping his fist, and waving his arms.

Waldman (in white shirt and vest) solicits cheers as the camera platform rises above him on a long arm.

Director Anspaugh listens in on the final huddle as photographers snap pictures.

The filmmakers later learned that there were various reasons why not many people turned out the first two nights. Some had work or school the next day and didn't want to stay up past midnight. Another factor might have been an unfortunate wording choice in the press release about the final game that was sent to the media. Several newspapers reported, "The only requirement for being an extra is to come dressed in early 1950s fashion." More people might have shown up if they had known that wearing period clothing was advised but not actually required. The costumers had many pieces of clothing and pairs of shoes available for the extras—just not enough to outfit the 8,000 people or more they originally thought might walk through the doors.

Cameos

Some notable Hoosiers had minor roles in the state-finals scenes. Ray Craft, a starting guard on the 1954 Milan Miracle team who became an assistant commissioner for the IHSAA, appeared twice. He played the official who welcomed the Huskers to Butler Fieldhouse, and in the locker room scene, he told them it was time to take the floor. Indianapolis mayor William Hudnut played a photographer. The public-address announcer was Tom Carnegie, the longtime PA announcer at the Indianapolis Motor Speedway and the state basketball finals. Well-known sports broadcaster Hilliard Gates served as the play-by-play announcer—just as he had done at the 1954 state finals and for many years afterward. Anspaugh wanted Gates to be in the movie, he said, because "To me, Hilliard Gates is the voice of the Indiana basketball tournament."

Ray Crowe, former coach of the storied Indianapolis Crispus Attucks Tigers, and Bailey Robertson, an Attucks player in the early 1950s, portrayed the coaches of the South Bend Central Bears. Attucks was a basketball powerhouse in the '50s. Under Crowe's leadership they became state champs in 1955 and 1956 and were state finalists in 1951 and 1957. Attucks won an additional state title under second-year coach Bill Garrett in 1959. Pizzo explained that casting Crowe and Robertson was "an homage to that legendary team."

Player number 45 on the South Bend team was portrayed by Indianapolis native Richard Robinson, who had played a couple years for the IUPUI Metros. He was a 1981 graduate of John Marshall High School, where he was coached by 1954 Milan team member Roger Schroder. He auditioned for his role in *Hoosiers* after one of his friends heard on the radio that the producers were looking for minority basketball players for the final game. Before the filming, the tall Bears were briefed on their style of play. They were instructed not to block shots or jump too high when defending against the shorter Huskers—a restriction the 6-foot-5 Robinson found difficult to follow.

The Final Game: Run and Gun, Not Stall Ball

The last game in the movie unfolds differently than the real-life 1954 state championship game did. The game in the movie is fast and physical, and the two teams fight it out to the finish, with Hickory winning on a last-second shot. In the real game, the pace slowed down as play progressed, with 25 total points scored in the first quarter, 15 in the second, 12 in the third, and only 10 in the fourth. In fact, the action practically ground to a halt in the last quarter. In those days a player was allowed to

> hold the ball—without dribbling, passing, or even moving—for as long as he wanted to. And Milan coach Marvin Wood decided to employ this very strategy in the game against the Muncie Central Bearcats.
>
> This was the second game of the day for both teams, and Wood feared his boys were running out of steam. The fourth quarter began with the Indians and Bearcats tied at 26, but Muncie quickly scored. Only half a minute into the quarter, Milan began stalling—passing but not moving toward the basket. With 5½ minutes to go and Milan still down by 2, Bobby Plump proceeded to hold the ball for just over 2 minutes. When he finally attempted a shot, he missed, but soon another Milan player tied the score. Then Plump was fouled, and he made both free throws to give the Indians a 2-point lead. But Muncie tied the score with 45 seconds left. Again Plump held the ball, until 18 seconds remained, and then Milan called a time-out. In the huddle, Coach Wood told Plump to take the last shot. With only 5 seconds to go, he drove toward the basket and hit the shot that lifted Milan to victory.

"I'll make it." —*Jimmy*

As the Friday night rehearsals progressed, Maris Valainis (Jimmy) kept missing as he attempted his game-winning shot. Because he had never been on a high school basketball team, playing in front of a multitude was an unfamiliar experience, and his nerves were getting the best of him. When Valainis would miss, the audience would groan with disappointment. Assistant director Harvey Waldman reminded the fans that, because they were being filmed, they were always to react as if the shot went in. He told them, "Remember, folks, this is the movies. Even when he doesn't make it, he makes it."

Growing impatient with Valainis's missed shots, Hackman suggested that Anspaugh have the cager move closer to the basket to take his final shot, instead of insisting that he shoot from the same spot where Plump did. Anspaugh usually was open to hearing Hackman's advice, he said, because it came from a creative place, not because the actor was intentionally creating conflict. But this time Anspaugh overruled Hackman. He thought to himself, "[Maris is] already shaky in terms of his confidence. If I tell him [to move closer], he'll think that I've seen him miss, then he'll think that I don't believe in him." So he had Valainis stay in the same shooting position. Right before the triumphant final field goal was to be captured on film, casting director Ken Carlson approached the player. He told him he'd noticed that Valainis hadn't been looking at the basket when shooting.

Anspaugh's faith in Valainis and Carlson's advice to keep his eyes on the hoop paid off. "When we got the cameras rolling and the extras on their feet," the director said, "first take, *boom*, nothing but net." Behind the scenes, said assistant director Adelman, he and Anspaugh were jumping up and down so much that they made the camera shake. Anspaugh described the eruptions of celebration on the court and in the stands as "pure, unbridled hysteria and joy" because the fans had been rooting for Valainis to make the shot in real life.

Valainis remarked, "It felt like I had just won the state championship." Even better, he had done so in front of the Chatard coach who cut him from his high school's preseason varsity tryouts three years in a row. Brad Long agreed with Valainis that it seemed as though his team had just won a real state title. "That's the closest I've been to seeing what it feels like to be in Hinkle in an actual game, and it felt real," he said. "It didn't feel like you were making a movie. I never got to experience it in real life. I got to experience it as a bit player in the movie." Although Steve Hollar maintained that winning a real-life state tournament was "100 times better" than filming a fictional championship, upon watching the movie's final bucket go in, "I got lost in the moment, and it was close. Both events really sent chills up my back."

Interestingly, the screenplay didn't describe Jimmy's making the last field goal, or anything that happened right afterward. As the scene was written, the ball arcs toward the rim, and the faces of the main characters are shown in quick succession. Then we're back in the empty Hickory gym months later, slowly zooming in on the large team photo captioned "Indiana State Champs 1952." Pizzo said he wrote those last two scenes as a way to avoid ending the film with "the cliché of the winning basket." But Anspaugh decided to keep the cameras rolling after Jimmy's final shot. The result was an incredibly real reaction, he said, adding, "That's part of the beauty of shooting a scene like that in Indiana."

Going into Overtime in Knightstown

Because they had fallen a bit behind schedule, the cast and crew needed to return to Knightstown to shoot a final home game, against Holland, after the Fieldhouse filming. This time students from Morton Memorial High School, located at the Soldiers' and Sailors' Children's Home in Knightstown, populated the stands.

Throughout the movie's production, Anspaugh and Pizzo had been fortunate enough not to have studio executives hanging around, questioning their decisions. But near the end of the shoot they came under pressure from the bonding company (the film production guarantor), which intended to ensure that the production would not overrun its schedule or budget. Demonstrating confidence in the filmmakers, executive producer John Daly decided to allow shooting to go on for a few extra days, even though doing so would cost additional money.

Anspaugh, Pizzo, and Waldman talk things over in Knightstown.

> **Keeping the Title**
>
> Although everyone in Indiana knows what a Hoosier is, execuvives at Hemdale and Orion disliked the movie's title because the term Hoosier is not widely known outside the state. They fretted that an obscure title would not pull in moviegoers. Pizzo complained that the executives were waging "a vociferous and unrelenting campaign against the *Hoosiers* title." Ever since Hemdale and Orion had agreed to produce and distribute the movie, they had been proposing alternative titles, including *The Last Shot*. But Pizzo wouldn't back down. "I'm going to fight for it all the way. I like it," he said. "I think in some ways [the title] may be [the movie's] strength rather than its weakness." As filming drew to a close, producer Carter DeHaven said, "We're 90 percent sure of keeping [the title] now. I think if we can build a campaign around what is a Hoosier and do something very clever with it and use the word to our advantage, I think we could sell it."

* * *

During the last days of production, Anspaugh and Pizzo took a moment to reflect on their work of the past few weeks. "If Andy's happy and I'm reasonably happy," Anspaugh said, "and the people who have worked on this film are proud of what we've done, and if the people of Indiana like it, then I couldn't ask for more."

7

The Final Cut: Editing, First Screenings, and Marketing Strategy

"I don't think I can cut it!" —*Shooter*
"You can cut it!" —*Coach Dale*

As soon as filming was completed, Pizzo had planned to relax and recover on a Hawaiian vacation. But he was too exhausted to go. The end of production in mid-December also left him disoriented. Making *Hoosiers* had been an insulating experience, he said, like residing on a cruise ship for a few weeks, and then suddenly it was over. Pizzo was depressed as well, because the tension and energy that had been their fuel were gone. Anspaugh felt physically and emotionally spent, as if he had just returned from war. But those feelings didn't last. At the beginning of 1986, the film's editors got to work assembling the footage into a rough cut, and they needed input from the director and writer/producer.

Even though Pizzo had deleted several scenes from the script during filming, the first cut of the movie still ran 3 hours and 15 minutes. When Anspaugh saw this initial version, his first impression was "It's too damn long. And boy, is this boring. People will be walking out in droves."

There was another issue as well. Film distributor Orion dictated that the movie's running time be no more than 2 hours. A longer running time would mean the film would be shown in theaters fewer times in a day, thus decreasing profits. So Anspaugh and Pizzo were forced to eliminate many scenes—something they did with much regret. "Those were painful cuts," said Pizzo. "It's never pleasant to cut anything out, especially in a movie that has turned out like this," Anspaugh said. "So much of it is so good. There's so much wonderful material in the film that has to be truncated, compressed, if not taken out of the film entirely. It's a really difficult experience. We know we can't release a film that runs 3 hours. You just have to be very careful and selective."

Anspaugh said that he and Pizzo screened the movie together and exchanged ideas and were pretty much in agreement about the scenes that should go. He added, "Maybe editing hurts Andy more than me." As a TV director, he had "experienced too many times where you set up a lovely shot, a wonderful scene, but when it comes down to it, that may not be the scene that advances the story."

Pizzo realized that he should have done some editing during the writing stage. "As a producer, I wasn't strict enough with myself as a writer," he said. "I should've cut the movie while it was still in script form." While writing, he had assumed it's better to have more to choose from than not enough. He was disappointed about being unable to retain every scene. He had "kind of lost track of what I [originally] thought the film would be like," he commented. "Putting together a film is such a long and involved process that after a while it takes on its own shape and definition." He had discovered that "once you've written a script, you have to let go. When you get the director, cinematographer, and art director involved, everyone brings some new ideas." However, the differences between his original vision and the finished film were significant enough to make him vow, "I will never produce my own script again. There are certain decisions I have to make as producer that don't make the writing side of me happy."

Differences in the Screenplay Versus the Movie

Pizzo's original script differed from the finished film in many ways:

- The screenplay describes Coach Dale as having worked at a steel mill for 12 years instead of serving in the Navy.
- The team is called the Cornhuskers.

- The previous year's squad had 12 players. After the former coach died, three transferred to Sunville (called Terhune in the movie), and two quit the team.

- Several of the players are mouthy and sarcastic. When Norman tells them at the first practice, "I'll be learning from you," Rade snaps, "I ain't no teacher!", and the others laugh. (Pizzo said he didn't want to portray the Huskers as sweet, innocent farm boys.)

- In the coach's class one day, a couple boys are absent. A student tells Norman they are at home digging postholes: "Fence got tore up. Cattle's gettin' out." Norman, who doesn't find this an acceptable reason to miss school, rolls his eyes.

- Cletus and Opal, two of Norman's early and most loyal supporters in the movie, take Norman to task for what they see as his stance of superiority toward the townspeople and their way of life. They warn him that the residents have noticed his bad attitude.

- Cletus's father, nicknamed The General, lives in another house on the Summers' property. The General hasn't left his house in two years, after getting into an argument with Cletus. Near the end of the story The General surprises the entire town by showing up at the caravan in downtown Hickory that is about to leave for the state finals.

- Instead of having a heart attack, Cletus falls off a ladder in his barn and breaks his leg.

- Jimmy has a brother named JP. Before Jimmy rejoins the team, one evening he and his brother are involved in a pickup truck accident. Norman and the Huskers come across the crash on their way to an out-of-town game. Jimmy suffers only a cut over his eye, but JP is more seriously injured. Norman volunteers to drive JP to the hospital and thus ends up missing the game.

> - Jimmy, not Myra, finds the incriminating newspaper article about Coach Dale. It's implied that he tells Myra about it.

For Anspaugh, who collaborated with film editors Tim O'Meara and Frank Urioste, the editing process was tedious and long, but fun. They never wanted to let go of it. Cinematographer Fred Murphy called O'Meara "a terrific editor, and very helpful and understanding in helping make *Hoosiers* work." The decision to condense many of the games into montages, Murphy said, "actually propelled the story in a terrific way that wouldn't have happened if we had shown all the basketball games [in their entirety]."

Fewer Tournament Games

The movie shows the Huskers playing only three tournament games on their way to capturing the state crown. But real Indiana basketball teams faced many more rivals than that, at four levels of tournament play—sectional, regional, semifinal, and state. Pizzo omitted the semifinal in the screenplay, he explained, because "there's enough basketball in the film, and, to people outside Indiana, it doesn't matter anyway."

The 1954 Milan Indians played three times as many tournament games as the Huskers. It took them nine victories to win the state title—three at the sectional, and two each at the regional, semifinal, and state. At those latter three levels, the Indians faced their first opponent in a late-morning or early-afternoon game. Then, after only a few hours of rest, they squared off against the winner of the other daytime game in the final that night.

At one point Hoosier rocker John Cougar Mellencamp was considered as the soundtrack composer. But the singer, whose hits included "Hurts So Good," "Jack & Diane," and "Small Town," had never written movie music. Also, the filmmakers wanted a sound that reflected the early '50s, Pizzo said. Furthermore, Mellencamp was probably too much of a rebel to be able to relate to the movie. "John never played basketball," Pizzo explained. "He was one of those kids who hated kids with letter jackets."

Even though the filmmakers supposed that their limited budget would preclude them from hiring a well-known soundtrack composer, producer Carter DeHaven nevertheless took a chance and approached prolific, award-winning TV and film scorer Jerry Goldsmith. "They didn't think they had the money for me when they started the picture," Goldsmith said. "Down the line when they finished, they realized they had something special, and they came to me." He said he often composed for "action, epic pictures; the small, intimate pictures I never seem to get." But his favorite kind of movie to work on was a movie with relationships, he said, because "the challenge of those pictures is trying to get the emotion into them."

Goldsmith agreed to view a rough cut of *Hoosiers*. DeHaven, Anspaugh, and Pizzo were present at the showing, observing from the back of the theater. "We didn't watch one foot of the movie," Anspaugh said. "We just kept watching Jerry to see his reaction. He never moved a muscle." Pizzo feared maybe Goldsmith had fallen asleep. At the picture's conclusion, the composer remained seated and silent, and the filmmakers assumed the worst. "Let's go; he's embarrassed," Anspaugh thought. "He doesn't want to say anything. We better get out of here and let him make a graceful exit." Then Goldsmith turned around, and they saw he was in tears. "You knew I'd fall for this movie," he said to DeHaven accusingly. Goldsmith ended up creating a soundtrack for *Hoosiers* that combined synthesizers and electronic instruments with traditional orchestral music. Said Pizzo, "We got a score that I think is extraordinary. [Goldsmith] captured a certain heartland quality—a Coplandesque feel—a symphonic score with a folk flavor."

Another part of the postproduction work involved looping—rerecording certain lines of dialog to improve their clarity or to change an inflection and thus create a cleaner voice track. Before Hackman came in for his looping session, he viewed a rough cut of the film for the first time. Given the difficulties Anspaugh and Pizzo had experienced with the actor during production, they were apprehensive about Hackman's reaction to the rough cut. But when he walked into the recording studio and asked, "How in the hell did you do that?", the director and writer/producer knew the movie had earned the lead performer's stamp of approval.

They Cheered and Laughed: The Test Screening

After trimming and deleting scenes during the editing process, Anspaugh and Pizzo had gotten the film's running time down to 2 hours and 12 minutes. Although Orion executives were displeased that the movie was still over 2 hours long, this was the version that Anspaugh wanted to test before an audience. A mall theater in Costa Mesa, California, was selected to host the first screening of *Hoosiers*. This Orange County city 37 miles southeast of Los Angeles was chosen because its population closely matched the age and race statistics of average moviegoers nationwide. The night before the June 24 showing was a sleepless one for Pizzo. If things didn't go well, he knew his first movie could also be his last. At the screening, Pizzo and Anspaugh sat in the back and waited anxiously to see how the test audience of 500 viewers, 70 percent of whom were younger than 20, would react. They were skeptical that youthful suburban surfer types would be able to relate to a film about the heartland in the 1950s.

"I think it's gonna work out." —Cletus

Much to the filmmakers' relief, the sneak preview went spectacularly well. The viewers cheered, laughed, stomped, and yelled, and gave the film a standing ovation. "The audience went nuts, and I went 'Wow!'" said Pizzo. "It wasn't until [that moment] that I realized what we had." Some of the audience members "noted how refreshing *Hoosiers* was," he added. "They said they rarely see films like it anymore." How could the writer/producer account for such an enthusiastic response to the movie whose quality he had doubted? During production, Pizzo explained, the filmmakers don't know how the film will come together in the cutting room or what the audience's experience will be. "Sometimes, magic happens," he said simply.

Hoosiers scored the highest preview rating in the history of Orion Pictures. "David and I were lucky in that we got to make the film we wanted to make," Pizzo observed. If the screening had gone badly, the studio could have demanded that the film be re-edited. Based on the test audience's overwhelmingly positive reaction, Pizzo hoped for "a first-class release" in 500 to 700 theaters. One question resurfaced, however—the movie's title. Of the 20 audience members selected for a discussion after the showing, nine didn't know what a Hoosier was. Pizzo had been telling Orion he was open to a title change if someone could come up with something better. The distributor finally gave in and agreed to go with the title *Hoosiers*. But in return, Orion asked the filmmakers to go back and trim more scenes, until the running time was less than 2 hours.

Changing Release Dates: Distribution and Marketing Strategies

When plans to film *Hoosiers* were first announced, its target release date was summer or fall of 1986. This was still the intent in February 1986, as the film was being edited. "We're working furiously to put this thing together," Anspaugh had commented. But experienced film producer Carter DeHaven understood the importance of choosing just the right date for a movie's premiere, as well as promoting it sufficiently. "The thing is, there's no guarantee of success," he said. "You could have the best script in the world and [your movie] could still fail because of bad marketing or timing."

After the triumphant California preview in June, the release was tentatively set for September 26. A little later, the premiere was moved to October. This was fine with Pizzo, who disclosed that the film's creators "had always sought a fall release because it seemed to fit the tone of the film more." But by late August, plans had changed again. "We are holding back on the film because, at this late date, we would not be able to maximize the publicity campaign," said Robert

Cheren, president of marketing for Orion Pictures. "It is in the best interests of the film, in terms of public awareness, that we wait until January." Pizzo agreed with this adjustment. "I'm pleased with the opening in January because I was worried we would not give this thing a fair shot and that we would have a problem getting it in the right amount of theaters ... [and] in good theaters, too, if we went in December," he said. Delaying the premiere until the first part of 1987 ensured that *Hoosiers* would not get lost in the annual Christmastime crush of blockbusters and family-oriented films.

"In the movie business, one thing that we never put in ink is the release date," said Fred Skidmore, vice president of publicity and promotion for Orion's Los Angeles office. "We don't know in advance what other films we may be up against, and that sort of thing. We always tell the film companies that we distribute for that we can *think* about a release date, but it can, and probably will, change."

Two weeks later, Indiana residents found out they wouldn't have to wait as long as they thought to see the film. Orion announced that *Hoosiers* would be released throughout the state on November 14, before being rolled out nationally. Orion hoped that people would flock to theaters to see *Hoosiers* over the four-day Thanksgiving holiday—the biggest moviegoing weekend of the year.

Pizzo asserted that a successful Indiana premiere was crucial because, even though Orion had a contractual agreement with Hemdale to release the film, Orion executives didn't believe in *Hoosiers*. He got this impression when Joel Resnick, chairman of Orion Distribution, remarked that Orion wanted to test *Hoosiers* to see how it would perform. "Obviously, the most favorable market for this picture is Indiana, so we decided to open it there," Resnick said. Pizzo was sure that Orion was ready to pull the film from theaters and cancel the national opening if Hoosier moviegoers didn't turn out that first week.

And even if *Hoosiers* did do well in Indiana, Pizzo said, Orion's marketing people were unconvinced that they could sell the movie to the rest of the country. He felt there was tremendous doubt about *Hoosiers*' ability to sustain interest outside Indiana and that Orion didn't want to spend millions on a national advertising campaign unless it was certain *Hoosiers* would be a hit everywhere. But Pizzo was confident that his motion picture could succeed on a national scale: "This is a movie about positive values, personal redemption, friendship, family, and community strength. You don't have to know anything about Indiana or basketball to appreciate that."

Orion's Modus Operandi

Hoosiers was not the first Orion film to be subjected to lukewarm marketing support and a wait-and-see attitude. In October 1984, Orion had allocated only enough money for a first-weekend push for *The Terminator*. The distributor figured that word-of-mouth marketing would take care of the movie after that. The lack of marketing support occurred in spite of (or perhaps because of) the film's strong test screening in front of a largely teenage audience. *The Terminator* grossed $38 million but likely could have done much better with more extensive advertising. Its 1991 sequel, *Terminator 2: Judgment Day*, grossed $204 million. Ultimately, the original *Terminator* spawned four sequels and a TV series, along with video games, toys, action figures, and collectibles. Orion cofounder Mike Medavoy noted, "Orion spent less money marketing its films during the '80s than other studios did. Our publicity department was small and not very effective."

Near the end of 1986, Orion employed a different money-saving marketing plan for another of its films. Oliver Stone's semiautobiographical Vietnam War drama *Platoon* was released in a small number of theaters on December 19 and immediately garnered positive reviews, just as Orion executives had expected. Opening before the year was out made *Platoon* eligible for Golden Globe and Academy Award nominations for 1986. Orion began *Platoon*'s national rollout slowly, starting with only 74 theaters on January 9. Throughout that month the film gathered steam, playing in more theaters each week. At the end of January, *Platoon* was the number-one film for the week. It

> stayed in the top five until early April. Ultimately, Orion's review-based marketing campaign for *Platoon*, which had a $6 million budget, resulted in box office profits of over $137 million. *Platoon* also cleaned up at the awards ceremonies. It was nominated for four Golden Globes and collected three, and it was nominated for eight Academy Awards and won four, including Best Picture and Best Director.

Sneak Previews for the National Press

In early October, sneak previews were held for a handful of movie critics. The resulting reviews were the first national publicity for the film. Pizzo trusted that positive early notices would help Orion begin to support *Hoosiers*. He wasn't interested to learn what critics thought about his freshman effort so much as he wanted *Hoosiers* to receive publicity that would help its marketing campaign. The filmmakers also hoped to cull some complimentary quotes that could be placed on the movie's poster.

Writing for trade paper *The Hollywood Reporter*, Henry Sheehan was unabashedly critical: "It's a thin line between bigger than life and less than believable, and it's a line that's crossed early on.... What could have been an engaging tapestry of Americana is blown up into ungainly mythic proportions.... [The filmmakers] seem more concerned with concocting a legend than creating psychologically plausible characters, and every possible line of development is subordinated to the beatification of the basketball team. Oddly, we find out little about them except that they have a date with destiny." Because he thought "there is little here for an audience to root for or identify with," Sheehan grimly predicted that "box office potential appears limited." Todd McCarthy of the trade paper *Variety* disagreed, writing that *Hoosiers* "will have to be groomed carefully, but there is likely an audience in Middle America for this solid, upbeat fare." He went on to call the movie "both rousing and too conventional" because "a carefully calibrated, closely observed character study of a driven man and his charges becomes a well-made but standard-issue sports yarn about the triumph of an underdog."

A capsule review in *Playboy* was a split decision. Awarding *Hoosiers* two bunnies out of four, Bruce Williamson said that "damned near running away with the picture is Dennis Hopper in a dynamic performance" and that "it's a notable achievement to steal a scene from Hackman." On the other hand, Williamson said, the film "is handicapped by familiarity more than anything else, despite all the local color soaked up by director David Anspaugh." A one-paragraph summary in *McCall's* was mostly positive, saying that "*Hoosiers* doesn't go far enough into the full dimensions of Hackman's rage, but it's still an acute study of a certain kind of man." The review in *Seventeen* raved that *Hoosiers* was "legendary" and "a real sleeper" that proved "there's no such thing as a cliché in the hands of real talent."

Gene Siskel on the TV show *Siskel & Ebert* complained that the film was too predictable, but Roger Ebert found it wonderful, exciting, and heartwarming. And he paid *Hoosiers* the ultimate compliment: "I think they ought to open this one in New York and L.A. to qualify for Academy Awards, because I think it's that good."

The *Seventeen* review was the first to hit print, and Orion's marketing people wasted no time in placing a quote from it at the top of the poster: "A legendary movie worth a dozen films."

* * *

Anticipating the movie's opening, Anspaugh commented, "I have a real responsibility to the production company. I would love to see them make millions on this film, if nothing else their reward for having made this film and giving us the opportunity." Pizzo mainly hoped that *Hoosiers* would garner enough attention to allow him and Anspaugh to work together on another movie someday.

A year after filming had begun, Indiana audiences had only a few more weeks to wait for the motion picture that bore their state's nickname. Pizzo and Anspaugh would soon find out if they had scored with real Hoosiers. Said Anspaugh, "Andy and I would like to come home again and not be known as the two guys that messed up the movie about Indiana basketball." But it would be a while longer before they knew if they had created a nationwide critical and/or commercial hit.

8
Endgame: The Movie Premieres

"There's a tradition in tournament play to not talk about the next step until you've climbed the one in front of you." —Coach Dale

In the fall of 1986, life had returned to normal for the members of the fictional Hickory team. Brad Long (Buddy) got married soon after filming ended and resumed his job with Jostens. Kent Poole (Merle) also got married and went back to farming. Wade Schenck (Ollie) returned to and graduated from high school. David Neidorf (Everett) landed a part in *Platoon* and traveled to the Philippines for the filming. Maris Valainis (Jimmy) moved to California to pursue an acting career. Brad Boyle (Whit) completed medic training for the National Guard and headed back to Ball State University. Scott Summers (Strap) transferred to Taylor University. And Steve Hollar (Rade) resumed classes at DePauw University, where his Sigma Nu fraternity brothers began calling him "Hollywood." He also joined the basketball team as a point guard.

But Anspaugh and Pizzo weren't yet finished with their work on *Hoosiers*. Three weeks before the Indiana premiere, they canvassed the state, doing numerous interviews in a final push to publicize the film. Pizzo said they contacted "every television and radio station and every newspaper reporter and talked about how important it was for people to go to the theater that first weekend." They also were preoccupied with how their film would be received in their home state. Pizzo said they were nervous because, despite the successful test screening in Orange County, California, they were certain Indiana would be a tougher audience. "In a movie called *Hoosiers*," he said, "you'd better get Indiana right."

Meanwhile, the Indiana Film Commission was planning the movie's world premiere at the stunning Circle Theatre. The almost-1,800-seat neoclassical venue was the ideal setting for the event. If Hinkle

Fieldhouse was Indiana's basketball palace, Circle Theatre had been Indiana's movie palace in its heyday. Built in 1916 on the circle in the center of Indianapolis, it was the first building constructed in the city for the purpose of showing feature-length motion pictures. By the 1970s, the theater had fallen into disrepair and faced possible demolition. But after getting listed on the National Register of Historic Places in 1980, Circle Theatre underwent an extensive $6.8 million restoration two years later. In 1984 it became the new home of the Indianapolis Symphony Orchestra.

The world premiere of *Hoosiers* would be invitation-only, for the filmmakers, actors, permanent extras, dignitaries, officials from Orion and Hemdale, and other special guests. Tickets would cost $100, and all proceeds would go to the Variety Club of Indiana to benefit the Jameson Camp for children.

The World Premiere

On Monday, November 10, as searchlights split the dark sky over Circle Theatre, the nearby Columbia Club hosted a pre-movie six-course dinner for the attendees. The get-together was like a homecoming for the reunited Husker teammates, said Long. Although Pizzo had again lost sleep the night before, Anspaugh was excited and optimistic about how the audience would respond to *Hoosiers*, feeling confident the filmmakers would hit a home run.

One by one, limousines pulled up to the brightly lit Circle Theatre marquee, letting their passengers out onto a red carpet lined with photographers, applauding fans, and onlookers. The Southport High School marching band played the Hickory fight song as the color guard waved red and yellow flags. Potted mums, balloons, and trees with twinkling lights decorated the sidewalks. A "Go Hickory All the Way!" banner used in the movie stretched across a nearby construction barricade. Among the moviegoers were about 35 New Richmond residents who arrived by bus, as well as three carloads of people from Knightstown, including Peg Mayhill. As she stepped onto the red carpet with her friends, under the lights, she felt like a movie star, she said.

Some regular Hoosiers wished the premiere could have been more like a normal movie showing, not an event with high-profile attendees and $100 tickets. Eyeing the festivities from Monument Circle outside the theater, they felt left out amidst the men in tuxedos and women in furs. "I watched the crowd going in, and it wasn't just the people in the movie," observed Jill Bruveris, who had been an extra in the film. "It was the money crowd." Glenn Butte of the 1954 Milan team also was irked by the expensive tickets. He and his fellow team members had been invited to the premiere—but not for free. "Heck, if it was about you, they would surely invite you to come up and see it without paying a hundred bucks," he said. Of the movie's three main actors, only Dennis Hopper attended. Gene Hackman was in England filming *Superman IV*, and Barbara Hershey was in Louisiana working on *Shy People*.

The viewers went crazy for *Hoosiers*, giving it a 10-minute standing ovation. Hopper said he "cried three times. When I left the theater, I felt good. These things are amazing to me, since I'm usually hardcore about this." Mayhill, after seeing her hometown gym on the big screen, was delighted that "something so familiar was elevated to something special." Wilma Lewellyn of New Richmond had been so busy watching for familiar faces and places that she couldn't concentrate on the plot.

The Huskers, some of whom had seen the movie for the first time at an earlier preview screening, had found themselves distracted during their first viewing. "It was very strange to see myself," said Long. "I couldn't help but think about what went on during filming of the entire scene." Hollar agreed: "I started thinking of all the people I met in Knightstown and trying to watch the movie at the same time." Poole was disquieted at his initial viewing: "I kept listening and wondering what everyone was thinking and if they liked it." Schenck said watching himself on the silver screen was "a lot different than seeing videotapes of basketball games from school. It was kind of hard to deal with at first." Long appreciated the movie more the second time around. "I was less focused on myself, and I just sat back, relaxed, and enjoyed it," he remarked. He was concerned, however, by the deletion of his scene showing how Buddy was allowed to rejoin the Huskers after being ejected from the first practice. "People will wonder how he got back on the team," Long predicted.

Anspaugh at the world premiere.

Watching his inaugural feature film play out in front of its first hometown crowd, Pizzo discovered "there's nothing more magical than being in a theater with an audience and your movie." For the film's director, the Circle premiere was one of the greatest nights of his life. It was, Anspaugh said, "a feeling of accomplishment, satisfaction, and pride, given the long, difficult journey." The audience's positive reaction reinforced his hunch about *Hoosiers*' chances of success: "If we can get people in [theaters] on the first weekend, word of mouth will take care of the film."

Some audience members asked about the possibility of a sequel. "I would be lying if I said we haven't talked about [it]," Anspaugh replied. But he believed that *Hoosiers* is unique and that sequels usually don't work.

Three marketing consultants hired by Orion flew in for the world premiere. The first part of the marketing plan, they said, was to "saturate the state with this film" so that it would "play in every little town." They hoped moviegoers would recommend *Hoosiers* to friends and relatives in other states. For the national rollout, the consultants said, the advertising would emphasize the film's "people" aspects—friendship, redemption, and father-son relationships—over basketball.

The celebration didn't end with the screening. The attendees returned to the Columbia Club for an afterparty. Lieutenant Governor John Mutz presented Anspaugh and Pizzo with the Sagamore of the Wabash award, the highest honor given in the state of Indiana. Indianapolis Mayor William Hudnut gave the two filmmakers the key to the city. Pizzo addressed the assemblage: "Individual dreams remain pipe dreams unless they are shared. Thanks for sharing our dream."

Sneak Previews in Indiana

A few towns were lucky enough to host sneak previews of *Hoosiers* just before the statewide rollout. Seven hundred people from Knightstown and the surrounding area attended two sold-out showings at the Northgate Cinema in Greenfield during Knightstown Night. The film was often interrupted by murmurs of recognition, applause, and even cheers for familiar faces and places. "People who are part of the location, as Knightstown was, really don't see the movie the first time around," Pizzo commented. "They have so much fun looking at the detail—the gym, the extras, and the street scenes—they'll miss the story." The attendees gave *Hoosiers* extremely favorable reviews. "Certainly the [school] board was leery when this all began," said school board president Kemper Rice of the filming. "Nobody really knew what kind of movie we would have, or how well it would reflect on the community." But, he concluded, "the movie was something we can all be proud of."

Especially gratifying for Pizzo was the preview at Bloomington's Indiana Theater—one of the sites where, in his youth, he had spent countless hours devouring movies. Pizzo's family and friends packed the house, where the writer/producer introduced his film and talked about how much the theater meant to him in his formation as a filmmaker.

The Toughest Audience: The Indiana Rollout

On Indiana's premiere day, November 14, 1986, Indianapolis saw a morning record-low temperature of 11 degrees. But the cold didn't keep people away from the five theaters showing *Hoosiers* in the capital city. People arrived long before showtime, and large queues were the rule at most screenings. The line outside Lafayette Square Cinema stretched well into the mall.

The movie was playing in 30 theaters across the state. In Vincennes, Showplace Theatre manager Harry Hutton expected sellout crowds throughout the weekend. Milan residents planned a celebration to coincide with the film's release. They held a pep session, reception, buffet supper, and tribute to the 1954 state champions. Then, in a caravan of Cadillacs for the 1954 players and buses and cars for everyone else, they headed north to nearby Batesville, where they had reserved the theater for the first showing. In Franklin, the historic Artcraft Theatre, built in 1922, was decorated in red and gold, and employees dressed as referees. Upon watching the film, the crowd often broke into applause—when the title appeared on the screen, at the first appearance of the Nineveh school, and during the basketball games, especially the state finals. Hickory Husker Brad Long was in attendance, signing autographs and meeting fans.

Hoosiers didn't face much box office competition that week. Its main rivals were fish-out-of-water comedy *Crocodile Dundee*, which had been the number-one movie since the first weekend of October, and pool-hustler drama *The Color of Money*, which had been in theaters for a month.

Hoosiers grossed an impressive $220,068 on its opening weekend—a per-screen average of $7,335—and $492,954 during the first nine days of its Indiana release. An Orion official noted that these 30 theaters across the state included "a lot of small-town houses that are lucky to gross $1,000 a week." The second weekend, *Hoosiers* was number 21 in the national box office earnings—even though it was still playing only in Indiana. Joe Koewler of Evansville's East Park Cinema said, "It's definitely got legs. It'll hang in there and play decently. It's not quite a *Crocodile Dundee*, but it's far above average." Mark Ferazza, a coordinator for Orion in New York City, commented, "It's doing better than we expected, even though we had a good deal of faith in *Hoosiers*."

Everyone's a Critic

The judgments about *Hoosiers* from the toughest audience were a mixed bag—often within the same review.

Rita Rose of the *Indianapolis Star* believed "the final basketball scenes ... tend to stray into *Rocky*-land," but she liked that "a homegrown morality ... holds the story together without being too preachy." However, she complained that the reasons for Myra's "bitter" attitude "are only hinted at and never explained" and that Myra and Norman's "enigmatic relationship ... is never developed."

The review in the *Indianapolis News* also was an amalgam. David Mannweiler called the movie a well-told story that was involving and solidly entertaining. He added, "The film doesn't demean Hoosiers or depict us as rubes or hicks. We won't be embarrassed when the rest of the country sees it." But he also deemed the players "interchangeable cardboard figures" and said that the movie "exploits the grip high school basketball has on Indiana but never adequately explains it." The reviewer for the *Knightstown Tri-County Banner* was critical of the "poor editing job which never allowed the relationships between [the coach] and the other members of the cast to be fully fleshed out."

Jim Gordon of the *Merrillville Post-Tribune* was of the opinion that *Hoosiers* "doesn't rank among the great sports movies." But Sandra Knipe of the *Evansville Courier* called *Hoosiers* a great sports movie. She thought the redemption theme was given shallow treatment, saying, "Much more time and care is given to choreographing and photographing the basketball games." In contrast to the *Indianapolis News* reviewer, she was most impressed by the young men who portrayed the Huskers. "The real stars of the movie are the Indiana boys who were cast as members of the basketball team—and not just because of the way they play ball," she wrote. "Non-actors when they were cast, they are natural even in the scenes played off the court. On the court, real tension and emotion show in their faces and their bodies. They represent the best of 'Hoosiers'—the movie and the people."

Bob Chase, who covered the 1954 state championship game as a radio announcer for WOWO, 1190-AM, in Fort Wayne, said *Hoosiers* was OK, but "I thought it was a little strange, adding the alcoholic guy into the middle of it," he said. "That, to me, didn't click."

Longtime Indiana sports editor and columnist Bob Hammel was generous in his assessment. He wrote, "When the movie was being filmed and its theme became known, my instinct was protective and resentful. Hollywood could not possibly capture the Milan story. It could not possibly grasp how very good an entire state ... could feel about itself and its passion.... [But my] initial fear that Hollywood would spoil a splendidly unspoiled story overlooked the loving and gentle care that was part of the project from the start.... Angelo Pizzo and David Anspaugh were Hoosiers whose basketball love and sensitivities motivated the whole thing. ... It was beautifully done, by ... artists who weren't old enough to see the Milan story happen and absorbed its wonder by osmosis."

Some people figured out that the character of gruff, demanding Coach Dale was partially inspired by controversial Indiana University basketball coach Bob Knight. Knight himself supposed that was the case. "I really think Angelo Pizzo and David Anspaugh owe me some dialog rights, if there is such a thing," he wrote in his autobiography. "I don't think I was the only one who recognized some of my coaching lines in Gene Hackman's dialog."

Two Experts: A Coach and a Player

The *Indianapolis Star* invited a coach and a cager to an early screening of *Hoosiers* and asked them to write a review.

Veteran high school basketball coach Ed Siegel noted that Coach Dale's requirement of four passes before a shot was typical of the more deliberate style of offensive play that was common in the East in the 1950s. Siegel also addressed the issue of zone versus man-to-man defense, mentioned in the barbershop meet-and-greet scene. "Many rural Indiana schools used zone defense," he wrote. Small-school teams "were not able to match up with more talented players of larger schools, and the zone defense protected a limited squad from foul trouble." Siegel disliked the Shooter subplot, maintaining that "selection of the town drunk to be an assistant coach is a little hard to believe." He also said, "I am afraid [the coach] would have spent a lot of time with his principal at the Indiana High School Athletic Association's office for bench conduct."

North Central High School basketball player Ken Turner could identify with wanting to win the state title. He suggested that the "Cinderella story" worked initially but eventually became "redundant and too pre-set." He liked the scene in which "number 25 [Rade] almost lost the game and in the locker room they talked about his selfishness, getting the point across of playing as a team. That was realistic to me." But Turner found unrealistic Hackman's pregame talks, as well as the relationship between Hackman and Hershey. "She looked entirely too young for him," Turner said of the 18-year age difference between the actors.

The Milan Reaction

The Milan townspeople also had conflicted feelings about the movie. Said resident Daren Baker, "It was really rural, and we're rural, but it was much more rural than we were. I think the people on the West Coast must think, 'Wow, what a hick place that must be.' They look at it and think that's probably the way we live in the Midwest."

Some Milan citizens were piqued because not only had their town not been used in the filming, but it also was never mentioned in the movie, not even in the closing credits. Milan 1954 team member Gene White said, "All of us from Milan were looking for a little more Milan. [People] ask me, 'Who were you?', and I couldn't find myself in there."

However, White also defended the moviemakers' intentions. He said the naysayers "didn't understand that [the filmmakers] just wanted to use the basis of the team, not the whole town. It portrayed the way basketball was in a small town."

Fellow team member Bobby Plump agreed. "I loved it," he said. "I thought it was great. The movie does a nice job of emphasizing the powerful influence a coach has on his players and community. Gene Hackman shows the same quiet, forceful, positive influence Marvin Wood gave us 32 years ago."

NCAA Controversy

Amidst the excitement of the successful Indiana premiere, Hickory Husker Steve Hollar received some bad news. The National Collegiate Athletic Association had declared him ineligible to play on his college team because of his participation in *Hoosiers*. The NCAA informed Hollar that he had violated Article 3, Section 1 of its manual, which stated that an athlete would lose his eligibility if he "has directly or indirectly used athletic skill for pay in any form in that sport." Several players on Hickory's rival teams also got caught up in the controversy. They included Hollar's DePauw teammate Griff Mills, Jim Rayl of Indiana University–Purdue University Fort Wayne, Mike Ricks of Wabash College, and Greg Eckstein of Rollins College in Florida.

Casting director Ken Carlson insisted that the issue had been addressed with the NCAA before filming began. "That question [of eligibility] came up in a casting meeting," he said. "I know someone cleared [the college players] … one of the producers. I don't know who it was. We were up front about it from the very start." But officials at the NCAA said no one from the movie ever contacted them. After he heard about the NCAA's objection, Carlson wrote the organization a letter, explaining that "we hired the boys as actors who had an ability to play basketball. I stressed they were *actors*, not basketball players." DePauw University basketball coach Mike Steele was inclined to agree. He noted that one of his best players, Phil Wendel, a member of the 1982 state-champion Plymouth team, tried out for *Hoosiers* but didn't make it past the first scrimmage. Steele speculated that Hollar was cast in the film "because he's smart, he looked young, and he did a good job reading the lines. I don't think he was chosen because of his basketball abilities."

All five college hoopsters faced not only the threat of suspension but also having to return to the production company any money they had earned from being in the movie. Mills, who received less than $50 for an afternoon's work ("I appear in the movie for about 3 seconds," he said) was unconcerned about the money. But the stakes were much higher for Hollar, who faced the possibility of having to give back his entire five-figure paycheck. "I don't have it," he said. "All the money I earned went toward my tuition." If he couldn't repay the money, he would have to quit the DePauw team. "I'm just very disappointed. In my eyes, I did nothing wrong," Hollar said.

A week later, the NCAA ruled that all five players would regain their eligibility after serving a three-game suspension. In addition, Mills, Rayl, Ricks, and Eckstein were to repay their salaries, which in each case amounted to union scale for a day's work. Hollar had to wait another month to find out what his monetary penalty would be. Just before Christmas, the eligibility committee ruled that Hollar would have to repay $632, which was 5 percent of his movie salary. They arrived at that amount by deciding that his role consisted of 95 percent acting and 5 percent basketball playing.

Hoosiers Heads West

"Welcome to Indiana basketball." —Coach Dale

According to Pizzo, executives at Orion surmised *Hoosiers* would impress audiences more than critics and therefore was an unlikely Academy Award nominee. But executive producer John Daly disagreed. To be eligible for Oscar consideration, a movie needed to open on either the East or West Coast before the end of the year and play for at least seven days. Daly paid for *Hoosiers* to be shown for a week in Los Angeles. It opened on December 12 at the UA Coronet.

His plan paid off right away in the form of a glowing review in the *Los Angeles Times* titled "Stand Up and Cheer for 'Hoosiers.'" Praising almost every aspect of the film, *Times* critic Sheila Benson called *Hoosiers* engaging and thrilling. "Certainly, between the pungency of Pizzo's script and the humanity and tenderness with which Anspaugh is able to invest his characters," she wrote, "these two would seem a debut team to watch." She concluded, "You can hate everything about basketball ... and still have a sensational time at 'Hoosiers.'" Another positive review appeared in the January 1987 issue of *The Film Journal*. Myron Meisel called the movie "a superbly observed character study" that was "distinguished by fine, subtle acting, a lack of condescension to its characters, and a seriousness of purpose that disguises the intensity of its low-key determination to please."

Encouraged by the favorable responses from nationally prominent movie critics, Orion began to display more confidence in *Hoosiers*. Ahead of the national premiere date, in January the distributor rolled out the film to 90 theaters in Western cities, including Tucson, Las Vegas, San Diego, and other southern California locations.

That same month, the filmmakers put *Hoosiers* through a major test as they screened it out of competition at the United States Film Festival (later renamed Sundance) in Park City, Utah. Anspaugh and Pizzo spent most of the showing pacing the lobby of the Egyptian Theatre and smoking outside. But their worries were for nothing, because the audience of independent-film fans and industry insiders adored *Hoosiers*, giving it a standing ovation. This response took them by surprise, Anspaugh said. He was starting to sense that maybe they had a nationwide hit on their hands.

"In my mind, I think it's already a success," Pizzo concluded. "The perception of the film within the film industry is that it's a success. We have their respect, and the validation has been phenomenal." When asked how much *Hoosiers* would need to earn for him to consider it a commercial success, he replied, "I'm hoping it will do $30 million in business, but if it does $15 million, I'll be happy."

The National Rollout

The national premiere of *Hoosiers* originally was planned for January 23. Then it was moved to February 13. Finally, the date was set for February 27. Joel Resnick, chairman of Orion Distribution, explained that Orion executives knew the movie would pull in people who loved basketball. Thus, their final decision had been to delay the nationwide rollout until late February or early March, when high school basketball season was at a fever pitch.

After playing in Indiana for eight weeks, *Hoosiers* had taken in a remarkable $1.5 million. Not even *Star Wars* or *E.T.* had done better business in the state. By the end of February, the rollouts in Indiana and on the West Coast had generated profits of almost $4 million. The movie's performance in these markets spurred Orion to plan for a strong national release on 1,039 screens. Contrary to what the marketing consultants had stated at the world premiere, the marketing campaign would focus on basketball action in an attempt to attract younger viewers, Pizzo said. "We've adjusted some things with the marketing, but it's basically the same," he commented. "Orion has tried to create television ads that appeal to the 14-to-21 core age group."

More good news was announced in February: The hoped-for Academy Award nominations had materialized. Dennis Hopper was nominated for best supporting actor, and Jerry Goldsmith for best original score. The successful Western rollout and the positive reviews in *Variety*, the *Los Angeles Times*, and other publications were not the only factors in the nominations. Orion and Hemdale Film Corporation had run full-page "for your consideration" ads in *The Hollywood Reporter* and *Variety* that promoted *Hoosiers* and its cast and crew as worthy Oscar nominees. In addition, Hemdale and Orion had hosted screenings of the movie for Academy members in January.

Hoosiers screening invitation.

Some movie critics thought Hopper should instead have been nominated for his role as a psychopath in the disturbing David Lynch film *Blue Velvet*. But Pizzo disagreed. "His role in *Hoosiers* demands greater range as an actor than *Blue Velvet*," he said. "*Blue Velvet* was a brilliant one-note. In *Hoosiers*, he had to play humor and tenderness and vulnerability and anger and hurt and drunkenness. There were a lot of different character colors that required more of him."

Goldsmith was no stranger to the Academy Awards. He had been nominated numerous times, and he won the Oscar for best original score for *The Omen* in 1977. But the American Federation of Musicians Local 47 in Los Angeles objected to his nomination for *Hoosiers*. Because nonunion musicians in Hungary had been hired to play on the soundtrack, the union asked members of the Academy of Motion Picture Arts and Sciences not to vote for Goldsmith.

Box Office Returns

Two other movies opened the weekend of February 27—teen love-triangle drama *Some Kind of Wonderful* and horror flick *A Nightmare on Elm Street 3: Dream Warriors*. *Hoosiers* debuted as the number 5 movie for the week despite tough competition. It was also up against the still-strong *Platoon*, as well as female-buddy farce *Outrageous Fortune*, dummy-comes-to-life comedy *Mannequin*, and the inexorable *Crocodile Dundee*. Cop thriller *Lethal Weapon* debuted the following week. Although *Platoon* would eventually gross almost $138 million, *Nightmare 3* $44 million, and *Lethal Weapon* $65 million, *Hoosiers* held its own against them, remaining in the top 10 for six weeks. Its box office receipts for those weeks were as follows:

Week	Rank	Screens	Gross
February 27	5	1,039	$3,653,562
March 6	8	1,048	$2,846,849
March 13	10	1,043	$2,443,955
March 20	8	1,038	$2,062,348

March 27	7	1,007	$1,743,278
April 3	8	995	$1,583,202

A film industry rule of thumb states that a movie must earn twice the amount of its budget before it can begin turning a profit. *Hoosiers* needed to bring in about $12 million to get to that point. It reached that milestone in its fifth week of nationwide release.

> ### See You in the Funny Papers
> *Hoosiers* got some publicity from the comics page in early April when the film became the subject of the nationally syndicated strip *Tank McNamara*. Over two days, the cartoon showed sports broadcaster Tank taking a date to see *Hoosiers*.

Critics' Comments

The movie reviews that rolled in from around the country were, on the whole, more positive than negative. Richard Schickel of *Time* wrote, "Someone remembered, or went to the trouble of finding out, how it felt to live in a small Midwestern town in the 1950s, when there was nothing better to chew on than last week's game and nothing better to savor than next Friday's." Said Rita Kempley of the *Washington Post*, "Much of the movie's validity stems from time and place recreated with such authenticity that you can sense the wet chill in the morning air and the new wax pungent on the old gym floor." And Janet Maslin of the *New York Times* wrote, "The quaintly innocent *Hoosiers* is irresistible…. This film's very lack of surprise and sophistication accounts for a lot of its considerable charm."

Gene Siskel of the *Chicago Tribune* disagreed, saying he "would have preferred to see the film contain darker, more unpredictable turns." Dave Kehr, also of the *Tribune*, derided the story's "aggressive clichés" and "often tortured mechanics." Ruminated David Ansen of *Newsweek*, "Have all those by-the-numbers inspirational sagas of underdog competitors dreaming the impossible dream so polluted the genre that it is past revitalization? Or can these same clichés, when handled with care and intelligence, rebound with cinematic life? In the case of 'Hoosiers,' there's no easy answer."

Writing

Paul Attanasio of the *Washington Post* sensed Pizzo's background in television production, observing that "much of the writing, particularly in the early going, is TV style—direct and underlined, rather than suggestive and oblique." Bruce Newman of *Sports Illustrated* called the movie corny but also thrilling while proclaiming that "*Hoosiers* gets it right." Myron Meisel opined that "the writing throughout sensitively finds the truest moments between the characters." He also held that Norman's "relationships with the players (each individual creations) may be classically familiar, but they avoid either cliché or sentimentality." Roger Ebert pronounced in the *Chicago Sun-Times* that Pizzo "knows small-town sports. He knows all about high school politics and how the school board and the parents' groups always think they know more about basketball than the coach does. He knows about gossip, scandal and vengeance. And he knows a lot about human nature."

On the negative side, many critics found Myra and Norman's love/hate relationship unbelievable and unnecessary. Ebert was on the right track when he said that "it feels like key scenes have been cut out of the romance." In fact, this storyline was the biggest casualty of the editing process and Orion's directive that the movie be less than 2 hours, as many of the scenes selected for deletion involved Myra and Norman. Pizzo acknowledged that the loss of these scenes made it seem as though the kiss came out of nowhere. He and Anspaugh insisted that if the film had shown all the interactions between these two lead actors that were originally written, their relationship would have made more sense, and their kiss would have seemed like a natural evolution of their relationship.

Considered on her own, the character of Myra provoked multitudinous disparaging adjectives. She was called harsh, mean-spirited, caustic, flinty, brittle, sterile, sour, cranky, chilly, icy, suspicious, moralistic, judgmental, severe, unfriendly, interrogative, insufferable, drab, one-note, perfunctory, and superfluous. She also was dubbed an old-maid schoolteacher, a frustrated spinster, a frigid schoolmarm, the town crone, and an angry prune. Although Anspaugh admitted that Myra was "not a terribly likeable character," he believed she never got a chance to fully develop because of the deletion of several of her scenes.

Directing

Of Anspaugh's work, Todd McCarthy of *Variety* wrote that he "paints a richly textured portrait of 1951 rural American life, both visually and through glimpses of the guarded reticence of the people." Meisel commented that "the drab rural Indiana milieu is carefully and sympathetically evoked" and that Anspaugh "shows a good, functional eye for setting up scenes visually." Said Kehr, "Anspaugh employs a discreet, even-tempered approach, letting his scenes unfold with a certain natural grace rather than whipping each sequence into a heart-pounding climax."

Noted cinematographer Fred Murphy, "One of the virtues of this movie is that scenes are often played out in one shot or just a few shots. Or often things are played out in groups; there's not a lot of cutting to individuals. And somehow all those shots work and have a strong sense of time and drama. They unfold at their own correct pace, without cutting to speed things up."

Ebert added that "Anspaugh's direction is good at suggesting Hackman's complexity without belaboring it."

Acting

The critics were united in their praise of Hackman. Schickel wrote, "Hackman is wonderful as an inarticulate man tense with the struggle to curb a flaring, mysterious anger." Maslin said he brought "shrewdness and a varied temperament to a man who might otherwise have seemed bland." Kempley maintained that "Hackman, with his decent face and bad haircut, gives the movie a credible core that offsets the corn." Said Meisel, "Hackman's reactions to the kibitzing of the local populace … are eloquent, complex and funny." Henry Sheehan of *The Hollywood Reporter* enthused that "Hackman truly is extraordinary, less acting than a transformation. Like a natural ballplayer, every move he makes—tossing a ball at practice, prowling behind the sidelines at a game, hiding beneath a nervous laugh—seems just right—succinct, unaffected and expressive." Sheila Benson of the *Los Angeles Times* deemed this role a high-water mark in Hackman's career.

Hopper also garnered compliments on his performance. David Sterritt of the *Christian Science Monitor* declared that the character of Shooter was Hopper's "best screen work ever." Benson called Hopper "demoniacally good." Kempley said Hopper was "convincing in this soulful role." Attanasio wrote, "Where Hackman's wounds have closed and crusted over, Hopper's are wide open, in the jagged eyes beneath his strong forehead." Steve Vineberg of the *Boston Phoenix* said, "Hopper is the movie's ace. ... There's ... a rumpled grandeur to the scene in which he boots Dale out of his house." Vineberg also called Hopper "fervently funny as ... he strains so hard to hew to the line [of sobriety] that his face gets all knotted up."

Despite critics' overwhelmingly unfavorable response to the character of Myra, some movie reviewers liked Hershey's performance. Benson called the actress radiant, and Kehr wrote that she displayed warmth and brightness. Schickel said Hershey put "a dispassionate face on a passionate nature." Siskel called her "refreshing simply because she doesn't have a cause." And Scot Haller in *People* said she "elevates what could have been a throwaway role." Anspaugh said he was very happy with Hershey's rendition: "She's a very good actress, and I thought she was cast beautifully." In contrast, Pizzo said he "was not particularly pleased with the performance, because I thought she lacked a certain humanity and warmth that I intended to be there for the character."

* * *

Monday, March 30 was the night of the 59th Academy Awards. It also was the night Pizzo and Anspaugh's alma mater, Indiana University, was playing Syracuse for the NCAA Division I basketball title in New Orleans. The two friends debated whether they should hop on a plane to Louisiana, or if they should attend the awards ceremony in Los Angeles and try to sneak in a Watchman and surreptitiously follow the game. Ultimately, they decided to skip the Oscars and throw a party at Anspaugh's house, where they watched both events on two TVs. "If it wasn't for Indiana basketball, I'd never have written *Hoosiers*. So that's what comes first," Pizzo said. "Once the game started, I didn't pay any attention to the Academy Awards." *Hoosiers* didn't collect any Oscars that night. But IU won 74–73 on a last-second shot, six years to the day of their last national title—the game that propelled Pizzo to begin writing *Hoosiers*.

9
Postgame Wrap-up: The Years After the Movie's Release

"I don't want this to be the high point of his life." —Myra

When *Hoosiers* left Indiana theaters in late May 1987, it had been playing in the state for over six months. Its final total box office gross was $28,607,524. Although this was a respectable number, Orion cofounder Mike Medavoy was somewhat dissatisfied. He believed that "*The Terminator* and *Hoosiers* were terrific films that could have done better at the box office had we spent more on marketing or gotten more publicity." When the film was released on videotape in September 1987, it experienced good rental numbers, climbing as high as number 3 on the weekly list of most-rented VHS tapes. But as *Hoosiers'* profits continued to accumulate, initially the two individuals who were the driving force behind the movie didn't reap many monetary rewards. "The movie generated money for a lot of people, but not for David or me," Pizzo said. The first-time filmmakers had lacked the leverage to negotiate a lucrative financial deal for themselves—although later they benefited from residuals.

The two men resumed their Hollywood careers. Anspaugh went on to helm his next feature, *Fresh Horses*, starring Molly Ringwald and Andrew McCarthy. And Pizzo kept writing screenplays. "I don't think there's anything more satisfying than to take 120 blank pieces of paper and fill them with characters and a good story that says something positive about the human condition and have it shared with an estimated 350 million people," he commented. However, Pizzo's main goal was to become a director—and to distance himself from his successful first film. "As much as I'm proud of it," he told a reporter in 1989, "I don't want to be introduced at cocktail parties five years from now as the guy who did *Hoosiers*. I would really like to see it behind me."

As David Neidorf and Maris Valainis pursued further acting roles, the rest of the Huskers resumed their regular, pre-Hollywood lives. (Poole did both, appearing in a supporting role in *Fresh Horses* before returning to farming for good.) During the filming of *Hoosiers*, when Wade Schenck was asked about his future plans, he said, "If someone called and asked me to do another film, I'd probably do it, but I'd much rather go back home and farm the land." When he returned to Lyons, he found that in his tight-knit community, "nobody treated me like a celebrity. And I didn't want to be."

The former Hickory Husker teammates stayed in touch. "All the guys on the team got pretty close," said Brad Long. Steve Hollar added, "I feel I can call any one of them and say, 'Hey, I need this favor for charity,' and they would come." Neidorf divulged that, on the sets of the other movies he appeared in after *Hoosiers*, "there were a lot of jealousies, people trying to grab the spotlight. [But with *Hoosiers*] there was a sense of togetherness." Poole said that, during production, "we just didn't realize what we were a part of. I don't think the writers and directors did either."

The Huskers were sometimes recognized by fans of the movie in the course of their everyday lives. "I wouldn't say it is daily, but it is continual," said Hollar. Even though Neidorf acted in hit movies such as *Bull Durham* and *Platoon*, his role as Everett became the one people remembered most. He said, "I was at a Dodgers game and heard somebody whisper, 'That's the guy from *Hoosiers*.'" Valainis commented, "I was in a line at a restaurant when this 6-foot-10 guy came up to me and said, 'Hey, you were in *Hoosiers*. You helped us win a state championship.'" Valainis appreciated what he called his subdued fame. "I enjoy the attention that comes with it," he said. "It's fun to embrace it."

Members of the 1954 Milan Miracle team and their families found themselves fielding questions about the film, such as how much of the movie was true, and who in Milan was the drunk.

> ### Directed by Jack Nemo
>
> The version of *Hoosiers* that is shown on network TV has some shortened and deleted dialog and scenes compared to the theatrical version. Making these changes let the movie fit into a 2-hour slot while allowing time for commercials. Anspaugh had no control over the release of the modified TV version of his film. Often the director is consulted when a movie is edited for television broadcast, he explained, but only to help decide what should be cut. He compared this process to "being invited to the execution of your child and getting to help decide how high to raise the blade!" Anspaugh expressed his disapproval of the chopped-up network TV version of *Hoosiers* by having his name removed from its opening credits. The fictitious "Jack Nemo" is listed as the director instead.

Anspaugh and Pizzo had assumed that, after *Hoosiers* completed its theatrical run, it would fade from people's memories, as most films do. But something unexpected happened: As the years rolled by, *Hoosiers* never went away. It remained as compelling as ever.

Coaches had their teams watch it before a crucial game. Milan Miracle team member Bobby Plump said he's never met a basketballer who hasn't seen it. References to *Hoosiers* abounded in sports articles—especially during the March tournament season—and often in relation to sports other than basketball. Parents sat down to watch it every year with their kids. Politicians mentioned it in speeches. The title *Hoosiers* became synonymous with or shorthand for basketball, traditional values, underdogs, Cinderella teams, David-and-Goliath matchups, courage in the face of daunting odds, and unexpected victories.

In April 2006, when the Final Four came to the RCA Dome in Indianapolis, Florida Coach Billy Donovan showed his players the film before they won the title. And when Indianapolis again hosted the Final Four in 2010, this time with the underdog hometown favorite Butler Bulldogs as one of the teams, references to *Hoosiers* proliferated throughout the media. Sports commentators couldn't resist drawing parallels between the Huskers and the Bulldogs. Not only was Butler the smallest school to reach the NCAA final game in the modern 64-team era, but the Bulldogs' home court also was the site of the Huskers' state championship game.

One of the most surprising non-sports-related references to *Hoosiers* appeared in the March 2013 issue of *Esquire*, in the article "The Man Who Killed Osama bin Laden ... Is Screwed." Phil Bronstein wrote that, on the night before the SEAL Team 6 mission to eliminate the al-Qaeda leader, "there was one last briefing and an awesome speech from [Vice Admiral William] McRaven [head of Joint Special Operations Command] comparing the looming raid and its fighters to the movie *Hoosiers*."

The movie was the subject of a unique tribute in July 2015, when the Indiana Pacers announced they would wear red-and-gold Hickory uniforms in select games over the next few seasons. The Pacers chose to honor *Hoosiers* and its upcoming 30th anniversary by creating these NBA Pride Collection uniforms, which celebrated a team's or region's unique history.

Another indication of the movie's staying power was the many lists on which it appeared:

- In 2001, *Hoosiers* was placed on the National Film Registry of the Library of Congress as a motion picture that is "culturally, historically, or aesthetically significant."
- In 2003, *Hoosiers* claimed the number 6 spot on *Sports Illustrated*'s list of "The 50 Greatest Sports Movies of All Time."
- The sportswriters of the *New York Daily News* named *Hoosiers* the second-greatest sports movie ever.
- The readers of *USA Today* and the *Los Angeles Times* chose the film as the best sports movie of all time.
- *Hoosiers* was number 1 on the ESPN.com list of "The 25 Best Sports Films: 1979–2004."

- The American Film Institute (AFI) put *Hoosiers* at number 13 on its list of "100 Years…100 Cheers: 100 Most Inspiring Films of All Time" in 2006.

- *Rolling Stone* also placed *Hoosiers* at number 13 on its list of "30 Best Sports Movies of All Time."

- Moviefone ranked the film at number 9 on its list of "Top 10 Inspirational Movies of All Time," at number 4 in the "Top 25 Sports Movies," and at number 1 in "Best Basketball Movies."

- The AFI put *Hoosiers* in the number 4 position on its list of "Top 10 Sports Films of All Time" in 2008.

"To me, the greatest award is to have [*Hoosiers*] entered into the Library of Congress," Anspaugh said. "It's so humbling. We say, 'My God, did we really do that?' We sure didn't plan on it."

The movie actually reached far beyond American borders. "Next to the world premiere in Indianapolis, my trip to the Soviet Union has been the most satisfying experience with *Hoosiers*," Anspaugh remarked. The movie was screened in 1988 in Moscow and Leningrad as part of a rare American film festival. "When the movie was shown, the Russian people cheered and laughed and cried," he said. "A Russian woman in the audience told me, 'People don't realize how similar we all are in our life experience. I knew all those characters in the movie.'"

Not Quite Lost in Translation

Because the term "Hoosier" can't really be translated, the movie's title was changed for foreign distribution. Here are some of its alternative titles in other countries:

- Brazil: *Momentos Decisivos* (decisive moments)
- Argentina and Peru: *Ganadores* (winners)
- England and Sweden: *Best Shot*
- Swedish TV title: *Basketligan* (basketball league)

- Finland: *Viimeinen Heitto* (last throw)
- Spain: *Más Que Ídolos* (more than idols)
- Portugal: *Raiva de Vencer* (anger to win)
- France: *Le Grand Défi* (the big challenge)
- Italy: *Colpo Vincente* (winning shot)
- Germany: *Freiwurf* (free throw)
- Poland: *Mistrzowski Rzut* (masterful throw)
- Czech Republic: *Hráči z Indiany* (players from Indiana)
- Hungary: *A Legjobb Dobás* (best shot)
- Serbia: *Odlučujući šut* (decisive shot)
- Bulgaria: Най-добрият изстрел (best shot)
- Greece: Παθος για το μπασκετ (passion for basketball)
- Turkey: *Kazanmak Arzusu* (the desire to win)
- Latvia: *Puiši no Indiānas* (boys from Indiana)
- Ukraine: Хлопці з Індіани (boys from Indiana)
- Russia: *Komanda Iz Shtata Indiana* (a team from Indiana)
- Japan: 勝利への旅立ち (journey to victory)
- China: 火爆教頭草地兵 (hot-tempered coach, meadow soldiers)

"Will you be back at Hickory next year?" —Reporter

In Indiana, the towns that served as filming sites held well-attended anniversary celebrations of *Hoosiers*. The summer after the movie wrapped, New Richmond decided to commemorate its role by hosting the first annual Hickory Festival. At the fifth and last festival in 1990, Anspaugh, Pizzo, the Huskers, the cheerleaders, and many extras showed up for the two-day gathering. In 1996, the Heartland Film Festival in Indianapolis marked the film's tenth anniversary by presenting Anspaugh and Pizzo with a Special Achievement Award.

Knightstown hosted a nine-day celebration for the 20th anniversary in 2006. Pizzo served as grand marshal for the parade, and the Huskers who attended rode in convertibles. Maris Valainis came all the way from California, where he had settled after appearing in *Hoosiers*. "I never imagined in my wildest dreams that I'd be back here 20 years later," he said. The parade was followed by an autograph signing at the gym, where *Hoosiers* fans from across the country lined up out the door. That evening a dinner and sports memorabilia auction were held. Other activities included a golf outing, a sock hop, and, of course, special showings of *Hoosiers*. From June 2010 to June 2012, communities around the state celebrated the movie's 25th anniversary. Events were held in Knightstown, Bloomington, Indianapolis, Decatur, Edinburgh, Nineveh, Elkhart, and Milan.

Anspaugh and Pizzo are popular invitees at events celebrating *Hoosiers*.

The Hoosier(s) Gym

The Huskers' home court narrowly escaped imminent destruction in 1988, three years after *Hoosiers* was filmed. After a new elementary school was constructed just north of Knightstown, the school board decided the old gym was no longer needed and should be torn down. But a group of residents were determined not to let that happen. They banded together to form

> Historic Knightstown and to save the gym from the wrecking ball. Eventually, the town took ownership of the building and chose a board of directors to manage it as a community center. The renamed Hoosier Gym got a second chance at life and opened its doors to visitors and *Hoosiers* fans from around the world. The beautifully preserved facility has welcomed current and former NBA greats, well-known sports journalists, and other celebrities. Each June, all-star basketball games showcase Indiana's top preps players. The gym has hosted high school basketball tournaments dubbed the Hickory Classic and the Norman Dale Classic. The night before these games, some of the participants prepared for their visit by watching *Hoosiers*. But the venue is more than just a gym. It is also the site of meetings, parties (birthday, bachelor, graduation), and even an occasional marriage proposal or wedding.

Anspaugh and Pizzo are at a loss to explain their modest film's runaway popularity. Pizzo attributes it to magic or serendipity, and Anspaugh calls it alchemy. They never expected *Hoosiers* "to be a hit, or to win awards—just something we would be somewhat proud of," the director said. "The fact that it's lived on blows my mind," Pizzo exclaimed. "I think for a movie like *Hoosiers*, there was a window of opportunity," he continued. "This movie would never be made today. If you reduce *Hoosiers* to [one sentence], it sounds banal, and marketing people will tell you that they can't sell it. The marketing departments run the creative departments much more than ever before. They would tell me: It's dusty. It's regional. It's rural." He speculated that because *Hoosiers* is a period piece, it never became dated, like most other '80s films. Anspaugh believes *Hoosiers* stands apart from modern-day films because "the movies that are made today are mostly special effects. When you leave the theater, nothing stays with you. That's not the case with *Hoosiers*."

When Gene Hackman was asked in 1988 how he thought *Hoosiers* had turned out, he said, "I felt good and also surprised. When I first saw the film, I was taken with it. It's not only a good human story, but it has a lot of action in it. It has a nice balance, so I feel in the end it was worth doing." Many years later, in another interview, he admitted, "I took the film at a time that I was desperate for money. I took it for all the wrong reasons, and it turned out to be one of those films that stick around. I never expected the film to have the kind of legs it's had."

The Deleted Scenes Resurface

Ten years after the release of *Hoosiers*, Anspaugh rummaged through his collection of tapes. He was looking for scenes that didn't make the final version of the movie to take to a special tenth-anniversary showing of the film in Indianapolis. Anspaugh didn't anticipate ever getting to make a director's cut of the film to restore all the scenes he and Pizzo had been forced to eliminate during the editing process. "I suspect [the original negative] has been destroyed," he said. "I don't even know who owns the film now."

But nine years later, in 2005, MGM Home Entertainment, which had the rights to *Hoosiers*, brought out a remarkable two-disc Collector's Edition DVD package. (Orion had filed for bankruptcy in 1991, and MGM acquired it in 1997.) The DVD reportedly sold out its first printing before its release date simply on the strength of pre-orders from vendors.

Instead of picturing the stars and scenes from the movie, as the earlier DVD releases had done, this DVD package was the color and texture of a basketball. As a special feature, disc 2 contained 14 deleted scenes, equaling almost 24 minutes of running time. The film's editor had found the footage while cleaning out his garage. Over the years, some of these scenes had been mentioned in the occasional article or website, but they had never seen the light of day. Some fans of the movie had long hoped for an extended version of *Hoosiers* with these scenes included that would answer their questions about certain plot holes and inconsistencies. The idea to put these scenes on the DVD originated with ESPN.com columnist and *Hoosiers* fan Bill Simmons. He wrote about some of the gaps in the movie, and Pizzo e-mailed him to explain that he and Anspaugh had been forced to eliminate many scenes. Simmons "asked why there wasn't a special edition, a director's cut," said Pizzo. "He then contacted someone who worked at MGM and told them they should do something about it."

The footage the film editor discovered was from an early rough cut of the movie. The original negatives of these scenes could not be located. Because the color and sound quality of the rough-cut scenes were less than ideal, these scenes didn't match the final print of the movie and thus could not be incorporated into a director's cut. Therefore, on the DVD Pizzo and Anspaugh introduce each scene individually. "Some of those scenes should stay deleted," Pizzo joked in a newspaper article about the new DVD.

But the most notable exception was the footage related to Buddy's mysterious reappearance on the team after he is dismissed from the first practice because of his disrespectful attitude. As Buddy storms out, he says something about going to play for Terhune. This neighboring town is mentioned several times in the original script. Its first appearance was to have been right after the opening credits, as Norman stops for gas on his way to Hickory. The next mention of Terhune would have come after Buddy's exit from practice; that scene had Coach Dale learning in class the following week that Buddy has indeed left Hickory High and transferred to Terhune. (That scene was lost sometime after the editing process and therefore could not be included on the DVD.) Yet another deleted scene shows Norman getting angry with Cletus for allowing Buddy to transfer. In a further deleted scene, a remorseful Buddy confesses that he couldn't bring himself to play for the Tigers. After listening to Buddy's explanation, Coach Dale implicitly allows him to return by saying, "If it's all right with Cletus, it's all right with me." So Buddy comes back to Hickory and is seen in the next game, at Cedar Knob. Terhune is not mentioned again in the movie until the Huskers face the Tigers in the sectional game of the tournament. Pizzo explained that the scene where Buddy asks to return was the last scene to be deleted; it was the one that got the film down to the 2-hour running time Orion executives had demanded. The filmmakers had been opposed to cutting this scene. Pizzo knew viewers would be confused when Buddy magically reappeared on the team, but the executives were unmoved.

Many of the deleted scenes depict Norman and Myra's developing relationship. Hershey was so unhappy with these cuts that she refused to do publicity work for the film around the time of its release and rarely spoke about *Hoosiers* in the years after. "She hates me and Angelo," Anspaugh said. "She felt we cut her out of the movie. She was wonderful in the movie, but we didn't get on at all, especially after she saw the film." Pizzo understood Hershey's disappointment. He admitted, "The fault is my own, because I tried to squeeze too much story into too short a time."

Another deleted scene shows Norman having dinner with Cletus, Millie, and Loetta, as the teen grills the coach about his personal life. That cheerleader Loetta is the principal's daughter is only hinted at in the film. She and her mother appear in a photo on Cletus's desk, and Loetta helps unload a box from Norman's car as he moves into a house on the Summers' property.

Laura Robling (Loetta) with her movie father, Sheb Wooley (Cletus), in New Richmond.

Also included on the DVD is the elaborate caravan scene shot on the crew's last day in New Richmond. It was reduced to 6 seconds of footage in the film. When assistant director Harvey Waldman first saw *Hoosiers* and noticed the virtual deletion of this scene, which had taken an entire day to set up and shoot, "I about fell out of my chair," he said.

Anspaugh and Pizzo's favorite scene that ended up on the cutting room floor shows all the characters working together to harvest a field of corn on a sunny autumn day. "I wanted to show what these people did other than watch basketball games and talk about them," Pizzo said.

The harvest scene was captured on one of the few sunny days.

The director and writer/producer weren't the only ones who mourned the loss of so much material. Said assistant director Herb Adelman, "I was disappointed that a lot of those personal scenes were deleted," because they were his favorite part of the story.

The Collector's Edition DVD also contains low-definition black-and-white footage of the 1954 Milan Miracle state championship basketball game. Because the game was filmed without audio, a play-by-play radio broadcast is used for the sound. Viewers could finally see the real game and teams that inspired the ultimate matchup in the movie.

The End of One-Class Basketball

"Let's win this one for all the small schools that never had a chance to get here."
—Merle

Indiana's final one-class, everyone-versus-everyone basketball tournament, which had made David-and-Goliath contests such as the 1954 state finals possible, took place in 1997. The IHSAA Board of Directors and the high school principals voted to divide the statewide basketball tournament into four classes based on school enrollment. These officials believed that having four state-champion teams each year instead of just one would be more fair and beneficial to schools with a small number of students. Few schools with low enrollments had ever progressed very far in the single-class competition. But even though the new format resulted in four times as many state finalists, it didn't produce more fans. In fact, tourney attendance and profits suffered. Five years into the multiclass system, just over half as many people were going to the tournament. By 2012, total attendance for the entire contest hit its lowest point ever, as that year only 22,820 fans went to the state finals. In addition, some schools saw a significant drop in the number of regular-season passes they sold. Pizzo didn't mince words when he said the transition to multiclass ruined the tournament and that he had "disdain and disgust for what they have done." Anspaugh felt the same, calling the decision disappointing and embarrassing for the state.

Pizzo recalled his days as a high school basketball fan. "I have very powerful memories of going to sectional games in Martinsville, where every team in the area, people who knew each other and who played against each other [since] grade school, engaged in a battle royal. Now, because there aren't enough teams in their classification close by, some have to drive upwards of 70 miles to play a Tuesday night sectional game against a school their fans have never heard of."

Some of the Hickory Huskers also weighed in. "Hollywood spent millions on a movie [about] the classless system of Indiana," said Steve Hollar. "I doubt if they will ever make a movie about class basketball." Brad Boyle asked, "If you win [the tournament] in a lower class, where are your bragging rights? I think a bunch of non-competitive people are trying to make it 'fair.' [But] Indiana basketball is about competition. The smaller team loves to compete against the bigger team. I would hate to not have a shot against the biggest team in Indiana." Brad Long had a slightly different view. "My heart says I'm sad about it. The salesman in me hears the small schools when they say they have no chance of beating [a large school like] Ben Davis High School," he said.

"[Single-class basketball] was something very, very special," said Purdue head basketball coach Matt Painter, who grew up in Muncie. "There's no doubt it's lost a lot of its mystique. It's not what it used to be." Commented Bobby Plump of the 1954 Milan team, "There's no interest [in the tournament anymore]. People don't care. Multiclass basketball just killed [the tournament]. I get asked all the time, 'Will Indiana basketball ever be what it used to be?'" Pizzo concluded, "I've yet to run across a single individual who feels strongly that the multiclass system is the way to go."

Opposition to the new system caused the issue to be revisited more than once. Three years after the original decision, the IHSAA Board of Directors reviewed and upheld the move to multiclass. In 2005, a survey of IHSAA member schools revealed that only 10.6 percent of them favored a return to single-class basketball. In the spring of 2012, town-hall meetings were held across the state to allow residents to voice their opinions on multiclass hoops and to vote on which system they preferred. Again the IHSAA declined to return to a one-class tournament. In the fall of 2013, the Indiana Basketball Coaches Association proposed a new format that was designed to correct some of the perceived problems with the multiclass tournament. The IBCA hoped to generate enough support from the state's high school coaches to be able to submit a proposal to the IHSAA detailing its suggested changes.

Attracting Productions to the Hoosier State

It was estimated that the production of *Hoosiers* pumped between $2 million and $4 million into Indiana's economy. About 200 cast and crew members worked on the film, approximately 80 percent of whom were from Indiana. Local residents were hired as day players, stand-ins, drivers, sign painters, seamstresses, assistants, and more. And the communities where scenes were filmed profited from the sale of goods, services, and souvenirs. Pizzo described filmmaking as "a very efficient, economic way of pulling money into a state."

To capitalize on the momentum generated by *Hoosiers*, the Indiana Film Commission created an advertising campaign targeted at people working in the industry. The IFC placed ads in *The Hollywood Reporter*, *Variety*, and *Adweek* with the slogan "Indiana leaves you with a lasting impression." In the following years, the IFC saw its efforts begin to pay off as more films were made in Indiana. Many of them, like *Hoosiers*, had a sports theme: *Eight Men Out*, *A League of Their Own*, *Rudy*, *Blue Chips*, *Madison*. Other productions shot in Indiana included the movies *Falling from Grace*, *In the Company of Men*, *Going All the Way*, and *Hard Rain*, as well as documentary/reality TV shows *The Shift, Breaking Down the Bars, 60 Days In*, and the short-lived *Armed & Famous* and *Porter Ridge*. One potential roadblock to filming in the state was the relative lack of people who could be hired for technical jobs such as camera operator, grip, and gaffer. "In *Hoosiers*, the vast majority of people we hired were from Indiana," Pizzo said in 2007. "However, the keys in every department came from either Chicago or L.A. [But] the crew base has become deeper here since we shot *Hoosiers*. And if the tax incentive bill passes, many of those students who were trained here in Indiana colleges would stay. And I know anecdotally a number of experienced crew members living in L.A. who would move back here."

Pizzo was referring to the state legislature's debate over giving tax credits to film, TV, and commercial production companies in order to lure more of them to Indiana. He was very much in favor of this move. "The economic benefits [to a state when making movies] are exponential," he said. "The film business differs from other industries [because] when a major film company comes to town, they spend a lot of money on restaurants, hotels, dry cleaners, and caterers, and other businesses don't do that. They're permanent. With permanent businesses, you have to support them through infrastructure and other expenditures." Disagreement arose among lawmakers over how much effort and tax money—if any—should be spent on luring filmmakers to Indiana. Other states spent significant sums on their film commissions and offered production companies generous tax breaks and incentives. In 2002 Louisiana became the first state to initiate a major incentives program. The high-grossing, Oscar-winning motion pictures *Ray* and *The Curious Case of Benjamin Button* were filmed there. In eight years the program generated thousands of jobs and more than $2 billion for the state.

A group of Indiana state senators and representatives worked to put together House Enrolled Act (HEA) 1388, the film industry production incentives bill, in 2007. It authorized a refundable tax credit for certain media production expenses incurred in the state. Productions that would qualify included feature films, documentaries, music videos, TV shows, and radio advertising. The Indiana House and Senate passed HEA 1388, but Governor Mitch Daniels vetoed it.

However, the House and Senate overrode his veto the following year, and the bill became law. Daniels released a statement expressing his disapproval: "At the very moment when we are facing a national economic slowdown, ... when any spare dollar should be used for property tax reduction, legislators have given out $30 million in corporate subsidies, most of which are likely to go to existing businesses and not bring a single new job to our state. It's truly an irresponsible decision, and I can't imagine what they were thinking."

Greg Malone, president of the Indiana Media Industry Network (IMIN), strongly disagreed with Daniels' viewpoint. "The incentives for production included in HEA 1388 are fair, reasonable, and necessary to counter the loss of production to states that have already enacted aggressive incentives," he said. "We are ready to attract our share of these high-paying, nonpolluting productions—both large and small—that will help fuel Indiana's economy."

HEA 1388 expired at the end of 2011 and was not renewed. In the meantime, most of the 39 U.S. states that did offer incentives reaped financial rewards. Said Greg Sorvig, director of marketing and public relations for the not-for-profit Heartland Film, "[TV series] *Breaking Bad* put New Mexico on the map for film production; *Walking Dead* did the same for Georgia. If we had just one in Indiana, it could be huge."

In 2013, filming began on *The Fault in Our Stars*, a $12 million budget movie whose story was set in Indianapolis; it was based on the wildly popular young-adult novel of the same name. Because Indiana was unable to offer the movie production any incentives, the state was passed over as a filming location—in favor of Pittsburg. The moviemakers were won over by Pennsylvania's 25 to 30 percent tax credit for motion-picture productions. *TFiOS* earned four times the amount of its budget in box office receipts after only its first weekend in theaters. Its final box office gross was almost $125 million. "This was the kind of film we needed to blow the lid off this topic in Indiana," lamented Sorvig.

In 2016, the Indiana Media Production Alliance proposed a new incentives bill for the 2017 session of the Indiana General Assembly.

It would offer a 30 to 45 percent tax credit to film, TV, and media productions, and it would not expire. In describing the need for this bill, Pizzo noted that, if *Hoosiers* were made today, the production company most likely would film it not in Indiana, but in a neighboring state that offered incentives.

An Ongoing Partnership

Anspaugh and Pizzo collaborated on more sports-themed projects based on true stories, again with Pizzo as writer/producer and Anspaugh as director. Following the release of *Hoosiers*, they set up a production company at Orion. "After the success of the movie, they asked us if we would like to make a home there for a while," Anspaugh said. Their first idea was to develop a motion picture based on the Indianapolis 500 and race car drivers. Pizzo immersed himself in the topic, spending time on the racing circuit and interviewing the drivers. But Orion put the brakes on the project after hearing about Paramount Pictures' plans for NASCAR drama *Days of Thunder*. When that 1990 film was released and "did lousy at the box office, measured against expectations," Pizzo said, "the comment we got after that was, [you have] a really good script, but if Tom Cruise can't sell a race car movie, how can you?" Nevertheless, Pizzo still thought the concept could work. He labored over the screenplay for years, seeing it through several incarnations while never abandoning the idea.

Although they didn't consider making a sequel to *Hoosiers*, the two friends did develop a pilot for a TV show based on the movie, titled *Hickory*. It was centered around characters other than the coach and examined their lives after the state championship. But Anspaugh and Pizzo were unable to interest a network in the concept.

In the fall of 1992 they returned to Indiana to film *Rudy* at the University of Notre Dame in South Bend. The story shared some themes with *Hoosiers*: love of and devotion to a sport (this time, Notre Dame football); the importance of hard work, determination, and faith in oneself; and achieving a seemingly impossible goal. Pizzo said both *Hoosiers* and *Rudy* "are about the state ... the people, the environment, the mindset, the values, the community." Anspaugh said he and Pizzo agreed early on that they would do *Rudy* only if they could film it at Notre Dame; they wouldn't film at another college and try to pass it off as the home of the Fighting Irish. Anspaugh believed their success with *Hoosiers* was why the administration gave them access to the campus. *Rudy* became the first movie shot at the school since *Knute Rockne, All American* over 50 years earlier. Unlike *Hoosiers*, Anspaugh said, *Rudy* was properly budgeted and scheduled. Although movie critics and moviegoers alike were divided on whether the final result was an inspirational, uplifting story or a trite feel-good flick, *Rudy* was profitable, earning $22,750,363.

Anspaugh and Pizzo teamed up again in 2003 for *The Game of Their Lives*, filmed partly in St. Louis; its story concerned a 1950 World Cup soccer match. Unfortunately, their third collaboration was a major letdown as they dealt with a slashed budget, a rushed schedule, fights with the production executives, a drug-addicted actor, difficulties with the shoot in Brazil, poor critical reviews, and dismal box office returns after a limited release. *TGoTL* was "significantly not the movie we set out to make," Anspaugh admitted. "It was a great disappointment," Pizzo agreed. "Having said that," he continued, "I'm still proud of the film. It's like all your films are your children. Even the ones that struggle, it takes them forever to walk, they're kind of the ugly duckling, you still love them. I still love this movie. I have a great fondness for it. And I see its flaws, and I see its weaknesses."

Back Home Again in Indiana

> *"You sound like my father. He thought it strange I ever wanted to leave town, kept telling me I'd be back. Course, he was right."* —Myra

Although Pizzo had lived in the Los Angeles area since the mid-1970s, he never really liked it there. He lambasted the city as being a "toxic environment of competitiveness and divisiveness"—a "soul-bruising place" where "you don't talk about anything other than the film business." He said, "You go to dinner or a party, and invariably the first question you hear is, 'What are you working on?' You constantly have to justify that you're still in the game. You constantly need to justify that you're still a success." Furthermore, "there was stratification, elitism, no mingling," he said. "What we were looking for we didn't find: a sense of community. I was coming back to Indiana 10 or 15 times a year, and it hit me that Indiana was my community. I never wanted to get on the plane [back] to Los Angeles." So in 2004, Pizzo and his wife and two sons left California and relocated to his hometown of Bloomington. "I love the Midwest, and I feel at home here," he said. "This is our tribe."

Witnessing Pizzo's satisfaction with his move caused Anspaugh to consider doing the same thing. Of Hollywood, Anspaugh said, "I was never cut out for that town. I never intended to live there. I never had the energy or the stomach for the place, and it nauseates me." In the summer of 2014 Anspaugh moved back to Bloomington. Though no longer a resident of Tinseltown, he stayed involved in his profession by teaching a class at IU, directing local theater, and serving as executive producer for locally made independent films. Anspaugh wanted his legacy to involve more than just sports pictures. "It's bothered me a lot from time to time," he said. "I'm very capable of doing other types of movies besides things with nets and balls and bats." He hoped to make moderately budgeted films with "stories indigenous to the Midwest, where people like Angelo and me would have full creative control."

Pizzo stayed busy penning screenplays, but he found the process didn't get easier with time. "Usually, I'm tortured when I'm writing," he said. "I'm not disciplined at all. I find writing arduous, difficult, painful." He believes a writer's work comes from "a deeper place, a place of vulnerability, a place of pain. I never met a writer who said he really loved writing and was really any good."

When the idea for *Rudy* was first pitched to him, Pizzo turned it down because he feared becoming pigeonholed as the Indiana sports movie guy. In the years following the triumph of *Hoosiers* and *Rudy*, he fielded numerous offers to write sports-themed screenplays, many of which he decided to accept. Becoming known for writing and producing *Hoosiers* and *Rudy* has been "both a burden and an opportunity," he said. "I get some great [offers] because of the success I've had." He was especially proud of stories he wrote about Mickey Mantle and the Harlem Globetrotters. One of his favorite scripts, a semiautobiographical story he wrote on spec, was set in 1941 in Logansport, Indiana, where his father grew up. It concerned an Italian-American family in which one of the sons idolizes baseball player Joe DiMaggio, who had a 56-game hitting streak that summer. But after he had spent more than 20 years penning athletics stories, Pizzo announced, "I can't do another team sport where a coach is involved. I am fundamentally incapable of writing another locker room scene."

The writer had to face harsh Hollywood reality as very few of his scripts completed the uphill journey to becoming finished films. "It's a miracle any movie gets made," he said. "There are so many gatekeepers." But he never gave up hope that his unproduced scripts would someday be turned into movies.

Even after completing approximately 25 screenplays, "I don't think of myself as a writer," Pizzo said. "I see myself as a filmmaker." He likened writing to directing, saying that composing a screenplay involves picturing images that will be translated into words and then back into images.

Three decades after *Hoosiers*, Pizzo realized a long-held goal with the release of his motion-picture directorial debut, *My All American* (aka *Courage*). This project, for which he also penned the screenplay, added yet another sports movie, and a second college football film, to his résumé. "I just wanted the opportunity to do the movie in my mind that I transcribed to the page and see it all the way through to the end," he said. Of his first time helming a film, he commented, "Early on, I was nervous. [But] once I stepped behind the camera, it felt like second nature. Directing this movie was an intense experience—14-hour days for 40 days. It was the most exhilarating but exhausting thing I've ever done in my life."

Above all, Pizzo is mindful of his legacy. "I always wanted to make films that my kids would be proud of," he said. "The works that I do should say something about me, about my values, the things I find important."

Reflections

During their graduate-school days at the USC film school, Anspaugh and Pizzo brainstormed about movies they'd like to make. Along with the plot that eventually became *Hoosiers*, they toyed with the idea of doing a movie about the fraternity experience during the height of the Vietnam War. "Angelo wanted to throw in a subplot about [IU's] Little 500," Anspaugh said. They ran these concepts past a professor who taught writing. He told them, "I know these experiences you had really mean a lot to you. But no one is going to care about some little bicycle race or about how some little farm team won the state championship."

"Six weeks later," Anspaugh continued, "*Variety* announced that 20th Century Fox had green-lighted *Breaking Away*. That's the last time we listened to anyone in authority." He declared, "Don't listen to anyone who tells you not to follow your dream."

Pizzo and Anspaugh found out just how hard it can be to live your dream from all the difficulties they faced in making *Hoosiers*. Anspaugh believed they benefited from not knowing what they were in for. "If we had, we probably wouldn't have done it. There was something to be said for that naïveté, not knowing what we were getting ourselves into," he said. "*Hoosiers* was a great experience I would not want to relive. If my agent gave me that script today and said I had five weeks to prep it and 39 days to shoot it, I would laugh and hand it back to him." Anspaugh concluded, "I don't know how in God's name we ever made that movie."

Anspaugh felt fortunate that the first motion picture he directed was one that had special meaning for him. "It wasn't as though I chose [*Hoosiers*] as my first movie; it just happened that way, and I was incredibly lucky," he said. "It's very rare that a filmmaker has a chance to do a movie that's that personal to them first time out. You usually have to make your bones either commercially or critically, or hopefully both, and you do two or three of those, and then you can sort of call your own shots."

"I never did think of it as a sports movie," he continued. "To me and Angelo, it was much more than that." *Hoosiers*, he said, is "about fathers and sons and community—and about defining yourself instead of having others define you." He feels that "it is a good movie, a good story, and well told, starting with Angelo's words, right down to the performances, down to the crew, down to the people of New Richmond." On the days of filming in Knightstown, the director recalled, "the fans cheered as hard at 7 p.m. as they did at 7 a.m." He added, "I will never make another movie as personal."

Pizzo commented that he and Anspaugh always wanted "to tell stories that touched us and that meant something personal to us. We never made a film with the thought, 'Gee, I think it's going to be a huge box office success.' It wasn't commerce that was driving us. It was passion. And I think that comes through."

Pizzo and Anspaugh visit the Hoosier Gym to commemorate the movie's 30th anniversary.

When the writer/producer ruminates on *Hoosiers*, although he's proud of its success, he doesn't concentrate on how much money it earned or the lists it's been named to. He contemplates how making the movie affected and changed him. "It's not the destination. It's the journey and the experiences along the way," Pizzo said. "Those months making the movie tested me. I was a changed person. It made me feel I could do anything."

During Pizzo's infrequent viewings of *Hoosiers*, "I look at all the faces in the crowd," he said, "and recall how much support we got from the people of Indiana. They are part of this." What he admires most about the film is not his own work, but the acting, direction, and music. These elements "made my words and story sing," he said. "Certain choices clearly improved what I had done."

At the same time, Pizzo has mixed emotions about his first feature: "Certain scenes I still enjoy. I want to see them over and over again. Other scenes embarrass me. They embarrassed me from the very beginning and get worse the more I watch it. They make me cringe. But I think part of my attitude toward the movie has been weaning myself and putting it in my past and thinking of it as an experience, and a terrific one, but one that's over." He concluded, "My focus is on the future. I never look back. I apply the same technique to my life as I do to my writing, which is to keep turning the page until I get to the end."

10
Legacy: *Hoosiers'* Lasting Appeal

"I hate to tell you this, Mr. Dale, but it's only a game." —Myra

Three tourist destinations are a testament to *Hoosiers'* persistence:

Even though New Richmond sits about 11 miles from the nearest interstate exit, curiosity seekers still manage to find their way there. They zigzag along county roads, past endless farm fields, until they reach the intersection of Wabash and Washington Streets. They stop in at the Hickory Café, whose walls are covered with photos of the filming, and they ply the locals with questions about the production. Across the street, the post office window still says "Hickory, Ind."

Nestled in a quiet Knightstown neighborhood of late 19th and early 20th century homes, the Hoosier Gym sits well back from the street. It blends in so naturally with its surroundings that it can be easy for visitors to miss. In the Gym's small lobby, they notice *Hoosiers* playing on a TV. Trophies and plaques listing basketball records and statistics from local teams long gone compete for space with *Hoosiers* souvenirs, photos, and memorabilia. Visitors exit the lobby by walking through the white double doors that lead into the Gym. They cross the lacquered playing floor with its outlines of 1950s-width free throw lanes and its gold H in the red center circle. They pass the gray-green bleachers where hundreds of fans cheered the Huskers at each home game. They descend the stairs into the cramped locker room. There they recall how Coach Dale growled at his players after the first home game: "What I say when it comes to this basketball team is the *law*, absolutely and without discussion!" They pick up a piece of chalk and inscribe a blackboard with their favorite quotes from the movie: "Welcome to Indiana basketball." "My team is on the floor." "I'll make it."

About an hour's drive to the southeast, a former bank building in downtown Milan stores not money but mementos—from both the 1954 state-champion basketball team and *Hoosiers*. The institution's name—the Milan '54 *Hoosiers* Museum—exemplifies the blurring of fact and fiction that has characterized the Milan story ever since the movie was made. Keepsakes from the 1954 team and tournament are intermixed with costumes and props from the film. The varicolored uniforms of Hickory's rival teams almost seem as if they were collected from the Indians' 1950s opponents.

Few motion pictures inspire permanent tributes like these. The definitive reasons why a certain film stands above others are impossible to pin down but fascinating to ponder. Anspaugh and Pizzo (a former student of film theory and criticism who ironically doesn't like to analyze his own movies) have seen *Hoosiers* undergo detailed scrutiny from multifarious people. Professional critics, journalists, scholars, basketball fans, and regular moviegoers have parsed the film, discovering various meanings in it. These include lessons about leadership and management, religious symbolism, and even statements about the politics of race and gender.

During production in 1985, Pizzo asserted that *Hoosiers* is "a film that goes against Hollywood's trend of targeting specific audiences like yuppies and teenagers." He predicted, "I think our film will appeal to everyone." And he was right. But just why has *Hoosiers* enjoyed greater and longer-lasting popularity than its creators ever expected? On the surface it's a low-key tale of an underdog sports team achieving greatness, flawed people seeking redemption, a look back at less complicated times. But it transcends its unvarnished story, creating meaning and symbolism that lead to many different interpretations. This chapter examines the sundry aspects and qualities that have resulted in the film's success and longevity.

Factors in the Filmmakers' Favor

Although Anspaugh and Pizzo faced many obstacles in creating *Hoosiers*, several circumstances worked to their advantage:

- The production was anchored by the strong bond between the director and writer/producer, their compatible personalities, and their shared vision for the film. A few people warned Anspaugh that working with Pizzo would ruin his friendship with the writer. But Anspaugh said actually the opposite occurred—their friendship was strengthened. He said of Pizzo, "When things got really stressful and tough, and I even felt like giving up at one point, he was right there to throw cold water on me and give me a good slap in the face. His presence was invaluable. I don't know what I would have done without him on that set. When things got really difficult with the schedule, the pressure was so intense, dealing with Gene on a bad day, I always had someone who helped me release some of that tension. Angelo was my sounding board." As Pizzo sees it, "David's like a brother. We complement each other's styles." Pizzo views himself as rational and linear and Anspaugh as instinctual and emotional.

- Executive producer John Daly was a major advocate of both the film and its creators. He gave Anspaugh and Pizzo the freedom to make the movie they wanted to without creative interference; he never came to the set. He also was one of the first to envisage *Hoosiers* as a potential Oscar contender.

- The filmmakers had a distribution deal with Orion from the beginning, so they didn't have to search for a distributor upon the movie's completion.

- The participation of thousands of Indiana residents provided inestimable value to the production.

- Although it wasn't part of the original plan, filming in different locations for the town, school, and gym meant that more people in more communities took part. This fact also generated increased media attention.

- Publications all over Indiana, not just those in the filming locations, carried stories about the production and premiere. From January 1985 through March 1987, over 225 articles about *Hoosiers* appeared in more than 40 newspapers and magazines statewide. The movie also was written about in campus newspapers, university alumni magazines, and even regional workplace newsletters. The amount of media interest impressed Gene Hackman, who said he had never appeared in a movie that received as much local press coverage as *Hoosiers* did.

- Positive reviews in the *Los Angeles Times, Chicago Sun-Times, New York Times, Washington Post, Sports Illustrated, Time, Variety,* and other widely read publications gave *Hoosiers* credibility as a motion picture with broad appeal. These notices were early evidence that the movie had turned out to be much more than a low-budget flick that would generate only regional interest.

Authenticity

Movie critics and regular viewers almost unanimously agree that *Hoosiers* exudes an undeniable genuineness. As production began, Pizzo and Anspaugh shouldered a huge responsibility in attempting to portray one of Indiana's most hallowed traditions—basketball—as well as depicting life in 1950s rural Indiana. Pizzo averred, "David and I really did take great care to be real and accurate and honest in our depiction and portrayal of people in this state." He said they wanted "to show the state off as we see it—with great love and great respect." Peg Mayhill, who witnessed much of the filming in Knightstown, noticed that Anspaugh and Pizzo were "very intent on getting everything right. They put their heart and soul in it and conveyed it to the audience."

Reviewer Paul Attanasio wrote that Anspaugh and Pizzo "have taken the tired 'go for it' dramatics of a David-and-Goliath story and revived it with the fervor of real experience. 'Hoosiers' demonstrates that it's not the tale but the telling." Wrote James Berardinelli, "The first shots of *Hoosiers* let us know that we're in the hands of a director who understands the material. As the opening credits roll and Norman's car trundles down rural streets amidst the swirl of falling leaves, we can *feel* the location. ... We are transported, and never during the next two hours are we tempted to go elsewhere."

A major decision that contributed greatly to the film's realistic ambience was shooting on location in Indiana, using area residents as extras. Key second assistant director Harvey Waldman noted that, for the extras, participating in *Hoosiers* "was an authentic expression for them. They weren't from the outside, commenting on it." He added, "They weren't blasé about the film project; it was something special."

The filmmakers' determination to cast real Hoosier hoopsters as the team members also paid off handsomely. Stated Pizzo, "No one can question the believability of this group winning ball games." Reviewer Pete Croatto appreciated that "the actors actually can play the sport, which gives the game scenes in *Hoosiers* a rarely seen realism. The athletic skills of the actors allow for limitless editing and cinematography possibilities." Bill Simmons of ESPN.com said the filmmakers' "attention to detail was superb. The [Huskers] shot the ball just like [players] did in the '50s."

Reviewer Leonard Pierce concluded, "Unabashedly sentimental and unrepentantly traditional, *Hoosiers* nonetheless is a winner, illustrating that you can avoid criticism for making a straightforward sports film by simply getting it right at every turn."

As many details as it gets right, however, *Hoosiers* at times comes perilously close to caricature with some hickish touches. The Fleeners' house is covered in peeling paint, and their barn looks ready to blow over in the next strong wind. They drive a rusty truck. Shooter's house has holes in the walls. Almost everyone in town uses improper grammar, even the high school principal. The pep band plays poorly and out of tune in the deleted state-finals caravan scene. A student is shown wearing denim overalls to school. The coach says his players have never seen a building more than two stories tall. Ollie's class report on items indicating progress mentions electricity and indoor plumbing. But these questionable details don't spoil the movie. Reporter Scott Miley, who covered the making of the film for the *Indianapolis Star*, addressed the issue: "In New

Richmond, a ghost town atmosphere leaks through dingy store fronts.... A muddied Hickory High bus looks ready to collapse. Names of movie characters include Shooter, Sheriff Sam, Buddy, Junior and Loetta—backwoods monikers. But, as one watches filming progress, the honesty at the heart of *Hoosiers* comes through." Enthused Attanasio, "Beneath the clichés lies a rich and detailed portrait of a time, a place and a way of life." But perhaps Evan West of *Indianapolis Monthly* put it best when he wrote, "Yes, it's replete with images of barns, cornfields, podunk towns and basketball goals on dirt courts—nearly every timeworn Indiana stereotype. ... [But] Hoosiers love to love *Hoosiers*, often in spite of ourselves."

Objectivity

Hoosiers also manages to portray its setting and characters with objectivity. Said critic Jeffrey Lyons, "Rather than being sentimentalized or glamorized, the look of the flat, drab farmland community is authentic." Todd McCarthy wrote in *Variety*, "The characters are neither sentimentalized nor caricatured." Movie reviewer Richard Schickel commented, "By laconically contrasting images of despair and hope—bleak winter fields and the throbbing heat and noise of a jam-packed gym in the fourth quarter when the game is close—Director Anspaugh achieves an admirable objectivity. He neither condemns nor justifies the sporting passion when it is distorted by claustrophobic pressure. He just tries to understand it."

Story Quality

Although Hoosier Hysteria was the primary inspiration for the screenplay, Pizzo didn't set out to make a sports movie. He crafted a story about characters and their struggles. Despite their flaws and shortcomings, they possess an innate goodness that's waiting to be uncovered and expressed. Although it unfolds in a relatively simple and direct style, the narrative doesn't lack subtlety or surprise. Movie critic A.O. Scott noted that *Hoosiers* "tells its story in a very straightforward and engrossing way, with a lot of momentum, and an absence of the kind of sentimentality and nostalgia that infuse depictions of small-town life." Wrote Tom Carson in *GQ*, "Unlike most sports flicks, *Hoosiers* doesn't hype the outcome by pretending that what's at stake is epochal—not to anyone but the people involved, anyhow—and that's what makes it affecting."

A Focus on Characters and Their Relationships

One of Pizzo's best insights when writing the script was to emphasize relationships more than basketball. Philosophy professor Michael L. Peterson viewed Hickory not as a basketball-crazy burg but as "a world where character breeds self-worth and achievement and where forgiveness makes possible amazing transformations." The characters' interactions, along with their wish for redemption and repaired relationships, are ultimately more important and gratifying than wins on the basketball court. The quiet personal moments also are a nice contrast to the noise, action, and raw emotion of the basketball games. Finally, the focus on relationships allows the characters to exhibit positive attributes that win over the viewers.

Straightforwardness of Motives

There's something refreshing and un-Hollywood about characters who don't have hidden motives or schemes they hope to carry out. All the characters in *Hoosiers* display this quality. Everyone is clear about what they want. No one acts with guile. No one has a hidden or less-than-honest agenda. In any other movie, Norman's speech to Jimmy, ending with "I don't care if you play on the team or not," would be a reverse-psychology trick. But Norman means what he says.

The characters act without apology, timidity, or tentativeness. Shooter goes to Norman's home uninvited to offer him an unsolicited scouting report. Myra is unapologetic about encouraging Jimmy to quit the team. Norman stands firm on his coaching techniques, even when challenged by the townspeople. Jimmy walks into the town meeting after the other players have been denied admittance and speaks his mind. He doesn't ask Norman's permission to join the team. And Jimmy also tells the coach he can make the last field goal at the state finals.

A Hint of Mystery

As straightforward as the plot and the characters' motives are, they are not without nuance. Pizzo accomplished this by including some mysteries in the storyline. Of course, we learn the answer to the first question that's introduced—why a successful former junior college coach would move to an isolated farming community. But other questions remain unexplored. What is the true source of Shooter's pain that leads him to drink? Will the Huskers get better college opportunities as a result of making it to the state finals? Did Myra tell anyone else about the newspaper article she found, such as Jimmy or her mother? Have Jimmy and Myra shared with each other their opinions of Norman?

The film also intelligently leaves a few key plot points unresolved. We don't know if missing the state finals will be the jolt Shooter needs to help him successfully complete his rehabilitation and stay sober, or if missing the game will push him further into despair. We also don't know what the future holds for Norman and Myra's fledgling relationship. When Myra asks Norman if he plans to stay in Hickory, he doesn't answer. At that moment, he doesn't know if he'll stay, and neither do we.

Responsibility

The characters in *Hoosiers* assume responsibility for their mistakes. Coach Dale was in exile for years after punching one of his college players. Whit apologizes for walking out of the first basketball practice. Norman gets thrown out of two games when he can't control his temper (and he also comes perilously close to losing his job). At the town meeting, Norman confesses, "I've made some mistakes," and then he adds, "but they're mistakes I take full responsibility for." And in the most heart-wrenching example, Shooter misses the most important basketball game in the town's history and in his son's life because he's in rehab.

Humility

Coach Norman Dale has an undeniably strong personality. If he didn't evince at least some humility, he'd be unlikable, insufferable—maybe even unbearable. The Huskers' leader understands that he must practice humility in order to receive his second chance. This down-and-out coach has simple goals—returning to coaching while hopefully achieving a winning season. Appropriately, his redemption takes place in the unpretentious environs of Hickory.

Although Norman knows he's lucky to have been granted a fresh start, he doesn't find it easy to adjust his attitude at first. It doesn't help that his initial attempt at deference doesn't turn out well. At the first basketball practice, when he states, "I'm gonna be learning from you, just like you learn from me," Buddy and Whit react disrespectfully by whispering and laughing. As the Huskers lose their first games and Norman becomes more alienated from the townsfolk, he realizes he can't succeed all on his own; he needs the help and support of others. One indication of this insight is when the coach humbles himself by asking Shooter, the town's biggest outcast, for help with the team. And Norman's admission at the start of his speech at the town meeting ("I've made some mistakes") is a lesser show of humility. Minutes later, he experiences a larger humbling moment when Myra and Jimmy act to save his job. Michael L. Peterson wrote that humility and surrender of false superiority are two components of giving to others exactly what we ourselves need.

Other characters display humility as well. Whit and Buddy humble themselves when they ask to return to the team. Jimmy shows humility by rejoining the Huskers and thus acknowledging that giving up basketball was the wrong decision. And Shooter is forced to own up to the fact that he needs professional help to stop drinking.

Respect for Others

The characters tolerate others' beliefs, even when they disagree with them. Norman doesn't fight Jimmy's decision to stay off the team. He also accepts the tradition of a prayer before the games and doesn't try to discourage Strap's individual prayers. Myra accompanies her mother to basketball games even though Myra herself has no use for the sport. Furthermore, she accepts Jimmy's return to basketball. The Huskers, with some initial reluctance, adopt Norman's unconventional basketball practice methods and his rule about four passes before a shot.

The Comfort of Nostalgia, Tempered by Serious Themes

Pizzo has a fondness for the decade in which the movie takes place; he calls that time period the last era of true innocence. "The early '50s have always interested me because, I suppose, it was the last era before television sort of homogenized the consciousness, the language of the subcultures of America," he commented. On the other hand, Pizzo acknowledged that "there's a fine line between sentiment and sentimentality." So he balanced the story's warm, nostalgic feelings with more downbeat elements, such as hostile townspeople, fractured families, and alcoholism. Observed Jeffrey Lyons, "Whereas most other sports movies about an underdog team are comedies, ... there is an undercurrent of wistfulness in *Hoosiers*."

The Art of Minimalism

Many people praised the story's conciseness and the artfulness of the film's simple, straightforward, almost spare mood. Indeed, this isn't the kind of movie that would have benefited from long stretches of dialog or a showy directorial style. Pete Croatto wrote, "Pizzo's script ... is a masterpiece of economy and balance. He's able to reveal volumes about a character with one line, and by doing so he creates a portrait of a team and a town consumed with winning. ... Shooter ... sums up his sorry life with a two-sentence story about missing a game-winning shot." Director Anspaugh opined, "The brilliance of Angelo [as a writer], I think, is his economy. He just allows me to fill in the blanks, to shade it in. He trusts his actors and director."

But the script didn't start out as a minimalist masterpiece. Originally it was a 230-page monster into which Pizzo had crammed too many plotlines and too much dialog. It was long on details and short on understatedness. Pizzo eventually realized his mistake had been in writing a complete story for every character. But several script revisions, numerous trimmed and deleted lines, and the painful elimination of some scenes during editing resulted in a tighter, more focused story. Not every character's background was explored, not every motive examined, not every feeling voiced.

Two deleted scenes included on the DVD that give some details about Shooter's and Norman's backgrounds don't really add to our understanding of the characters. Another cut scene shows Norman and Myra right after the town meeting, where she decided at the last minute not to disclose the secret in Norman's past. He tells her, "What you did took a great deal of strength and courage. I know how hard it was for you. And that, more than anything else, means a lot to me." Far better is the scene that made it into the movie, where Norman's only reaction to Myra's charitable action is the expression on his face.

In yet another deleted scene, Opal explains to Norman the importance of advancing past the sectional in the tournament: "Winning the sectional is like taking grand prize around these parts. Most little farm schools can't match up to those city schools in regionals. First school we play is more than 15 hundred kids. ... The fact is, no one from this section ever reached the regional finals." In the film, Shooter conveys this concept much more succinctly: "Sectional champs? I know what that means to these folks around here. A lot. I remember what it meant to me." His facial expression and tone of voice give these lines greater impact than Opal's bit of dialog that is over twice as long. And it doesn't need to be spelled out that Hickory will compete against much larger schools as it progresses in the tournament. We can sense this from the increasing size of the gyms.

Anspaugh's uncomplicated directorial style also served the movie well. Mike Pearson wrote that *Hoosiers*' "quiet approach yields an unexpected emotional force." Commented film critic Michael Phillips, "*Hoosiers* isn't really a classic sports movie in terms of technique: There's nothing flashy or attention-getting about any of its moves, either on the court or behind the camera. ... [But] because basketball (particularly high school basketball, whatever the era) is such a great spectator sport, it works like gangbusters on-screen."

Visual minimalism is evident in the movie's concluding shot, as the camera zooms in on the team photo in the gym while a lone boy shoots baskets. This scene presumably takes place only a short while after the state championship. However, if not for the 48-star American flag hanging on the wall, we could imagine that this action is occurring in the present day—or maybe even in the future. Thus, the movie ends on a simple and timeless note.

Literalism Versus Symbolism

It's tempting to view the movie in a strictly literal way, simply because the literal elements, such as the basketball games, are rendered so effectively. But other themes are more symbolic, such as redemption, forgiveness, and grace. The film's symbolic meanings elevate plot points that, in another movie, would come across as either unbelievable or unoriginal. Strictly speaking, Norman's asking the town drunk to be his assistant coach isn't that believable. But this action perfectly exemplifies the movie's redemption theme. Ollie's free throws at the end of the regional when considered literally can seem banal—the clumsiest player ensures a key victory. But viewed symbolically, this scene proves that the team can't do without even its weakest member. Basketball is the literal vehicle through which many of the movie's themes are realized.

Two of the best symbolic meanings occur during the opening credits. Norman begins his trip to Hickory at sunrise, signaling not just the beginning of a new day but also a second chance for the coach. Sunbeams breaking through cloudy skies seem to offer hope for a better future. The shot where Norman stops his car at a rural intersection occupied by only dried cornstalks and a tiny white chapel indicates that he's at a crossroads in his life. This visual symbolism occurs long before we learn about Norman's troubled past and his need to start over, and it serves as muted foreshadowing.

The black coaches of the opposing team in the state-finals game can be viewed as symbolic of coming changes. In 1951–52, the years during which *Hoosiers* takes place, the very few black coaches in Indiana were found at all-black high schools such as Indianapolis Crispus Attucks. However, this situation would change in a few years. "Jumpin'" Johnny Wilson, Indiana's Mr. Basketball in 1946 and a Harlem Globetrotter in the early and mid-'50s, became head basketball coach at the integrated Indianapolis Wood High School at the end of that decade.

The pep session scene also includes symbolic meaning. What's supposed to be a fun basketball season-opening event quickly turns uncomfortable as the crowd begins chanting for Jimmy. After Coach Dale silences them and finishes his speech, in that scene's final image, he stands alone in front of the entire town. The team stands behind him, literally—and also figuratively, because they are becoming some of his first supporters in the community.

Quality of Acting

One of *Hoosiers'* greatest strengths is the performances of the actors—especially the three leads. They are so well cast that it's hard to imagine anyone else in their roles.

Gene Hackman

Hackman is an actor of great understatement, as he demonstrated brilliantly in the 1974 film *The Conversation*. In *Hoosiers* his everyman appearance and low-key acting style helped him disappear into the character of Coach Norman Dale. James Berardinelli wrote that Hackman's "performance is letter perfect, from the competitive heat he shows during games to the reflective sadness that emerges in quieter moments. The film doesn't have to give us a detailed backstory for Norman; Hackman's acting provides us with a full definition of his personality."

Hackman's acting style allowed him to communicate his feelings through his expressions and reactions. In the scene where Myra informs him of the town meeting that will decide his fate, you can sense his deep hurt as he searches for a reply. You also can perceive his sorrow and dispiritedness during his speech at the meeting, even as he says, "I apologize for nothing." And in the scene where Myra reads Norman the article she found, detailing his lifetime suspension from the NCAA, Hackman's face displays a whole range of emotions.

Paul Attanasio said, "Hackman anchors the movie with a performance of remarkable control. You see his hurt in his glances at his shoes, his little phony chuckle; you can feel him carrying his secret—it's a rage held together with rubber bands." Myron Meisel wrote, "Hackman creates an entire physical vocabulary for this man that expresses more than any amount of dialog could convey." And Scott Tobias wrote, "Whenever the schmaltz threatens to ooze over, [Pizzo and Anspaugh] have a secret weapon in Gene Hackman, whose no-guff performance as a coach with a checkered past seems lived-in and genuine."

Barbara Hershey found Hackman easy to work with. "I was totally unselfconscious acting with him, which isn't easy to achieve," she said. "He was so good that I became caught up in what he was doing. We were electric—that's what I felt." Meisel thought the scenes with Hershey and Hackman "comprise wonderful examples of two players of superbly mature skills volleying off one another." Hackman's talent and professionalism also rubbed off on the newbie actors who played the Huskers. Wade Schenck called Hackman "the kind of actor who makes everyone around him look good."

In a 2004 interview with Larry King, Hackman revealed why he sometimes gave directors a hard time: "I have trouble with direction because I have trouble with authority. I was not a good Marine. I made corporal once and was promptly busted. I just have always had trouble with authority."

Anspaugh acknowledged that working with Hackman hadn't been all bad: "I learned a lot from him—things I could incorporate into my directing."

Barbara Hershey

The lead actress brought a toughness and determination to the most difficult role in the movie. The part required a strong performer who could make an impression in a small number of scenes. A younger or milder woman couldn't have done as well.

Said director Barry Levinson, who worked with Hershey on *The Natural* and *Tin Men*, "She stays with her convictions. Her instincts are very true. She has a great deal of credibility in just the way she presents herself. In her heart and soul, she is a really serious woman and actress." Dave Kehr of the *Chicago Tribune* called her "one of the most appealing performers in American movies."

Hershey worked on the character of Myra "from the inside out," she said. "I tried to find the parts of me that were in her—she's very angry and she's very repressed and she's very unhappy. She never took the chance to leave the town and evolve. And because of that she lives vicariously through her students."

Dennis Hopper

"Out of all the characters I wrote," Pizzo said, "[Hopper] added the most color and dimension to the part." During the writing process, he said, "I really didn't think of [Shooter] as much more than a dark soul. When Dennis showed up, he brought all these different colors like humor, whimsy, playfulness, heart, and kindness and things I hadn't intended in the script. He made a much more dimensional, much more multifaceted character than I sketched out. That was one of the great experiences for a writer—to see what an actor can bring to make something you've written so much better."

Commented *Rebel Without a Cause* screenwriter Stewart Stern in 1988, "The performance in *Hoosiers* was the best thing that I've seen from Dennis. I long for Dennis to start dealing with the things that really have touched him ... the farm in Kansas, his grandparents. I saw some of that in *Hoosiers*, a vulnerability. And I wish that he would let himself be moved again by his own childhood. There's a side of him which is authentic and America at its most traditional."

Richard Schickel of *Time* noted, "Hopper brings some fresh, forceful observation and a jittery melancholy" to his role. The actor's long battle with drug and alcohol addiction helped him understand exactly what his character was going through. As a recovered substance abuser, Hopper knew the toll that addiction takes and everything the addict loses, as well as the commitment that is necessary for a successful recovery. Thus, his simple lines in the hospital are convincing and deeply affecting.

Wrote Paul Attanasio, "In creating Shooter, who missed the key shot in the big game and has been down and out ever since, Hopper seems to have drawn on all those years when he was down and out himself." Hopper's own life somewhat paralleled that of Shooter, a high school basketball star whose later life took a turn for the worse, eventually rendering him an outcast in his community. Hopper's addictions almost wrecked his career. At the time *Hoosiers* was filmed, he had been sober for only a couple years. "I did the part without drinking," he said. "If I had done it before, I would have been drinking and performing. My mood swings would have been unbearable." One of the favorite scenes of Hopper biographer Elena Rodriguez was when a hospitalized Shooter confesses, "I feel real empty inside, and I have some bad visions." She wrote, "To look at Hopper's face at that moment is to look at a man who has felt that emptiness and seen the horrors lurking there." Reviewer Robert Spuhler said, "Hopper strikes just the right note between being in control and out. [Shooter's] alcoholism controls him, but Hopper knows how to avoid caricature and is believable, even as he jumps up and down on the bed celebrating at the end of the film."

Actor James Dean was a major influence on Hopper's acting style. Dean became a mentor and informal acting coach for the younger actor during the filming of *Rebel Without a Cause* and *Giant*. Hopper said that Dean employed "spontaneity" and "real emotions" and would act "from a moment-to-moment reality rather than a preconceived idea." With this acting technique, "you stop indicating," Hopper said. You "stop presupposing or guessing what's going to happen, working it out technically. You let it happen to you."

Anspaugh appreciated Hopper's humility. "When actors come up with suggestions, there's a lot of ego at stake," the director remarked. "Dennis could come up with six ideas, you could say no to all of them, and he wouldn't be bothered by it."

Although he didn't receive an Academy Award, Hopper won a Los Angeles Film Critics Association (LAFCA) Award for his role as Shooter. He also was nominated for a Golden Globe.

Supporting Actors

The actors in the smaller roles also created engaging characters.

Jeffrey Lyons thought the young men who played the Huskers "project stoic, believable screen presences." James Berardinelli also was impressed by the first-time actors, saying that they "acquit themselves admirably." He also picked up on one of Pizzo's strategies, noticing that "the filmmakers are savvy enough not to tax them by providing them with complicated storylines requiring displays of range." Wrote Steve Vineberg in the *Boston Phoenix*, "After [several] miserably fraudulent high school sports movies of the last few years, it's a relief to see teenagers on-screen who were obviously cast because they look like emissaries from the real world and because, when their distinctive personalities knock up against one another, they produce a believably messy mix." Said Hackman of his team, "They were terrific kids, and you can see it in the film. There's a wonderful innocence in the boys ... they conveyed a kind of wonderful cleanness and kind of a naïveté. They were really well cast."

The team members differentiated themselves well despite their limited dialog and screen time. Scott Summers did an excellent job of bringing Strap to life, exuding a peaceful benevolence. His character's minimalist description in the script says only that he "smiles a lot for no apparent reason." And the fear and uncertainty in Ollie's face at the regional seem quite real. The Huskers convincingly emanated emotion, passion, and intensity on the playing floor by drawing on their real-life athletic experiences. Pizzo said if he had known what good actors the Huskers would become, he would have written more substantial parts for them. "All of us exceeded our capabilities in the movie," opined Husker Wade Schenck. As for his own role as Ollie, he added self-effacingly, "I was just in the right place at the right time. Anybody could have done it."

Opal stood out in her few scenes as Myra's basketball-loving mom. Reviewer David Mannweiler called actress Fern Persons "plucky" and a scene stealer. Chelcie Ross, as the troublemaking George, struck just the right notes as one of Norman's biggest critics. And Robert Swan was quietly forceful as Whit and Rade's steady, caring father and the Huskers' coaching assistant.

The Three Main Characters

Despite *Hoosiers'* basketball theme, Norman, Myra, and Shooter are the heart of the movie. Of course, the coach is the most important of the three. But without either Shooter or Myra, the story would be incomplete.

The movie doesn't provide a wealth of information on any of them. In some ways this creates a more involving story, because our imaginations can fill in the details and make up the backstories.

As different as these primary characters are, they have things in common. Each one is both an outsider and an insider. Norman has an insider's knowledge of basketball but is an outsider as the newest member of the community. Having lived in Hickory his whole life, Shooter technically is an insider in his community, but his alcoholism has rendered him an outsider (and an outcast because of his public drunkenness). As another Hickory native, Myra also is a community insider but is an outsider to the town's mania for basketball.

In addition, all three characters find themselves residing (or possibly trapped) in a small town. Reviewer Holly E. Ordway wrote that one of the film's "timeless and thought-provoking themes" is "an exploration of the idea that choosing to live out one's life in a small town is an indication of personal failure."

A final characteristic the three share is that each one needs to change in order to get to a better place in life. Norman knows he needs to change (by controlling his temper) in order to take full advantage of the second chance he's been given. Shooter also knows he needs to change, but he either doesn't know how or doesn't think he can. Myra needs to address her decisions and attitudes that have contributed to her frustration with life in Hickory. The story's elegant structure involves a logical balance of give and take between the three. None of them is really a redeemer of anyone else, because they all need, give, and receive grace. As a result, everyone both changes and is changed by others.

Coach Norman Dale

"I apologize for nothing." —Coach Dale

From the start, Hickory's new coach projects an air of confidence and an unflagging belief in his convictions, even when he's confronted by skeptical team members and doubtful townspeople. He intends to achieve success not through consensus, agreement, and compromise, but by following his own judgment. Norman manifests this trait early on by refusing to humor the suggestions of the "barbershop boys" or to accommodate the residents who want to watch the basketball practice sessions. It might have made more sense for the man who admits that Hickory represents his last chance to exercise some caution when he first comes to town. He could have been more friendly and less harsh, could have considered more suggestions and been less opinionated. After all, his stubbornness almost gets him kicked out of Hickory. However, wrote Shaun O'L. Higgins and Colleen Striegel, "By refusing to compromise, [Norman] underscores the importance he places on his job." For the audience, there's something comforting about a man who believes he's right and who is ultimately vindicated. It's gratifying to watch him win over the townspeople one by one—and win games along the way—simply by sticking to his principles.

But Norman isn't a sage savior of the backward hicks. He's brusque and impatient. When Shooter drops by the coach's house unexpectedly, instead of welcoming him, Norman asks pointedly, "Isn't it a little late to be calling on folks?" When George offers to help at basketball practice, the coach attempts to dispatch him with "Your coaching days are over." And when Norman visits Shooter at home and proposes making him an assistant coach, the conversation quickly deteriorates when Norman tells Shooter bluntly, "You're embarrassing your son."

Despite Norman's occasional heedlessness, we sense his underlying dejection and remorse; therefore, we like him and want him to succeed. Randy Williams described Hickory's new coach as "a difficult mix of compassion, suppressed anger, intense desire to win, and a strength of character with an everyman feel, a complexity that adds up to being quite human." Norman is able to pack up and leave behind his old world in only two days. He's eager for a new start and a chance to get back into coaching. And his stay in Hickory also will offer him an opportunity to become a better person.

At the start of the movie, Coach Dale is a solitary figure, opposed by nearly everyone. John Clemens and Melora Wolff wrote, "Everything about him announces his displacement and perpetual isolation." In one of the film's first images, Norman pauses at a deserted rural intersection on his journey to Hickory. At the season-opening pep session, the coach stands as a lone figure facing off against the unfriendly crowd. Later in the season, you discern his dissociation from the entire town as he sits by himself in the Hickory locker room after being ejected from a game. But Norman is never really alone. Everyone in the community is inextricably interconnected. Norman must learn to trust others as much as he trusts his own experience and instincts.

Initially Norman has only one supporter—Cletus, a friend from long ago. He gathers a few more—Rollin, Opal, Shooter. Before long, all the team members are on his side. Myra comes around. Then Jimmy rejoins the team. And as the victories pile up, the townspeople become fans of the coach as well. As the team racks up tournament victories, people throughout the state begin to take notice. This is shown by the crush of reporters following the team in a couple scenes. By the final game, Norman has seemingly every basketball lover in Indiana on his side, as evidenced by the packed Fieldhouse and people scattered throughout the state listening to the game on the radio. By the time the Huskers have claimed the state crown, Coach Dale has accumulated an army of supporters.

Is Norman a Bad Coach?

Although most fans of the movie praise the character of Norman Dale, the coach also has his detractors.

Movie critic Henry Sheehan of *The Hollywood Reporter* complained that Norman's coaching methods are not adequately elucidated: "It's never clear exactly what Dale has taught these kids or what they're doing out on the court. Their key to success remains as cloudy as the origins of the word 'Hoosier.'"

Hoosiers devotee and sports journalist Bill Simmons proclaimed Norman overrated. He said the state-finals game was "one of the worst coaching jobs of all time. Jimmy's missed one shot the whole game, and you decide to use him as a decoy for the biggest play of your season."

Other critics of the Huskers' leader find additional reasons to conclude that Norman is a bad coach. Writing for ESPN.com's Page 2, Barry Locke cited the following examples:

- During the Cedar Knob game, "instead of being the calming influence his team needs," Norman, "a coach with a history of assault," instigates a fight by slapping the hand of an opposing player.

- At the regional, Norman instructs Strap not to shoot. Luckily, Strap doesn't listen and proceeds to go on a scoring binge to put Hickory comfortably ahead. Then, when Norman is forced to put Ollie in the game, he gives "no instructions or strategy to keep the ball out of the little man's hands" and "the lead evaporates." Near the end of the game, Norman doesn't tell the Huskers what to do if Ollie misses his free throws.

- In the state-finals game, as the Huskers fall behind early on, "Dale is left searching for a game plan," forcing Merle to suggest one. For the final shot, when Norman says they will use their star player as a decoy, "the team is left speechless, and Jimmy calmly tells his coach what everyone [else] already knows: 'I'll make it.'"

Drew White of the *Michigan City (IN) News Dispatch* raised a final point:

- "In the regional finals, when Strap has to replace the injured Everett, why does Dale call a time-out right after the seldom-used post player has made back-to-back shots on consecutive possessions? ... If you've got a guy that inexplicably catches fire ... you don't throw water on the fire in the form of a mid-quarter time-out during a rally."

Shooter

"I know everything there is to know about the greatest game ever invented!"
—*Shooter*

Said by anyone else, that line would sound boastful. But rendered by Wilbur "Shooter" Flatch, with a hint of a smile at the end, it's simply the truth. And his encyclopedic knowledge of basketball may be the only area in which he shows some confidence. Shooter's alcoholism is ruining his life, causing estrangement from his wife and son and a crisis of confidence. We're never told the exact reasons for his drinking. The movie suggests that Shooter's basketball talent and knowledge never materialized into any lasting achievement. This story thread is vital to the film, because it brings weight and seriousness to what otherwise might have been just a rah-rah story of underdogs beating the odds.

Shooter finds himself as a spectator to his own life—and his son's. Becoming an assistant coach will allow him to put his vast basketball knowledge to use and also reconnect with Everett. But he must face the most difficult challenge of his life when he fails in his attempt to remain sober and must enter rehab. In a story in which the characters offer each other hope and second chances, Shooter must complete his rehabilitation on his own.

Author Randy Williams wrote that Shooter is "a welcome blend of humor and empathy, and [he brings] a crazy-like-a-fox dimension to the story. His melancholy portrayal of a man constantly fighting his demons delivers some keen insights on and off the court, and leaving his character arc unresolved by the film's end enhances the story."

Pizzo viewed Shooter as an indispensable part of the story. He was convinced that if this character had never existed, *Hoosiers* would not have been made, because financier and executive producer John Daly identified with Shooter's situation the most.

Myra

> *"I have high hopes for him. ... He could do better."* —Myra

As the lone Hickory resident who doesn't relish basketball and even finds it a waste of time, Myra is the most unsympathetic character and the hardest to identify with. Many movie critics and *Hoosiers* fans view her unfavorably. As she clashes with Norman upon their first meeting and subsequently, she becomes a one-person representation of the barbershop boys—the group of unfriendly men who dislike the new coach.

We learn little about Myra. She seems to accept living in Hickory with some resignation. We don't know if she stays in her hometown because she aspires to be a positive influence on the students of her alma mater, or because she's afraid to go anywhere else. When she speaks with Norman outside and looks out across the green pastures, she confides, "I used to play in these fields. I used to wonder what it would feel like to start walking and just keep going." This comment seems to indicate either that she's long felt trapped in Hickory, or that she used to have more of a sense of adventure. When Myra tells Norman early in the movie her theory that he's in Hickory because he has nowhere else to go, perhaps she's subconsciously expressing her own frustrations with feeling trapped and not having the courage to leave her birthplace.

We don't know how Myra feels about her teaching job—whether she finds it fulfilling or whether it's one more thing she's resigned to. She is certain Jimmy can have a future outside Hickory. Perhaps she often pushes her talented students to strive for more than small-town life. A scene showing her teaching or interacting with students could have been enlightening.

We don't know how the students and townspeople view Myra. You'd assume they would resent her for influencing Jimmy to give up basketball. Instead, they seem to blame the new coach for Jimmy's reluctance to rejoin the team. When Jimmy enters the town meeting and announces, "I figure it's time for me to start playing ball," George triumphantly exclaims, "I told you—once we got rid of *him*!" and looks at Coach Dale.

Finally, we don't know if Myra accepts or fights against the fact that her unpopular viewpoints make her an outsider in Hickory. Perhaps to her, being an outsider is an acceptable trade-off if she can convince her students to aim high when considering their futures.

The fact that Myra figures out Norman is harboring a secret indicates her intelligence and powers of perception. But we don't know if she's just more insightful than average or if her life experiences have shaped her ability to read people.

As smart and intuitive as Myra is, she fails to realize that it's a mistake for her to pressure Jimmy into denying his love of basketball. She no doubt believes she's doing what's best for him. But she fails to realize she's doing the same thing of which she accuses Norman and the townsmen: forcing aspirations onto Jimmy instead of encouraging him to choose his own path. Perhaps in Hickory Myra feels marginalized, underestimated, and underappreciated, and she sees trying to help Jimmy as a way to make a difference in someone's life. She appears to be the only Hickory resident who has contemplated Jimmy's long-term prospects. Everyone else in town seems to think no further ahead than the next ball game. On the other hand, perhaps Myra merely sees Jimmy as her best chance to bring someone around to her (unpopular) outlook—and she fears Norman will take away this opportunity. She'll feel justified in her beliefs and vindicated if Jimmy rejects basketball, embraces his studies, receives an academic scholarship, and attends college out of town. Her rationale is "I've seen 'em, the real sad ones. They sit around the rest of their lives talking about the glory days when they were 17 years old." And although Myra doesn't say so, Shooter exemplifies this statement. However, even though presumably basketball's failure to provide him a future is at least one factor that led to Shooter's alcoholism, it's basketball that redeems him. And Jimmy realizes that by rejoining his teammates and embracing the sport he loves, he can both save Coach Dale's job and help the team start winning. So Myra's stance is indeed proven wrong.

Or is it? Myra's character gives voice to skepticism about how much importance basketball and sports in general should be assigned. Maybe she's a reminder that, as much as basketball means to the people of Hickory, other things are more important.

Relationships Between the Main Characters

The script sets up a clever set of relationships between the three protagonists that creates the interesting and vital structure upon which the story is built. None of the three acts alone or stands alone. The structure isn't triangular in shape, because Shooter and Myra don't interact with or influence each other. Instead, it's more of a straight line, with Norman in the center as the strongest point. Both Myra and Shooter need Norman's help to transform themselves. Norman wants to help Shooter reconnect with his community. Perhaps he can help Myra do the same, to relieve some of the bitterness or hopelessness she feels about her situation. And Myra and Shooter end up changing the coach as well.

Norman and Shooter

Author Norman K. Denzin commented, "Without Shooter there would be only the story of Hickory and their new coach. His presence adds another dimension to Dale's character." Coach Dale undoubtedly recognizes the traits he and Shooter share. Both men have been letting their hoops expertise go to waste for years. Both have impulse control issues: Shooter drinks, and Norman loses his temper. And both are outsiders in their community. Norman needs to gain insider status, and Shooter needs to regain his.

With Shooter, Norman recognizes an opportunity to give someone a chance, just as he has been given a chance. As an assistant coach, Shooter will be able to impart his roundball conversance to the coach and team. At the same time, he can build his confidence by trying out the roles of leader and authority figure—skills that will come in handy if he intends to mend his relationship with his son.

It's likely that Norman doesn't naively imagine that his gesture of kindness toward Shooter will magically transform Shooter's life. Movie critic Roger Ebert observed that Norman probably knows his efforts to rehabilitate Shooter won't completely succeed. However, Ebert wrote, "by involving Shooter once again in the life of the community, he's giving Shooter a reason to seek the kind of treatment that might help."

Instead of condemning Shooter for his poor choices, Norman offers him a logical reason to get sober—the reasonable and seemingly reachable goal of becoming assistant coach. Shooter even gets a taste of what it's like to be head coach during the two home games from which Norman is ejected. If Shooter can succeed to the point where he can become a role model and authority figure for the team, he can begin assuming these same responsibilities with his son. When Shooter ultimately fails in his efforts to stay sober, again Norman is supportive rather than critical.

But it's not a one-sided friendship; the opportunity to help goes both ways. Shooter wisely approaches the coach in a friendly, non-threatening way that contrasts with Norman's earlier encounters with the other citizens. Norman is smart enough to realize that Shooter's understanding of Hickory's rivals can be of use to him, and he's humble enough to ask for Shooter's assistance.

Denzin wrote that "the film offers simple solutions to complex problems. But it does so in such a direct and unpretentious way that its moral message seems incontrovertible; somehow Hickory's miracle will become the miracle of Dale and Shooter."

Norman and Myra

Many movie critics and analysts are negative not only about Myra but also about her relationship with Norman. Paul Attanasio called it "a love story that goes nowhere." John Nesbit said the romance was "seemingly tossed in under Hollywood orders to create something for female audiences." Deborah Tudor believed Myra was portrayed as a sexually repressed woman who just needed to relax.

However, a positive interpretation of the relationship is also possible. It isn't that Myra needs a man's romantic attention to ease her anger and make her life complete. Rather, her self-image improves because an outsider sees qualities in her that no one else does. Myra has always lived in the same town with the same people, and they formed their opinions of her long ago. That the town's newest resident shows interest in her even though initially she is unkind toward and suspicious of him improves her self-image. Like all the other townspeople, she benefits from the new perspective that outsider Norman Dale introduces.

Certainly Norman doesn't chase after Myra because she likes him and is sweet and supportive. The fact that he pursues her so early on and so persistently clearly shows that he needs her. This fact softens his character somewhat. Although Norman displays almost complete self-confidence, he's not invulnerable. Part of him is needy. This is exemplified visually twice in the movie. When Norman enters the Hickory gym for his first game, the continuous shot from the locker room all the way across the playing floor is broken only by Norman's glance at Myra in the stands. A parallel shot occurs at the state-finals game after Jimmy's winning basket. Despite all the chaos and celebration on the floor, Norman remembers to look for Myra in the crowd. These shots also serve as a reminder that relationships trump basketball.

The relationship isn't about Norman's wanting to prove Myra wrong or win her over as a personal challenge. He recognizes that both of them have deeply held beliefs they're willing to stand up for, even in the face of strong criticism. In her he sees the same stubbornness, determination, and outspokenness he possesses. He appreciates her intelligence and resourcefulness, as evidenced by the scene in which she tells him about the newspaper article she found. He reacts not with anger or annoyance, but with a steady gaze and the barest hint of a smile. In addition, they are both teachers who hope to have a positive influence on their students. They want the kids to have goals and aspirations. But Norman and Myra are opposites in another way. Whereas Norman is a basketball insider and community outsider, Myra is the reverse. This mixture of similarities and differences offers them a unique opportunity to help each other. But both must drop their tough exterior to take a chance on being vulnerable in order to create new possibilities in their lives.

Norman, like Myra, benefits from and is changed by the relationship. Ebert called it "the rehabilitation of his heart." Pete Croatto said Myra helps unearth the likable streak in what should be an unlikable man. This process begins with her simple act of faith—deciding not to reveal Norman's secret at the meeting and asking that the others give him a chance. By the movie's climax, Coach Dale has become more patient and less harsh, even telling his team "I love you guys" before the final game.

Although Myra's early suspicion of the new coach causes her to dislike and distrust him, we see her viewpoint gradually begin to change. Tudor derided the Hollywood cliché in which "initial dislike often masks 'real love' and evaporates in the face of undeniable attraction." But we see real reasons for Myra's change of heart. She approves of how Norman silences the fans' chants of "We want Jimmy" at the pep session. She appreciates Norman's honesty and his refusal to make excuses for his behavior when she asks him why he hit one of his players during his college coaching days. And she sees him becoming more caring and less obsessed with winning when he benches an injured Everett during an important game. Myra's shift in attitude isn't illogical or sudden. In fact, it occurs in fits and starts. This proves that Myra isn't enamored of the coach—she's just willing to grant that maybe she misjudged him.

Myra and Shooter

These two individuals are the polar opposites in the triad of main characters—the two points at opposite ends of the line. Shooter is aimless; we don't know if he's even employed. He also is estranged from his family. Myra has a stable career and is a supportive and responsible daughter. He is a repository of basketball knowledge; she has no use for the game. The fact that the two don't interact or even so much as cross paths highlights their differences. At the same time, they actually have things in common. Just as Shooter has a difficult family situation, Myra has a somewhat strained relationship with her mother and probably feels conflicted about living with her. Both Myra and Shooter are dissatisfied with their lives—albeit to different degrees. And both know Norman's secret and have decided to keep it quiet.

Other Characters

Although their roles are small, the supporting characters round out the town and add depth and richness to the story.

The Huskers

Like the citizens, the Huskers are resistant to change, as shown by Jimmy's early absence and Whit and Buddy's leaving the first practice. But the players who remain run the drills as they're instructed to, even though they gripe that it "ain't no fun" and "feels like we're in the Army." Further resistance occurs as Rade defies the rule about four passes before a shot. But the team members are the early adopters of the change that Coach Dale introduces to the town. And they demonstrate the transformative power of embracing change and the success that results.

They're a fractured group when Norman arrives in Hickory. But by the end of the film they are a cohesive unit—of one mind. This is clearly evident by their expressions when Coach Dale tells them

Merle will attempt the final field goal in the last game. No one says anything at first, but we can see they're all thinking the same thing. And when Jimmy says "I'll make it," we know they agree with him.

Norman succeeds in teaching the Huskers a more disciplined, team-oriented style of play. But just as important, or perhaps more important, are all the things the Huskers teach him. Strap's lengthy prayers before and during games force Norman to develop patience and show tolerance for others' beliefs. In time, Norman can even joke with Strap about his religious fervor. When the coach removes the hurt Everett from the regional final, he decides to put his player's welfare ahead of the game's outcome. Everett's problems with his father teach Norman to care about his players' personal lives.

Jimmy

From the beginning, Coach Dale emphasizes the need for the Huskers to work as a team, with "no one more important than the other." As Norman tells Cletus, it's his experience that nobody's irreplaceable. However, *Hoosiers* actually embraces the opposite philosophy—that each member of the Huskers is indispensable. This detail is palpable as Ollie, the worst player, steps up to help secure a key victory. But the better and most obvious example of each player's invaluable nature is Jimmy. This team has been playing together for years—not just in high school, but since grade school. When one of their members is missing, they are unable to function to the best of their ability. It's not that Jimmy is the best player and the Huskers can't win without him. It's that the team is incomplete without any one of its members. The team is a miniature community of diverse individuals, each of whom has something essential to contribute. When even one person is missing, the group can't achieve its goals.

Jimmy's zeal for basketball is unmistakable, represented in images rather than words. He shoots baskets when no one else is around. He lurks outside the gym during practice and sits up high in the bleachers at the games. He bounces a basketball on his way to the town meeting. Although Jimmy has accepted Myra's seemingly sensible argument that if he drops basketball to concentrate on academics, he can get a college scholarship and depart Hickory, his true passion can't be denied. He needs to look past his sadness and Myra's goals for him and acknowledge what he loves—basketball.

The character of Jimmy might reflect Pizzo's life philosophy that you should never give other people the power to define you. As soon as Jimmy is ready to admit what he really wants and needs, he realizes that by returning to the team he can rescue the coach's career. And this turns out to be the perfect solution to both his and Norman's dilemmas.

Pizzo wisely made Jimmy a bit of an enigma by mostly relegating him to the background for much of the first half of the movie and by giving him so few lines. Jimmy doesn't speak until halfway through the film. And when he finally does, his "I play, Coach stays; he goes, I go" statement changes the course of the story.

The Townspeople

Reviewer Mitchell Hattaway wrote, "You get the sense that many of the townsmen played [basketball] while they were in school, had their moments of glory, and are now living vicariously through their children." This mindset is clearly shown in the barbershop scene. The first and most important concept the barbershop boys want to drive home to the new coach is their long-standing devotion to the team. They illustrate their interest with remarks such as "We were 15 and 10 last year, and we got all our boys back but one." Longtime Boone County resident Sharon Louks found these characters quite familiar. When she attended Lebanon High School in the '60s, her basketball team had a group of loyal followers similar to those in the movie. In her town, these men were known as the "downtown coaches."

The barbershop get-together, disguised as a friendly meet-and-greet, is actually the citizens' first opportunity to let the new coach know they're willing to give him a chance—if he plays by their rules. "Zone defense is all we've played in the past, and it's the only thing that'll work this year," they state unequivocally. They don't just want him to win; they want him to teach basketball and win games using the traditional, time-tested methods. And the barbershop boys will attend each home game and maybe even some practices to make sure Norman understands and complies.

The Movie's Themes

Although the film's most obvious subject matter is basketball, the many other themes, such as redemption, family, and achieving your dreams, make *Hoosiers* much more than just a sports flick.

Basketball

Pizzo and Anspaugh's inspiration for the story was to depict the fanaticism for basketball in Indiana and everything the sport means to Hoosiers—especially on a local level. *Hoosiers* unquestionably succeeds as a captivating sports movie. Stanley Kauffman said, "The test of this genre is simple: Knowing exactly what we are watching, are we nevertheless swept up? *Hoosiers* passes the test easily; we get taut, tearful, gleeful." Pete Croatto concluded, "It's very simple. When you talk about the best sports movies of all time, there is *Hoosiers*, and then there's everything else." But basketball goes far beyond being just a sport; it serves many purposes in the story.

A Community Tradition

Norman has only just arrived in Hickory when, in one of the deleted scenes, Cletus makes clear the importance of basketball by equating it with the academic subjects: "We give 'em a good old-fashioned 'four R' education here: readin', writin', 'rithmetic, and roundball." Although this would seem to be an extreme statement, the film in no way exaggerates Hoosiers' ardor for the game. Eight of the ten largest high school gyms in the U.S. are located in Indiana. The biggest, in New Castle, seats 9,325—over half the town's population. In 1990, a world-record crowd of more than 41,000 attended the final game of the high school boys' tournament in the Hoosier Dome. Furthermore, typical Indiana communities find public ways to inform passers-by and remind residents of some amazing basketball feat accomplished by their local team. Quite a few towns whose team has won the state championship have a sign posted at the city limits, signifying this fact. After the Milan Miracle, that town painted its water tower to say "State Champs 1954." And even though tiny Swayzee High never made it to the state finals, a large sign just outside the town boasts of another notable basketball accomplishment—that squad's victory in a nine-overtime game. That 1964 state record still stands, but the high school was consolidated into Oak Hill only a couple years after its remarkable feat.

But just why are Hoosiers so preoccupied with this particular pasttime? In the first half of the 20th century, before school district consolidation, every Indiana town, no matter how sparsely populated, had its own school and, thus, its own basketball team. These young men were the local heroes, the representatives of their town's sense of identity and pride, its standard-bearers into battle with the town's neighboring rivals. The citizenry lived vicariously through the boys' athletic exploits, and their goals and victories became the town's. As well, before the era of television, basketball games were one of the few forms of entertainment in isolated communities on winter weekends. Pizzo believed that, for Hoosier towns in the 1950s, the weekly high school basketball game was "a release point. It was a time in the winter in which people, locked up because of the cold, with a limited amount of things to do, could let it all go."

Movie reviewer John Nesbit noted, "One of the best aspects of *Hoosiers* is how well the local community spirit and attitudes are portrayed." A good example is the caravan scenes, in which a long line of cars filled with loyal supporters follows the team bus to away games. The last scene in the Hickory gym with the hoops-loving boy making baskets also suggests a feeling of tradition, as do the images throughout the film of townspeople of all ages enjoying basketball.

A Unifying Force

Film critic Roger Ebert, who started his career as a sportswriter, averred that "there is a passion to high school sports that transcends anything that comes afterward; nothing in pro sports equals the intensity of a really important high school basketball game." Former

NBA player Rick Fox, who played high school ball in Indiana at Warsaw for two seasons, agreed: "It was very special. You had this opportunity to represent your town. It was pure in that you were all really rooting for each other. Once you step out of the high school arena, you lose that sense of community."

History professor Troy D. Paino wrote that "the rise of high school basketball's popularity in Indiana can also be seen as an effort by Indiana communities to discover cohesive forces amidst modernity's tide of economic and social fragmentation." Opined professor Dayna B. Daniels, "If a culture's values and beliefs are seen to be present in sport, then sport and the athlete will be seen to be a positive aspect of a society. Therefore, sport represents a positive way for children to be socialized into the norms of that society." Aaron Baker stated, "The team operates as a social structure to foster the development of self-reliant individuals." Pizzo had a simpler explanation: "In these farming communities, where everybody lived in outlying regions from the main community center, [basketball games were] an excuse for everybody to come together."

A Constant

Although their lives and town will inevitably change over time, the residents can rest assured that the basketball tradition will never die. After all, high school boys' basketball has been a part of Hoosier existence since the beginning of the 20th century. It seems inconceivable that there could ever be a time in the future in which high school basketball doesn't exist.

The final scene of the kid shooting baskets in the empty gym conveys both tradition and constancy. It stands in stark opposition to the changes that are creeping in and slowly transforming the town. This scene also is reminiscent of the two scenes of Jimmy shooting baskets alone—on the Hickory court and on the outside court—providing a further impression of an enduring constant.

A Path to Healing

We can sense Jimmy's regret at not being on the team from his hidden observances of practices and his attendance at the games, in the last row of bleachers. But he's able to step out of his mourning period by rejoining the team.

Shooter and Everett use their shared fondness for basketball to begin repairing their relationship. When Shooter is forced to take over coaching duties during the game with Dugger, he's at a loss for words during a time-out. As the players wait for Shooter's instructions, Everett breaks the tension by speaking first: "Reckon number four'll put up their last shot, Dad?"

The Thrill of Victory

The most joyous moments in *Hoosiers* result from the team's triumphs, especially in the final game. Pizzo understood the need to conclude the movie on a high note. And most viewers and critics approved of ending *Hoosiers* with a win. James Berardinelli believed that "this isn't the sort of film where a bittersweet finale would have provided satisfaction." John Nesbit agreed, saying, "Audiences would feel ripped off and heartbroken if the ending was different."

Throughout the movie, the basketball victories move in parallel with and intertwine with individuals' victories. The characters' personal triumphs end up meaning more than the numbers on the scoreboard.

The Agony of Defeat

Remarkably, as much as the movie is about winning and realizing goals, it doesn't shy away from showing the devastation of losing and the dissatisfaction of not completely succeeding. Coach Dale comes close to being fired. Shooter falls off the wagon a couple of times. And at the conclusion of the final game, the opposing team's dejection is heartbreakingly clear.

One unfortunate side effect of the realistically rendered state-finals game was that it brought back bad memories for the real-life 1954 state runners-up. Jimmy Barnes was on the Muncie Central team defeated by Milan in the state finals. He recalled, "Nobody could imagine us losing that game to a small team like Milan. That's what made the thing so devastating." His teammate Bill Tinder commented, "To this day, I don't know what happened. How in the world did we lose that game?" The first time he watched the movie, he was reduced to tears at the recollections brought back by *Hoosiers*' final matchup. Fellow Muncie team member Philip Raisor said, "Long ago I put that game behind me, until the movie came out. Then the questions began. 'What was it like being on the losing team?' 'Was the game really like that?' 'Was the Milan coach like Gene Hackman played him?' I couldn't remember. I made up stories. ... In 1993 both the Milan and Muncie players [received] Indiana's highest service award, the Sagamore of the Wabash. I got mine for being on a losing basketball team."

Betty Crowe, wife of former Crispus Attucks coach Ray Crowe, also disliked the final game scene. She was unhappy with her husband's role as the head coach of the movie's defeated South Bend Central Bears. "My husband was never a loser," she insisted.

Issues of Race

Carrying on with the goal to imbue *Hoosiers* with an authentic flavor, the filmmakers showed a racially integrated team as the Huskers' final opponents—the fictional South Bend Central Bears. The real-life 1954 Muncie Central Bearcats also had both black and white players. But the racial makeup of the team in *Hoosiers* stirred up a bit of controversy and criticism from certain viewers and analysts.

Some people found it surprising, even jarring, to see black players in the last and most important game after none had been shown throughout the movie. This fact led these viewers to conclude that the black players were meant to be viewed unfavorably. Rodger Sherman of the sports website SB Nation opined that the filmmakers "hoped that by making Hickory's opponents black, we'd immediately assume that they are stronger and faster and better than the small-town white kids. They used the black skin of Hickory's opponents as an indicator telling viewers to root against them." Interestingly, many of those who complained that the fictional South Bend Central Bears were represented negatively incorrectly described this team as being made up of only black players. Writing for the *Arkansas Democrat-Gazette*, Philip Martin stated that Hickory defeats "an all-black team" that he termed "an arrogant and obnoxious bunch." He further stated that "to have cast an all-black school as a privileged powerhouse in 1950s Indiana seems bizarre." Wrote Aaron Baker, "An all-black team from the city becomes the threatening Other that must be defeated in the climactic contest in order to reaffirm the traditional white values that matter in this film."

Other viewers took issue with what they saw as the movie's under-representation of black players. In the early 1950s, African-Americans were emerging as a powerful force in basketball and were transforming the sport. Wrote Troy D. Paino about two state-finals games in the mid-'50s, "The 1954 game between Muncie Central High School and Milan High School in many ways represented the state's past, while the 1955 game between Indianapolis Crispus Attucks and Gary Roosevelt [two all-black schools] represented its future." Some movie viewers got a bad vibe from the virtual omission of black players in *Hoosiers*, concluding that the filmmakers were trying to make a statement. Ron Briley wrote that the movie "attempted to render invisible the racial context of black basketball in Indiana." A review from *TV Guide* said "the film clearly functions as wish-fulfillment for the kind of people who are nostalgic about all-white basketball, leaving a nasty aftertaste." Said filmmaker Spike Lee, "[In the mid-'80s] the NBA was becoming rife with black players…, so what do you do? You fill a nostalgic need with a fantasy, turn back the clock to a much simpler time … when a state championship was won by a tiny small-town lily-white high school."

Actually, controversy about *Hoosiers*' paucity of black players had arisen as early as the summer of 1985, when the film's cagers were being cast. Some members of the African-American community were disgruntled that the press release announcing the open casting call specified that those auditioning should be white.

A final criticism came from viewers who questioned why Milan, with its lone state crown, had been chosen as the inspiration for a feature film instead of multiple titleholder Crispus Attucks. During the decade in which *Hoosiers* was set, Attucks won the state championship three times and was a state finalist two other times. This school turned out NBA stars and Harlem Globetrotters such as Bailey

Robertson, Willie Gardner, Oscar Robertson, and Hallie Bryant. Some people referred to Attucks as the black *Hoosiers* or the forgotten *Hoosiers*.

But not every commentator who addressed the race angle was pessimistic about the championship game. Wrote Scott Tobias, "the racial makeup of the Muncie team, which is initially discomfiting, is confirmed by the real-life game footage, and there's no attempt to posit one playing style above another." And Mark Royden Winchell wrote, "In the climax of *Hoosiers*, the farm boys play against a racially mixed city team for the state championship.... The point of the story, however, is not a racial one but rather the transracial truth that David sometimes can slay Goliath. That fact alone makes this picture a welcome departure from tendentious racial politics and a reaffirmation of values routinely scorned by the adversary culture."

Redemption and Second Chances

One of *Hoosiers'* most important themes is redemption. As Pizzo explains it, "Every principal character has a failure of nerve in some way [and] they are given a second chance. Redemption is one way to look at it—or to chart a different course." According to the screenwriter, the characters' redemption must be aided by other people, because the only way the characters can see themselves in a new way is through someone else's eyes. This central focus on hope and second chances nicely contrasts with and helps relieve the film's sometimes-downbeat tone. As sad as the story can be, it's also highly optimistic with its depiction of people's faith in each other and their power to change others and themselves. Pizzo describes *Hoosiers* as "a dark film with people in pain, but they come out the other side of that in a positive way—they are liberated from their pain."

Hickory Husker David Neidorf was personally affected by the movie's theme of redemption. "Like a lot of sons," he said, "I have a complex relationship with my dad. He really connected with the redemptive part of the movie. When I told Dennis Hopper that I loved him, my father felt like I was telling him. This film brought us closer together."

Michael L. Peterson wrote that when we have committed a wrong and are in need of redemption, "we long for something that will release us from condemnation and restore broken relationships." Two crucial components of this process are forgiveness and grace.

Forgiveness

Peterson described forgiveness as "overcoming negative feelings and judgment toward an offender ... by endeavoring to view the offender with benevolence and compassion, while recognizing that he or she has abandoned the right to them." When Everett visits Shooter in the hospital and speaks of his hope for a better future for the two of them, he's taking the first steps toward forgiving his father for their estrangement.

Pizzo cited another example of this trait in the story. When Myra "saw the value in what this coach was teaching and what he stood for," Pizzo said, "[not revealing his secret] was her measure of forgiveness" for his misdeeds and shortcomings. Peterson wrote that Myra and the others who show faith in Norman and give him a second chance "demonstrate the human ability to transcend the strictly moral categories of justice, obligation, and retribution and move our thinking to a higher plane."

Giving and Receiving Grace

Grace is an unmerited act or instance of kindness, mercy, or compassion, given freely. Brant Short and Dayle Hardy Short wrote that, in *Hoosiers*, "redemption does not result from doing good works or by suffering, but instead by grace. The emphasis upon redemption by grace helps explain why audiences remain inspired by a film that appears, at least on the surface, to be another predictable movie about sports."

In the story, one act of grace leads to another, until they have multiplied. The several instances of grace being given and received include Cletus's hiring of Norman, Norman's "hiring" of Shooter, and Shooter's silence about Norman's past. But perhaps the clearest moments of grace being offered occur in the town meeting. When Myra goes to the pulpit to speak, she begins, "I think, in order to be fair ..." as she prepares to tell everyone about Norman's scandalous past. But emotion wins out over equity as she suddenly changes her mind and tearfully concludes with "I think it'd be a big mistake to let Coach Dale go. Give him a chance." And then Jimmy comes in and echoes Myra's sentiments. The Shorts observed that even though "no one act [of grace] appears to call forth any other, ... all fit together in such a way that the viewer is left with a feeling of hope and generosity."

A Simple Matter of Faith

Usually when a team isn't winning, the reason is poor coaching, or untalented players, or a lack of effort. But for the Hickory Huskers, things begin to turn around when Myra and Jimmy publicly evince faith in the new coach at the town meeting. In the screenplay that Pizzo described as "everybody gets a second chance," for each character who receives another chance, that opportunity starts with another person's showing faith in that individual.

The numerous simple acts of faith are the heart of the movie. By vocalizing confidence in the coach at the town meeting, Jimmy asks—insists, even—that the townspeople do the same. Another good example of faith occurs in the time-out huddle before Ollie attempts his free throws that could send Hickory to state. "After Ollie makes his second shot—and you *will* make your second shot ...," Norman says emphatically to the petrified player. And the coach's faith in his weakest team member pays off handsomely. Ollie's winning shots are not "a product of luck," wrote Higgins and Striegel, "but of the hours of practice Dale has spent [teaching Ollie and the others] fundamentals." If Norman had written off and ignored the seemingly unpromising Ollie, they wrote, "the outcome, predictably, would have been a loss."

But faith doesn't come only from other people. The characters also must have faith in themselves, because this is the first step in achieving their dreams. In *Hoosiers*, having faith in yourself means trusting your instincts. Coach Dale does so even in the face of residents' frequent bellyaching early on. Ollie must believe he can make the charity tosses that will send the Huskers to the state finals. Shooter must believe he can remain sober. Jimmy shows faith in himself on two occasions. He decides that returning to the team is the right decision for him, and he tells Norman and the team that he can make the shot that will win the state championship.

Reaching Your Goal and Achieving Your Dream

By winning the state finals, Coach Dale and the Huskers experience a transcendent moment. They accomplish more than they ever imagined. And their success is all the sweeter because they didn't expect it. The increasing size of the gyms—starting with the Huskers' Hickory home and ending with Butler Fieldhouse—is a sublime representation of the team's progress toward greatness. This meaning is obvious, but the film gives it freshness as we see it through the players' eyes. The gyms' growing magnitude and greater number of fans also serve to heighten the tension in the game scenes.

Initially Resisting but Ultimately Embracing Change

Hickory's residents acknowledge, accept, and defend their town's unchanging nature, as well as their own resistance to change. The mayor makes this attitude clear by announcing "This town doesn't like change much" at the barbershop meet-and-greet. Even Myra speaks glowingly of this aspect of life in Hickory: "During all those years [I was] away, there were a few things I missed.... Knowing that nothing ever changes; people never change. It makes you feel real solid." In the deleted corn-harvesting scene, farmer Rollin tells Norman he prefers to have the stalks cut down by hand because "I'm just one of those old mules tryin' to keep threshin' days alive. Just like the way things been. 'Fraid of what they could be." Although the townspeople take comfort in this constancy, Pizzo believes "sameness can be stifling." So his story forces the characters to confront the question of whether it might be beneficial for them to change their lives.

At first the locals are suspicious of outsider Norman, opposed to his different ways of doing things, and resentful of his attitude. However, his fresh perspectives—not just on coaching, but also on Shooter and Myra—end up being a positive for the community. Norman's presence in Hickory indicates the inevitability of change and the importance of accepting it.

Personal Change

It's important that the characters "find moments of clarity of how to unstick themselves in a situation where they've been stuck for many years—maybe their lifetimes," Pizzo explained. "And there's victory and character growth. What we're rooting for is [for] our characters to move beyond the place where they're stuck." The protagonists must be different people at the end of the story. They won't solve all their problems or reach a state of perfection. But they must make an effort toward improvement.

Why do the characters encounter so many challenges and confront a fair amount of sadness? A clue might be found in Pizzo's attitude toward change. "You don't grow and change in good times," he said. "I don't think anybody does."

The characters must admit that they need to change if they are to receive redemption. Encouraged by someone else's faith in them, the characters are able to overcome their flaws. The keys to their success are expressing humility and acknowledging that they need to change. The process continues with commitment.

In an early draft of the script, Norman concedes that before he came to Hickory, "my need to win and win my way were the only two things that mattered." Two pregame locker room talks signal his change in attitude. At the regional game, instead of pushing the goal of victory, he tells the team to just play to their potential and be the best they can be. If they do that, he says, "I don't care what the scoreboard says at the end of the game—in my book we're gonna be winners!" And before the state finals, he asks the players to share what's on their minds. This request elicits heartfelt comments such as Everett's "I want to win for my dad" and Merle's empathetic "Let's win this one for all the small schools that never had a chance to get here." Even Norman himself opens up: "I want to thank you for the last few months. It's been very special for me." At this moment, and with this admission, the coach has reached his destination—not participating in or even winning the state finals, but the transformation of his character.

Societal Change

Hoosiers suggests that, just as individuals must accept the need for change, so must communities. Hickory won't stay the same forever. Even the game of basketball, despite its representation in the movie as a constant, is always changing and evolving. This point is nicely represented by the racially integrated South Bend Central Bears, the Huskers' state-finals opponent.

Perhaps Hickory's state championship is a last hurrah for little schools and a final tribute to a vanishing way of life. Sportswriter Bob Cook observed, "You notice a sense of melancholy lurking beneath the inspiration. It's clear that what's happening is a fluke, that the real world is perched on the edge of town, ready to make Hickory—the town as well as the school and its basketball team—obsolete."

Teamwork and Self-Sacrifice

"The idea of the power of team over individual," said Pizzo, "whether it be family or athletic team or community, is very meaningful to me and thematic in my life." In *Hoosiers*, playing basketball is an ideal way to learn about teamwork. "The five players on the floor function as one single unit," Norman advises the Huskers at the first practice. "Team, team, team." He compares them to "five pistons firing together." And to operate most effectively, the team must obey their coach. Norman reiterates this directive in the locker room after their first home game, which they have lost: "What I say when it comes to this basketball team is the *law*, absolutely and without discussion!"

Self-sacrifice goes hand in hand with teamwork. Norman wants his team to see sacrifice as a necessary component of victory. Norman tries to instill the concept of self-subordination in his players with his four-passes-before-a-shot instruction; he doesn't want them to act impulsively and selfishly on the court. And the coach doesn't hesitate to bench Rade for defying the "four passes" rule in the first game, ultimately leaving a deficit of Huskers on the floor. He is even willing to accept a loss (and risk angering the fans) to accentuate his insistence on teamwork and submission.

But Norman doesn't expect self-sacrifice from only his players. He too embodies this attribute when he causes himself to be ejected from the Dugger game to allow Shooter to take over coaching duties. By being kicked out yet again, Norman risks looking as if he still hasn't learned how to control his temper. He might have damaged the progress he's made in earning the trust and confidence of the team and townspeople. Shooter also makes a major sacrifice in the course of the story: By deciding to enter rehab, he ends up missing the latter part of Hickory's amazing run to the state finals.

Family and Community

Most of the families in the film are surrogate or symbolic. Because Norman lives on the Summers' property, Cletus and his wife and daughter become his substitute family. The basketball team is a group of brothers, with Norman as the father. The team provides familial structure and support for Everett and Jimmy, the players who have fractured families. Myra serves as a sort of surrogate mother to Jimmy. The town of Hickory is the largest family, with all the disagreements and conflicts but also the genuine caring, concern, and emotions experienced in a real family. Everyone needs and is needed by someone. Norman obviously needs a place to belong—and a purpose. Within mere days of being contacted by Cletus, Norman hits the road and heads to Hickory. Furthermore, no one in the community stands alone—not even Norman. The team needs their coach to lead them and take them to a higher level. He needs them in order to realize his second chance. The town needs the coach to carry on their basketball tradition. He needs their moral support. Living in Hickory also offers Norman the opportunity to care about others and to be cared about, and potentially even to love and be loved.

The community is an important element of the movie's redemption theme. According to Pizzo, "It's not enough to have a second chance. It's important that someone other than yourself provide that second chance." Only through the community will Norman's transformation be complete—and perhaps Shooter's as well. If Shooter knew that more than just a couple people were rooting for him to complete his rehab and stay sober, his chances of success might improve. In Pizzo's words, one of the movie's themes is "individuals succeeding through the help of each other."

Small-Town Life

"The appeal of the 1950s for me," Pizzo said, "is that it's the last era that allowed true regionalism. Before TV homogenized the nation, you could have an enclave with its close, special bonds." Anspaugh related a story about how, a couple months after *Hoosiers* came out, he received a call from a California resident who had just seen the film. The man said *Hoosiers* reproduced a communal experience he had never known and that his daughters would never know either. He told Anspaugh that seeing the movie made him nostalgic for something he never had.

Movie reviewer Philip Martin recognized that "what's great about *Hoosiers* is the way it captures the often claustrophobic, sometimes comforting feeling of living in a small conservative town." The crowded gyms, packed to the rafters with fans, are one good representation of the lack of privacy. And the minimal number of townspeople makes it a safe bet that everyone knows everyone else's business.

Hickory seems like a supportive town in which to grow up and live. However, to an outsider such as Coach Dale, Hickory is more like an exclusive private club with strict membership requirements. Norman must overcome a crucial hurdle before being accepted into the community—one that an ordinary newcomer to town wouldn't face: He must win games.

Some critics sensed something less than positive in the portrayal of Hickory. Ron Briley contended that the town symbolized "conformity and loss of individualism." Aaron Baker said the film celebrates homogeneity, and Pat Graham believed the film's primary goal was "feeding white-bread fantasies." Deborah Tudor thought Hickory represented a "fantasy about a time and place where societal problems do not exist." Furthermore, she argued that the community was a stifling environment in which people like Myra "who challenge the system of values simply do not have the power to withstand the recuperative force of dominant culture."

Religion

It's not hyperbole to say that, in Indiana, basketball is a religion. In the movie, this fact is cleverly symbolized: The bus belonging to Preacher Purl doubles as the team bus, and the town meeting deciding the coach's fate is held in the church. The intertwining of basketball and religion also is made clear through Norman and Myra's discussion of how high school basketball players are treated like gods, and the reading of Bible verses before games. Reverend Doty leads a group prayer before games, and Strap drops to one knee for individual prayers. These supplications seem to work. After praying more than usual at the regional, Strap begins playing with new life. And after Strap's extra prayer for Ollie, the team's least-talented member proceeds to shoot two game-winning free throws.

Pizzo commented, "I wanted to have the church and the spiritual life of small towns included. In my research, and in my understanding of small towns, the church played a major role." Applying the religious motif with a light, gently humorous touch prevents the tone from becoming too serious or preachy. During one of Strap's longer prayers, Norman finally advises him, "Strap, God wants you on the floor." And Reverend Doty has a funny line in the barbershop scene. He says to Norman, "We trust that you're a fine, upstanding, God-fearing man with Christian morals and principles who will set an example and a standard of leadership for our boys. Tell me—do you believe in man-to-man or zone defense?"

Three Key Scenes

A trio of scenes stand out as best encapsulating the movie's themes: Norman's handling of Jimmy's decision not to play basketball, the referendum on Norman's removal as coach, and the last time-out huddle at the state finals.

Dealing with Jimmy's Early Absence

The first situation the new coach is forced to confront is Jimmy's decision to quit the team. As Rooster the barber tells Norman firmly at the barbershop meet-and-greet, "We don't get Jimmy Chitwood back playing ball, we don't have a prayer," and the other townsmen nod in assent. The following morning, Myra informs Norman that she's the one who convinced Jimmy to give up basketball. Rather than arguing with the barbershop boys and Myra over Jimmy's future and letting the situation fester, the coach decides to face the issue head-on. When he spots Jimmy practicing at the outdoor dirt court one afternoon, he takes the opportunity to speak with the young man:

> *You know, in the ten years that I coached, I never met anybody who wanted to win as badly as I did. I'd do anything I had to do to increase my advantage. Anybody who tried to block the pursuit of that advantage, I'd just push 'em out of the way. It didn't matter who they were or what they were doing. But that was then. You have a special talent, a gift. Not the school's, not the townspeople, not the team's, not Myra Fleener's, not mine. It's yours, to do with what you choose. Because that's what I believe, I can tell you this: I don't care if you play on the team or not.*

By confessing that he's decided to adjust his previous mindset, Norman exhibits two characteristics of a good leader: humility and a willingness to change. Having spoken his mind, he walks away. He's closed the chapter on Jimmy and is ready to move forward with his existing team.

But some analysts read restrained motives into Coach Dale's brief talk. Deborah Tudor theorized it is "a deliberate attempt to upset Jimmy, to break through his reserve" and that it is "ambiguous, apparently leaving Jimmy freedom of choice." She continued, "The mention of Myra, however, indicates that Norm wants Jimmy to consider a choice other than her goals for him."

Clemens and Wolff maintained that Norman's speech "creates the unthreatening, attractive environment Jimmy needs. ... There's no art of the deal here, no transaction, no quid pro quo. Just laserlike and unconditional focus on what really counts—Jimmy's ownership of and responsibility for his own talent and potential. ... Coach Dale has created a new vision for Jimmy that transforms him."

The Town Meeting

The residents' loyalty is to their team, not the new coach. When Norman doesn't live up to their expectations, the fans don't hesitate to boo him at the games. Eventually they run out of patience, because he hasn't produced wins or even managed to get his temper under control. The scene in which a referendum is held to vote on Norman's removal as coach effectuates the greatest number of the movie's themes. It occurs halfway through the film and changes the story's direction. Ironically, the lowest point of Norman's time in Hickory is the high point of the film. All of the movie's most vital elements and themes are present in this scene: humility, responsibility, conviction, forgiveness, grace, redemption—and, best of all, surprise.

The town meeting also is the scene that best exemplifies the art of minimalism. Coach Dale's speech in which he defends himself is concise—only 54 words long:

> *I've made some mistakes, but they're mistakes I take full responsibility for. I was hired to teach the boys the game of basketball, and I did that to the best of my ability. I apologize for nothing. You may not be pleased with the results, but I am. I'm very proud of these boys.*

Likewise, Jimmy's dialog at the meeting—the first time he speaks in the movie—also is succinct:

> *I don't know if it'll make any change, but I figure it's time for me to start playing ball. One other thing—I play, Coach stays; he goes, I go.*

When Myra touches Jimmy's arm after he speaks at the meeting, this little gesture of support says a lot. She conveys not only that she cares about him, but that she accepts his decision, even though she might not agree with it. Likewise, other characters' reactions communicate a wealth of sentiment: Norman's face when Myra asks the town to give him a chance, Preacher Purl's expression after Myra's comments, Opal's glance at her daughter after Myra's remarks.

The outcome of the meeting is Norman's first victory—and it doesn't occur on the basketball court.

The Final Huddle

Another scene that is packed with meaning and emotional impact is the last time-out of the state-finals game, where Norman tells the team that Merle will take the last shot. From their expressions it's obvious the boys disagree with their coach. When he demands, "What's the matter with you guys?", Jimmy delivers just three words: "I'll make it." It's the film's best representation of the team's unity and single-mindedness. The meaning would have been completely different if Jimmy were the only player who thought he should endeavor to make the final field goal.

With this straightforward, minimalist declaration, the reticent player makes it clear that, just as the townspeople showed faith in Norman and gave him a chance, now Norman can return the favor. He can signify his faith in Jimmy (along with the rest of the Huskers, who agree with their fellow team member) by letting him attempt the last basket.

This scene also offers examples of leadership. When the coach agrees to let Jimmy attempt the shot, wrote Higgins and Striegel, Norman masters "a new major leadership trait. He has delegated decision-making and shown that he knows when to let the team make the call." And when Jimmy expresses his desire to go for the game-winner, he's stepping up and assuming responsibility for his team's victory or defeat.

Finally, "I'll make it" could also be taken to mean that Jimmy knows he'll have a successful future outside Hickory, just as Norman and Myra had hoped.

Other Interpretations

Still further meanings can be found in *Hoosiers*. Some viewers see Coach Dale as an example of a strong leader from whom lessons can be drawn. Other critics have addressed the lack and negative portrayal of female characters in the film.

Lessons in Leadership and Management

Some analysts and authors of management texts find that *Hoosiers* reflects the application of sound leadership principles. Norman displays his unbending style of leadership as he sticks to his convictions and doesn't heed his detractors. In the face of almost constant criticism and questioning, he never backs down. However, despite his toughness, Norman doesn't lack compassion. In fact, he employs his own experiences and emotions in understanding and leading his team. One of the film's more subtle themes, dealing with a sense of loss, is something the coach understands well. Clemens and Wolff wrote that Norman "is navigating an enormous sea of losses," including "his career ... and his ticket to the world he loves, and he wants it all back." Facing his own failures, they said, makes him "a kind of expert reader of individual loss and isolation." Therefore, he is able to sympathize and deal with others' struggles and what they are missing in their lives. These problems include the team's mourning of their previous coach, Shooter and Everett's almost nonexistent father-son relationship, Shooter's lack of self-esteem, and the Huskers' need for cohesion and identity. Norman purposely creates an unexpected situation of loss for his team when he is deliberately kicked out of a game. He wants to show them that they can handle even the absence of their coach.

By helping his players achieve their goals and better themselves, rather than reaching for his own personal glory, Coach Dale embodies the spirit of servant leadership. One quality of this style of leadership, wrote Ken Blanchard, is humility. This attribute is characterized by the realization that leadership is not about the leader; it's about the people who are being led and what they need. Another quality of humility is the desire to move from success to significance—from getting to giving. One way Norman bespeaks servant leadership is by trying to help heal the rift between Everett and his father. Asking Shooter to be an assistant coach is a risky and perhaps impractical and unwise move. If Shooter falls back to his old ways, the negative consequences could be significant. But Norman feels that the possible positive outcomes are worth the risk. The coach also shows concern for his players' futures when he voices his conviction that athletic achievements will offer the boys the most likely way out of Hickory.

Higgins and Striegel noted that Norman also succeeds in helping the Huskers develop into leaders: "By the end of the movie, every player on the team has demonstrated leadership by encouraging a fellow player, taking personal responsibility for the outcome of a game, or shoring up team spirit in a moment of doubt." Norman guides Shooter toward a leadership role as well. The assistant coach hesitatingly but ably takes over and leads the Huskers to victory in the game where Norman is ejected on purpose.

Gender Issues

The movie's story about a high school boys' basketball team is nearly bereft of female characters. The only others besides Myra are her spirited mother, Opal (Fern Persons created an unforgettable character despite limited screen time); principal Cletus's wife, Millie; and the cheerleaders (their scenes with dialog ended up on the cutting room floor). Professor Dayna B. Daniels suggested that "sport is traditionally seen as a male activity and, therefore, the role of girls and women is tenuous at best."

Even the story's female lead, Myra, has a relatively minor part. In addition, her character is almost always perceived negatively. Because she temporarily steps into the traditionally male role of school principal, wrote Ron Briley, and because she "block[s] Jimmy's relationship with a surrogate father in Dale," Myra "clearly poses a menace to the masculine order." In such a masculine world, he continued, "the patriarchy must be restored in order to assure a sense of stability." Therefore, by the film's resolution, Briley concluded, Myra has taken on the stereotypical role of a woman on the sidelines, rooting for her man.

ESPN.com writer Bill Simmons also disliked Myra. He derided the "sports movie tradition [in which you] put your down-on-his-luck hero on the road to redemption, then toss in a woman to make him miserable along the way. These females always jump on the bandwagon near the end, as soon as fortunes change for our tortured hero."

Making a Personal Story Universal and Relatable

When Pizzo shared with his graduate-school professors and classmates an outline for a movie that years later would become *Hoosiers*, they were unenthusiastic. They told him, "Just because you experienced it and you enjoyed it doesn't mean anybody else will." But Pizzo didn't let that criticism derail his dream of making a movie centered around Hoosier Hysteria. He and Anspaugh figured out that they needed to take a story that was personally meaningful to them and make it appealing to a wide audience. This is probably the biggest factor in *Hoosiers*' lasting success. The film effectively interweaves diverse universal themes such as redemption, healing, the need for family and community connections, and the joy of victory for an underdog team.

It's ironic that Anspaugh and Pizzo, who grew up enthralled by epic films and blockbusters, gained their fame by creating a low-budget production. As Pizzo transitioned from a film fan into a filmmaker, he realized that he wanted his own movies to have strong characters and compelling stories at their core. As he developed his screenwriting skills, Pizzo came to understand that his scripts must, as he put it, "have a personal emotional resonance and a locus where the screen story and my own story meet." Furthermore, he said, "I hope as a writer I am able to access the place that has feelings, and the place that has heart. That core well was dug in Indiana, in the Midwest, and hopefully will never go away." *Hoosiers* was a milestone in Anspaugh's career and life. He commented that the film "will probably be for me the most personal movie I will ever make in terms of where I came from and the people I knew and the place that I love so much."

Although Anspaugh and Pizzo had modest hopes for *Hoosiers*, they saw it become far more popular and endure longer than they ever imagined, taking on a life of its own. In 2007 film reviewer Mitchell Hattaway dubbed *Hoosiers* "the grandfather of the modern underdog sports movie." This is a particularly apt description considering that the film was completed years before its current college-age and younger fans were even born.

Milan Miracle team member Glenn Butte was referring to his former teammates, but he may as well have been speaking for all of Indiana, when he said, "I think the movie *Hoosiers* did more than any of us will ever realize to solidify our niche in history."

Epilogue

"I'm sure going to the state finals is beyond your wildest dreams...." —Coach Dale

Whenever I watch *Hoosiers*, I find a lot to like. Pizzo and Anspaugh skillfully captured the thrills and amazement associated with witnessing a small-town team building momentum and eventually winning the state championship. I know this because I watched my hometown team, Vincennes Lincoln, win the boys' state tournament in 1981. I can even identify with the fans of the losing team in the movie's final game, because my hometown team also lost the state final, in 1984. But the basketball scenes aren't the only high point in *Hoosiers*. The movie's old school and gyms remind me of those in my hometown. I even believe the slight awkwardness of Norman and Myra's relationship adds a nice bit of realism. Throughout the movie, the filmmakers' attention to detail, knowledge of and devotion to their subject, and commitment to getting it right really shine through. Although making the film proved difficult for Pizzo and Anspaugh, it was a labor of love. Anspaugh described the production this way: "It was an effort on everyone's part that was just beyond anything I've ever experienced, either before or since. It was like a crusade of some sort; it was just infectious, in every department, people working day and night [who] believed in this story."

This small film's huge success has taken its creators by surprise. Movie reviewer A.O. Scott of the *New York Times* puzzled over *Hoosiers*' long-lasting attraction: "Even if you've seen movies like this thousands of times before, somehow this is the one that you want to watch again and again and again. And I find myself wondering why that is, what aspect of this movie accounts for its extraordinary power and its hold on people's imaginations. I still can't quite say what it is that makes this movie great. Sometimes a Cinderella team makes it all the way to the finals. And sometimes a little movie has a very big impact."

Although the reasons for *Hoosiers*' unexpected acclaim and staying power remain somewhat elusive, perhaps the purity of the filmmakers' intentions is part of the answer. Anspaugh and Pizzo were united in their determination to produce a heartfelt movie about the sport and the state they loved.

In his review of the film, Jim Gordon of the *Merrillville (IN) Post-Tribune* stated, "Hickory is hardly a place from which dreams are likely to spring." But, in fact, that's exactly what happened. This fictional town and its residents were the catalyst for a dream and a path to fame for two aspiring filmmakers. Pizzo and Anspaugh achieved their goal of making a movie based on universal themes and conveyed in an authentic and emotional way. In so doing, they created an incredibly inspiring story—the making of *Hoosiers*.

Images

INDIANAPOLIS.........WANTED: Caucasion males, 18-20 years old, possessing <u>excellent</u> basketball playing skills to audition for the role of the "home team" in the movie, "Hoosiers."

    Written by Bloomington native, Angelo Pizzo, and directed by Decatur, Indiana native, David Anspaugh, "Hoosiers" was inspaired by the miracle Milan high school basketball squad and their 1954 state championship victory.

    The $6 million film will be produced by Hemdale Films and Carter DeHaven Productions of Los Angeles.

    The Indiana Film Commission is assisting the Ken Carlson Casting Agency of Chicago in conducting auditions for basketball players to play the part of the "home team." Open auditions will be held at the IUPUI Natatorium on Monday, August 26 and Tuesday, August 27 from 9 a.m. to 3 p.m. (Enter the main entrance located on the building's westside.)

    Cast requirements set by the Ken Carlson Casting Agency are looking for young males, 18 t0 20, who look high school age and are no taller than 6'2". (Potential actors currently playing basketball are encouraged to check their ogranization's regulations for maintaining their amateur status.)

    Open auditions to demonstrate individual basketball playing skills are expected to be time consuming; participants are advised to expect to wait.

    Filming is scheduled to take place in Indiana in October, November and early December.

    The Indiana Film Commission is a part of the Indiana Department of Commerce which is directed by Lt. Govenor John Mutz.

* May be as old as 22 as long as you still look younger!

The press release telling of the open casting call to find the Huskers.

```
TO:        David Anspaugh
           Carter De Haven
           Andy Pizzo
           Graham Henderson
           Fred Murphy
           David Nichols
           Rick Schmidlin

FROM:      Herb Adelman

SUBJECT:   LOCATIONS YET TO BE FOUND

DATE:      October 11, 1985

To date, the following scenes have yet to find homes:

DAY    DATE    SCENE(S)      SET

X1     10/18   3, 4          Ext. Various Roads

X2     10/19                 Ithaca Team Photo

1      10/21   49,50,61      Int./Ext. Deer Lick Library
               46Pt.,53Pt.   Ext. Country Roads

2      10/22   46Pt.         Int. Team Bus/Moving

8      10/29   14            Int. Coon Hunter Lodge
               1, 2          Int./Ext. Buffalo Apartment

16     11/7    102,106       Int. Jasper Locker Room
               56            Ext. Needmore Gym

19     11/11   64            Int. Shooter's Domain

20     11/12   45, 83        Int. Norm's House
               100           Ext. Myra and Norm's Ridge

27,28  11/20
       11/21   74-80         Int./Ext. Church

31     11/25   63, 96        Ext. Shooter's Forest

32     11/26   97,108        Int. Hospital
               92, 94        Int. Deer Lick Locker Room

36     12/2    84Pt.,
               113Pt.,
               54, 55        Int. Team Bus/Moving
                             Ext. Accident Scene

37     12/3    115           Int. Fieldhouse Locker Room

In Addition, I haven't even started to address the locations or
scheduling of the second unit -- more to follow. Stay tuned.
```

This memo, dated the week before principal photography was to start, indicates the time pressures the crew faced.

```
                        GAMES LIST
              SCRIPT DATED: October 21, 1985

                                                   LOCKER ROOM/
   SCENES     GAME                    LOCATION     GYM/EXTERIOR

   35 - 40    OOLITIC (PURPLE/GREY)   Hickory      LR/Gym

   47 - 48    CEDAR KNOB (GREEN/GOLD) Cedar Knob   Gym

   56         NEEDMORE                Needmore     Ext. only

   65 - 67    VERDI (ORANGE/ROYAL)    Hickory      LR/Gym

   69 - 72    LOOGOOTEE (RED/BLACK)   Hickory      LR/Gym/Ext.

   81         HOLLAND                 Hickory      Gym

   84         MONTAGE (Fish Fry)
              Stinesville             ?            Gym
              Decatur                 ?            Gym
              Bloomington             ?            Gym
              Paragon                 ?            Gym

   85 - 89    DUGGER (MAROON/WHITE)   Hickory      Gym
   -----------------------------------------------------------
   STATE TOURNEMENT

*  91 - 93    Franklin (GOLD/PURPLE)  Deer Lick    LR/Gym/Ext.
*             Birdseye (SCARLET/WHITE) Deer Lick   Gym
*             Holland                 Deer Lick    Gym

   94 - 95    TERHUNE (NAVY/CREAM)    Deer Lick    LR/Gym
   -----------------------------------------------------------
*  102 - 104  Evansville Bosse        Jasper       LR/Gym
              New Albany              Jasper       Gym

   105 - 107  JASPER (ORANGE/OL.BLUE) Jasper       LR/Gym/Ext.

   114 - 121  SOUTH BEND CENTRAL      Butler FH.   LR/Gym/Ext.
              (ROYAL BLUE/WHITE)
```

An initial list of Hickory's opponents and their colors.

14	2 5/8	The "Boys" question Norm.	1,3,18,19,20,21	INT/N
4TH DAY				
15	1 6/8	Myra and Norm talk at school.	1,2	INT/D
16	4 5/8	Norm confronts George about coaching. George leaves. Buddy gets kicked out and he and Whit leave. Jimmy watches in the b.g.	1,6,7,8,9,10 11,12,13,18 19?,20?	INT/D
17		OMIT		
18		OMIT		
5TH DAY				
19	3/8	Montage of team practicing.	1,7,8,10,11,13	INT/D
20	2/8	Norm lets Rade shoot a basket.	1,7,8,10,11,13	INT/D
6TH DAY				
21	2 1/8	Cletus and Norm meet Shooter on the street. Cletus gives him some money but Everett makes him give it back.	1,3,4,7,18	EXT/D
7TH DAY				
22	3/8	The team, feeling like they're in Norm's army, stand at attention.	1,7,8,10,11,13	INT/D
23	2 2/8	The "Boys" enter the gym to watch practice. Rollin brings Whit in to apologize. Rollin makes the "Boys" leave.	1,5,7,8,9,10, 11,13,18,19,20	INT/D
8TH DAY				
24	4/8	The Reverend blesses the threshing	1,3,5,6,7,8,9, 10,11,12,13,14, 18,20,21	EXT/D
25	3/8	Montage of the threshing.	1,5,6,7,8,9,10, 11,12,13,14,18, 20?,21?	EXT/D
26	4/8	Ollie gives Norm some whiskey.	1,13,18	EXT/D
27	3/8	Montage of threshing. Norm and Rollin drive away in the tractor.	1,3,5,6,7,8,9, 10,11,12,13,14, 18,20?,21?	EXT/D
28	7/8	Rollin tells Norm how he is trying to keep threshing alive.	1,5	EXT/D
29		OMIT		

Page 2 of the list of scenes, showing the day, scene number, how many pages the scene takes up, the actors needed, and whether the scene is interior, exterior, day, or night.

TOTAL SETS	SCRIPT P. NO.	LOCATION SET NO.	EXT/INT	DESCRIPTION	DAY/NIGHT	
1	1	1	EXT	NORM'S APT., "STEEL MILL TOWN"	D	F
2	1	1A	INT	" "	D	F
3	1	2	EXT	ON RAMP — TPK.	D	F
4	1	3	EXT	RURAL COUNTRY ROAD — "WELCOME TO INDIANA"	D	F
5	1	4	EXT	SMALLER ROAD, ROLLING HILLS	D	F
6	1	5	EXT	ENT. SUNVILLE, OLD BRIDGE & HOUSES	D	F
7	1	6	EXT	JUNIOR'S GAS & GEN. STORE (HOOP)	D	F
8	3	7	EXT	COVERED BRIDGE WITH "HICKORY, POP 640" SIGN	D	F
9	3	8	EXT	HICKORY MAIN ST. — DRIVE THROUGH	D	F
10	85	8A	EXT	" " " TRANSFORMATION	D	W
11	104	8B	EXT	" " " CARAVAN	D	W
12	112	8C	EXT	" " " EMPTY	DAWN	W
13	112	8D	INT	" " " HOMES - SHOTS OF PEOPLE AROUND RADIOS & TVs.	N	W
14	3	8E	EXT	" " " RUSSEL'S GUN SHOP	D/N	F/N
15	3	8F	EXT	" " " ROOSTER'S BARBER SHOP	D/N	F/N
16	45	8G	INT	" " " " "	D	F
17	46	8H	EXT	" " " GENERAL STORE, DRY GOODS, FEED	D/N	F/N
18	71	8I	EXT	" " " LOADING DOCK, TRAIN STA	D	F
19	73	9	EXT	CHURCH	N	F
20	73	9A	INT	"	N	F
21	10	10	INT	COON HUNTER LODGE	N	F
22	3	11	EXT	HICKORY HIGH SCHOOL	D/N	F/N

Page 1 of the list of sets.

```
P. 71.   LIVE STOCK CAR
         LARGE BELL
         HOGS.
         TRAIN PULLING OUT.

P. 73    LADDER

P. 82.   TEAM BUS.  ✓
         SMALL TROPHY AND PLAQUE

P. 85.   BLUE AND GOLD
              RIBBONS / BUNTINGS

         ROYS CAR - SIREN SCREAMING
              LIGHTS IN CARAVAN.

P. 86    ICE BLOCKS.

P. 86    16 SETS OF COLORS.

P. 87    CHAMPIONSHIP TROPHY  (SECTIONAL FINALS)

P. 104.  CARS  "AS FAR AS THE EYE CAN SEE"
         VEHICLES
         SHERIFF ROYS CAR.
         SUNVILLE BUS
         CROSS PLAINS BUS.
         WHEEL CHAIR (UNION)

P. 105   POLICE CAR, FIRE ENGINE.

P. 108   BUTLER FIELD HOUSE
              TV CAMERAS.
```

Part of the list of props.

"HOOSIERS"

PICTURE VEHICLE BREAKDOWN 288 VEHICLE DAYS

NORM'S CAR   sc 2,3,4,5,6,7,8,14,19,21,23, 30,32,41,50,52,58,76,78, 88,96

HICKORY BUS   sc 45,70,86,101,107,108

OPAL'S TRUCK   sc 43,50,52,71,88,96,107,108

SHERIFF CAR   sc 7,55,71,76,88,107,108

HUDNUT CAR   sc 8,14,19,21,107,108

MYRA'S CAR   sc 8,30,76,96

SCHOOL BUS #1 sc 70,107,108

SCHOOL BUS #2 sc 107,108

FIRE TRUCK HICKORY sc 7,107,108

FIRE TRUCK #2 sc 107,108

BAKE TRUCK   sc 55,56

A. NEW RICHMOND VEHICLE GROUP
   15 ROTATING CARS/TRUCKS
   sc 7,8,21,23,32,41,45,55-56, 70,71,73,74,76,78,88,107,108

B. INDIANAPOLIS CARAVAN GROUP (30 ROTATING CARS/TRUCKS)
   sc 107,108

C. SPECIALTY GROUP /DRIVE BY/KNIGHTSTOWN/NINEVA/SUNRISE
   sc 4,5,6,8,88,101 ALSO 46,55,56

E. GARY INDIANA GROUP (20-25 VEHICLES FROM GARY)
   sc 2,3.

Vehicle list.

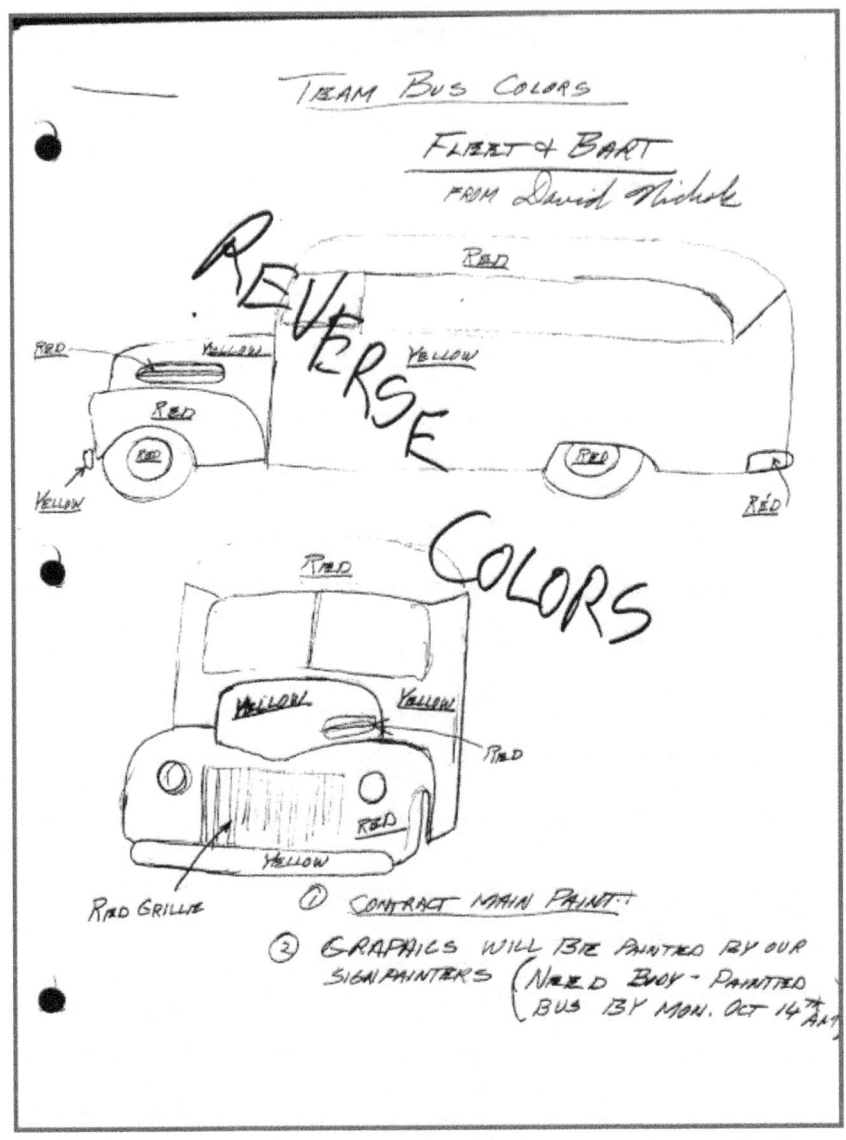

A drawing of the Hickory team bus with painting instructions, from production designer David Nichols.

Images

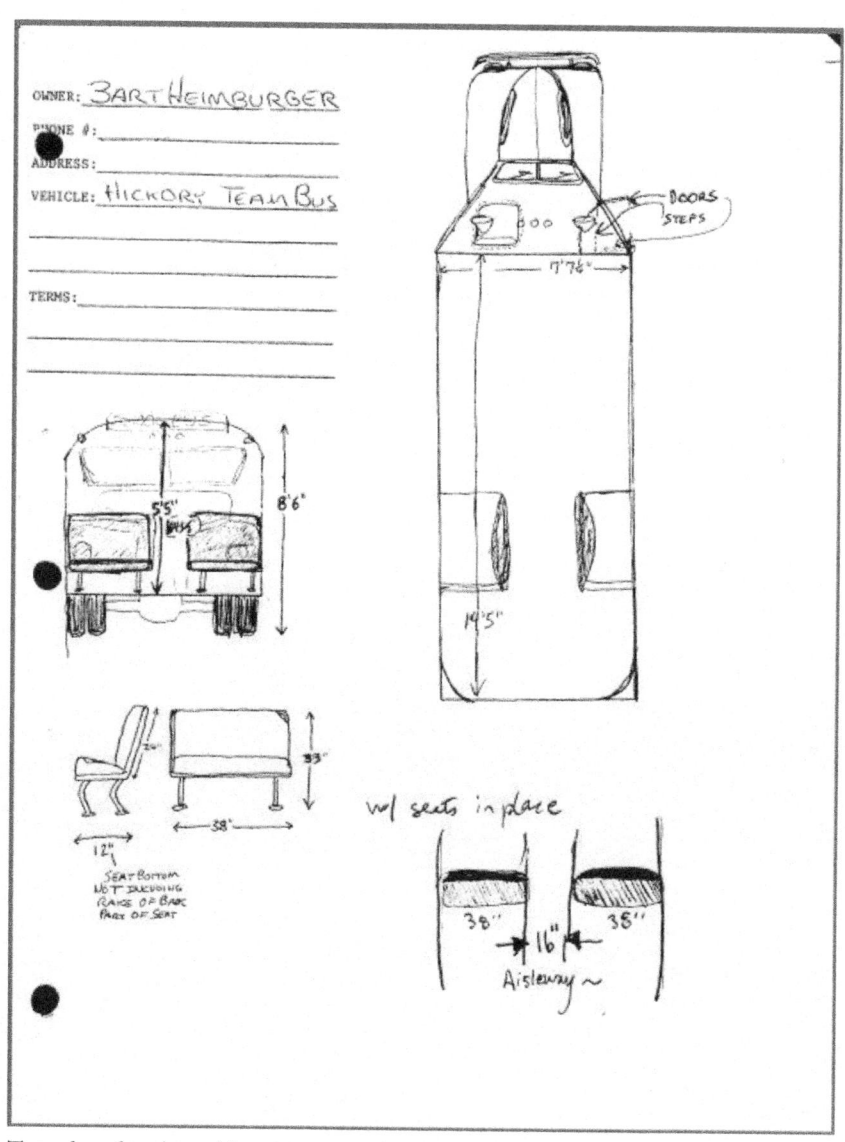

235

Team bus drawing with measurements.

```
                          "HOOSIERS"                    Date: 10/26/85
                       SHOOTING SCHEDULE                Page: 35
--------------------------------------------------------------------
DATE            SET/SCENES              CAST            DEPT. BREAKDOWN
LOCATION
--------------------------------------------------------------------
DAY 13          INT. HICKORY HIGH GYM

MONDAY          Sc. 16                  #1  NORM        PROPS
11/4/85         Day - 4-1/8 pg.         #6  JIMMY*      Basketballs
                                        #7  EVERETT     George's whistle
LOCATION:       Norm relieves George as #8  RADE        Norm's whistle
Knightstown     coach -- Buddy and Whit #9  WHIT        Towels
                walk.                   #10 MERLE       Water
                                        #11 STRAP
                                        #12 BUDDY       SPECIAL EFFECTS
                                        #13 OLLIE       Smoke
                                        #18 GEORGE
                                                        NOTES
                                                        Makeup: Sweat
                                        *Seperate call
                                                        GRIP
                                        ATMOS           Scissor lift
                                        1   Standin (Norm)
                                        4   Standin (M)
--------------------------------------------------------------------
                INT. HICKORY HIGH GYM

                Sc.  19, 20             #1  NORM        PROPS
                Day - 1-4/8             #7  EVERETT     Norm's whistle
                                        #8  RADE        Basketballs
                No shooting! Drill!     #10 MERLE       Towels
                Drill! Drill!           #11 STRAP       Water
                                        #13 OLLIE
                                                        SETS
                                        ATMOS           8 Chairs
                                        1   Standin (Norm)
                                        4   Standins (M) SPECIAL EQUIPMENT
                                                        Camera: 2 Cameras
                                        NOTES
                                        Make-up: Sweat  SPECIAL EFFECTS
                                                        Smoke
--------------------------------------------------------------------
                INT. HICKORY HIGH GYM

                Sc. 122B                                SETS
                Dusk - 1/8 pg.                          Hickory Championship
                                                        Photo
                CAMERA MOVES into empty gym
                and focuses close on photo              NOTES
                of the 1952 State Championship          Grip: Zevs or Electra
                team.                                         Crane
--------------------------------------------------------------------
                END DAY 13      TOTAL PAGES             5-6/8 PAGES
```

A page from the shooting schedule. These three scenes were filmed in Knightstown on November 4, 1985.

The call sheet for the town meeting scene.

238   THE MAKING OF HOOSIERS

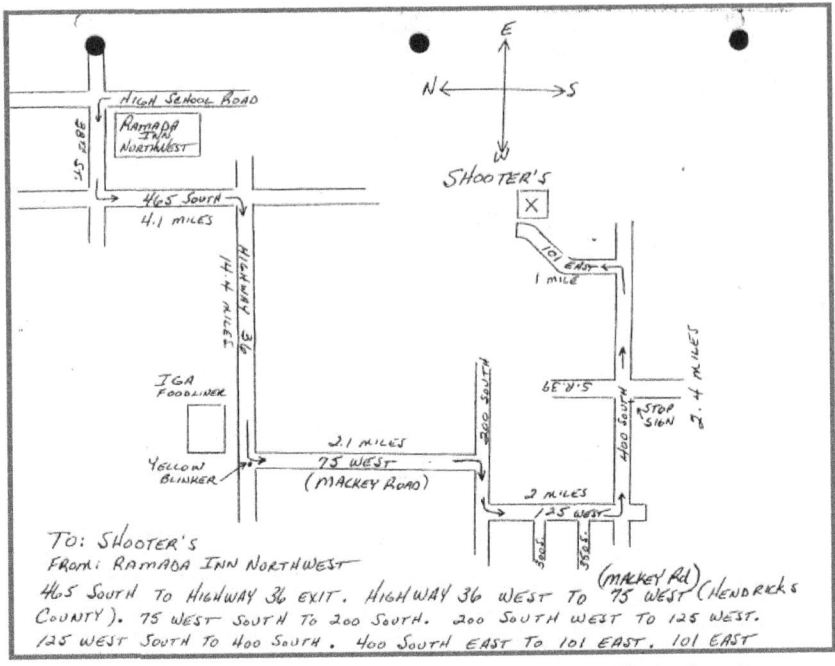

Detailed hand-drawn maps directed everyone to the various filming locations.

Orion created an advertisement promoting Dennis Hopper after he was nominated for a Golden Globe Award for Best Supporting Actor.

"For your consideration" advertisements placed in *The Hollywood Reporter* and *Variety* encouraged members of the Academy of Motion Picture Arts and Sciences to nominate Dennis Hopper for an Oscar. Orion also placed FYC ads promoting the other lead actors and primary crew members.

Norman drives into downtown Hickory and parks.

To relieve boredom, Kent Poole shoots free throws and David Neidorf rebounds.

The Steadicam captures Norman telling Shooter to take over coaching duties.

Gloria Dorson, Gene Hackman, and Barbara Hershey at the town meeting.

Cedar Knob game rehearsal.

Anspaugh briefs the actors during the sectional game.

The extras rehearse rushing the floor at the end of the regional game.

Only a couple hundred extras showed up for the first two nights of filming at Hinkle Fieldhouse.

The actors before the harvest scene, which ended up being deleted.

Norman and the Huskers are questioned by reporters and bid farewell by family and townspeople as they prepare to depart for the state finals. This scene was shortened to only 6 seconds and placed in a montage in the movie.

Acknowledgments

Many people assisted me as I wrote this book, and I'm forever grateful to them. The wonderful staff of the Carmel Clay Public Library helped me as I began my research. The Indiana State Library and the Indiana University Libraries supplied me with a number of microfilms. Reporters for the *Indianapolis Star*, the gone-but-not-forgotten *Indianapolis News*, and the scores of other newspapers and publications cited in the text and endnotes have provided excellent coverage of *Hoosiers* over the years, and they greatly aided my fact-finding. Insightful book editor Cheri Clark gave me valuable feedback and suggestions.

Special thanks to former Hoosier Gym president Mervin Kilmer, as well as Roger Kunkel and Wilma Lewellyn of New Richmond. They and other Hoosiers offered additional information for my research, helped me find people to interview, and served as tour guides at several of the filming locations. Thanks to everyone who gave me pictures and videos from behind the scenes. I'm also indebted to all the generous folks who let me interview them, as they shared their memories of and experiences with the movie.

Finally, a huge thank-you to David Anspaugh and Angelo Pizzo for their kindness and help. Angelo in particular demonstrated almost preternatural patience in answering my endless questions. Thanks, Angelo and David, for getting the (basket)ball rolling all those years ago by having the perseverance to follow through on your dream of making *Hoosiers*.

Image Credits

Joe Boswell: pages 56, 57, 61, 100, 108, 109, 157, 240 (top), 244 (bottom)

Bob Garner: page 168

Steve Hollar: page 227

Chris Hushour: pages 75, 78, 82, 240 (bottom), 241 (top)

Roger Kunkel: pages 97 (middle), 228–238, 242 (bottom), 243 (bottom)

Wilma Lewellyn: pages 58, 80, 93, 113, 241 (bottom), 242 (top)

Nancy Long: pages 48, 71, 97 (top), 158, 243 (top), 244 (top)

Notes

Chapter 1

3   four-stage: Sectional, regional, semistate, and state. This tournament format began in 1936. At least one school smaller than Milan won the state crown in the tournament's early years (the 1910s), when fewer schools participated.

"Every year…": Greg Rice. "DePauw student brings real championship experience to the movie set in Hoosiers." *Alumnus* (DePauw University), volume 50, issue 2, Winter 1986, 32.

"In a certain…": Ann All. "'Hoosiers' memories of a Midwestern myth." *Indiana Statesman* (Indiana State University), November 7, 1986, 4.

Pizzo grew up…: Nelson Price. "Arts awards honor Indiana filmmaker, cellist, others." *Indianapolis News*, February 22, 1995, E8; Bonnie Britton. "Pizzo 'back home again' for award. Producer and screenwriter is in Indiana for the Governor's Arts Awards presentations today." *Indianapolis Star*, February 21, 1995, D1; Nelson Price. "Pair plots next moves. 2 filmmakers took 'Rudy' to White House." *Indianapolis News*, October 25, 1993, B1.

He often watched…: Angelo Pizzo. Online chat with HeraldTimesOnline.com, March 6, 2007.

Pizzo didn't play much…: Angelo Pizzo. Interviewed by Peter Noble Kuchera. *Profiles*, WFIU HD1, June 25, 2006.

4   Mickey Mantle…: Angelo Pizzo. Interviewed by the author November 12, 2012.

He relished westerns…: Nelson Price. *Indiana Legends: Famous Hoosiers from Johnny Appleseed to David Letterman* (4th ed.). Cincinnati: Emmis Books, 2005, 230; Angelo Pizzo. Interviewed by the author November 27, 2009.

Some of his favorites…: Linda Thomas. "Angelo Pizzo: beyond 'Hoosiers.'" *Bloomington (IN) Herald-Times*, October 13, 1989, D5.

His mother sometimes…: Angelo Pizzo. Interviewed by Peter Noble Kuchera; Yaël Ksander. "Happy Patti Pizzo Day, Bloomington!" Indiana Public Media, January 22, 2013.

At University High School…: Angelo Pizzo. Interviewed by the author November 12, 2012.

Pizzo struggled…: Andrew Tallackson. "Creator of sports movies gives glimpse into process." *Michigan City (IN) News Dispatch*, October 12, 2003; Angelo Pizzo. Interviewed by the author November 27, 2009.

"I felt success…": Hank Nuwer. Interview with Angelo Pizzo.

He would have liked…: Angelo Pizzo. Videoconference at the Challenger Learning Center, Brownsburg, Indiana, March 3, 2009.

5   "That was the temple…": David Anspaugh. Interviewed by the author January 13, 2010.

At IU Anspaugh…: Nelson Price. "Spotlight on Hoosiers. Film director to receive Governor's Arts Award." *Indianapolis News*, January 31, 1991, F-1.

Whenever Anspaugh drove…: David Anspaugh. Interviewed by Andy Hunsucker and Jason Thompson. *A Place for Film: The IU Cinema Podcast*, episode 28, April 8, 2011.

They took…: Angelo Pizzo. Videoconference.

"I think [it was] called…": Jonathan Streetman. "Q&A with David Anspaugh." *Indiana Daily Student* (Weekend edition) (Indiana University), September 28, 2011.

They viewed many…: Spyridon Stratigos, interviewed by the author August 24, 2013.

Although at the time…: Mike Penner. "Inspiration Points." *Los Angeles Times*, February 20, 2004, D-1.

6   They wondered…: "'Hoosiers' opens here Friday." *Vincennes (IN) Sun-Commercial*, November 9, 1986, Life Along the Wabash 9.

By the time…: Angelo Pizzo. Interviewed by the author November 27, 2009; Angelo Pizzo. Interviewed by Peter Noble Kuchera; Linda Thomas.

"The energy…": Bill Kauffman. "Hoops. Hoosiers. Hollywood. Home." *The American Enterprise*, vol. 17, no. 2, March 2006, 40.

So he outlined…: Mike Penner.

7   During his third year…: Mike Pearson. "How 'Hoosiers' got from script to filming." *Bloomington (IN) Sunday Herald-Times*, November 17, 1985, D1; http://www.imdb.com/title/tt0075507/episodes; Angelo Pizzo. Interviewed by Peter Noble Kuchera; Sandra Knipe. "Hoosiers. 'Miracle of Milan' was inspiration, but movie's not just about sports." *Evansville (IN) Courier*, November 7, 1986, B14; Angelo Pizzo. Acceptance speech at his induction into the National Italian American Sports Hall of Fame, November 15, 2014.

On March 30…: Bob Hammel and Kit Klingelhoffer. *The Glory of Old IU*. Sagamore Publishing, 2000, 193.

Time Life had…: Sandra Knipe.

"I was devastated": Eric Harper. "Angelo Pizzo: Screenwriter and film producer." MavenStar Consulting blog, March 23, 2013.

8   "I think I started writing…": Ibid.

"I wanted the writer to know…": Read Pizzo's interesting and detailed account of writing the script and then searching for financing in Lydia Wilen and Joan Wilen, *How to Sell Your Screenplay: A Realistic Guide to Getting a Television or Film Deal*, Garden City Park, NY: Square One Publishers, 2001, 156–160.

"it was Bloomington…": Angelo Pizzo. Ibid, 157.

"I saw my hometown…": Bill Kauffman, 42.

"I put the search out…": Angelo Pizzo. Interviewed by Randy Williams. *WGA's Written By*, October 2005.

"For some projects…": Randy Pease. "Utopia. The New Harmony Project strives to serve writers who celebrate the human spirit." *Evansville Living*, May/June 2006.

Because Pizzo felt…: Bill Kauffman, 40.

When Coach Marvin Wood…: For details on the 1954 Indiana state-champion Milan Indians, as well as what happened to them, their coach, and their town in later years, see Greg Guffey. *The Greatest Basketball Story Ever Told: The Milan Miracle* (50th Anniversary ed.). Bloomington, IN: Indiana University Press, 2003.

9   Pizzo began his research…: David Mannweiler. "After 'Hoosiers,' it's race cars for Pizzo." *Indianapolis News*, November 6, 1986, F-1; Aaron Baker. "The Indiana movie Hoosiers." *The Ryder Magazine*, December 1986, 16.

He also interviewed…: Mike Penner.

10 "I knew I didn't…": Bill Kauffman, 40.

conflict is…: Joe Hodes. "Going for the Cup: Interview with Screenwriter Angelo Pizzo." PLAYBACK:stl, August 31, 2003.

He felt he was remaining…: Sandra Knipe.

"in the course…": Hank Nuwer.

"I didn't want…": Mike Penner.

For additional inspiration…: Andy Graham. "Pizzo comes full circle." *Bloomington (IN) Herald-Times,* July 14, 2016.

"was to really capture…": Mike Leonard. "Buddies: Filmmakers Angelo Pizzo and David Anspaugh. Back in Bloomington where it all began." *Bloom,* October/November 2014, 92.

"This is not…": Scott L. Miley. "Movie creators goal of authenticity has some real Hoosiers' on defensive." *Indianapolis Star,* December 1, 1985, 1B.

11 As he retreated…: Angelo Pizzo. Videoconference.

"I started thinking about…": Eric Harper.

"the idea of…": Angelo Pizzo. Lydia Wilen and Joan Wilen, 156.

In the cold…: Angelo Pizzo. Videoconference.

"it was a terrible experience": Evan West. "Basketball diary." *Indianapolis Monthly,* vol. 27, no. 8, March 2004, 131.

"everything I thought…": Angelo Pizzo. Videoconference.

"the rational…": Angelo Pizzo. Interviewed by Peter Noble Kuchera.

"There was always a critic…": Eric Harper.

Eventually TV writer…: Angelo Pizzo. Lydia Wilen and Joan Wilen, 157.

12 "specifically clear…": Angelo Pizzo. Read more about Pizzo's writing strategy and insights in Lorian Tamara Elbert, *Why We Write: Personal Statements and Photographic Portraits of 25 Top Screenwriters.* Beverly Hills, CA: Silman-James Press, 1999, 207–210.

Pizzo remembered hearing…: Angelo Pizzo. Videoconference.

"a protagonist…": Angelo Pizzo. Online chat with HeraldTimesOnline.com.

"a theme that's been around…": "'Hoosiers' opens here Friday."

have to be a part of you: Angelo Pizzo. Videoconference.

But he also knew…: Andrew Tallackson.

"take on a life…": Hank Nuwer.

who was inspired…: John Carlson. "'Hoosiers' writer says film is about character." *Muncie (IN) Star Press,* February 20, 2004, special section 12.

13 Originally the alcoholic Shooter…: Hank Nuwer; Angelo Pizzo. Interviewed by Mickey Maurer. *Mickey's Corner,* JCC Indianapolis, January 16, 2008.

Pizzo described Myra's purpose…: Angelo Pizzo. Interviewed by the author November 12, 2012.

Pizzo envisioned…: Ibid.

"The guys on the team…": Sandra Knipe.

14 Mandelker stated…: Angelo Pizzo. Lydia Wilen and Joan Wilen, 157–158.

Eight months later…: Angelo Pizzo. Interviewed by the author November 27, 2009.

"your first draft…": Hank Nuwer.

Berg helped him…: Angelo Pizzo. Interviewed by Peter Noble Kuchera.

Pizzo decided to focus…: Angelo Pizzo. Interviewed by the author November 24, 2009.

Berg's feedback…: Angelo Pizzo. E-mail communication, April 18, 2013.

After graduating…: David Anspaugh. Interviewed by the author.

15 Anspaugh wished…: Ibid.

But then he took a class…: Mike Leonard, 91.

Anspaugh's first…: Nelson Price. "Spotlight on Hoosiers."; Scott L. Miley; http://www.filmreference.com/film/16/David-Anspaugh.html; Marc D. Allan. "Governor honors filmmaker. 'Hoosiers' director wins one of seven arts awards." *Indianapolis Star*, February 6, 1991, B11; David Davis. "Kicked! How the IU grads who created *Hoosiers* and *Rudy* got beaten in *The Game of Their Lives*." *Indianapolis Monthly*, vol. 28, no. 9, April 2005, 156.

"The odds that one…": Steve Bell. "Fast breaking away. Plans for a basketball movie stir up an early epidemic of Hoosier Hysteria." *Indianapolis Monthly*, October 1985, 72.

"The more work you do…": Frank Gray. "Film about down-and-out coach could ease TV director into movies." *Fort Wayne (IN) Journal Gazette*, December 23, 1984, 5D.

16 he knew they shared…: Nelson Price. *Indiana Legends*, 231.

Anspaugh's ego…": Angelo Pizzo. Interviewed by the author November 27, 2009.

Pizzo couldn't think…: Angelo Pizzo. Interviewed by the author November 12, 2012.

"David is not…": "Hoosier History: The Truth Behind the Legend." 2004. MGM Home Entertainment LLC.

He thought it was…: John Carlson.

He was convinced: Lynn Ford. "'Hoosiers' creating early hysteria." *Indianapolis Star*, November 11, 1986, 8.

His favorite kind of movie…: Frank Gray.

After completing…: Angelo Pizzo. Lydia Wilen and Joan Wilen, 158–159; "Where are they now? Angelo Pizzo." As told to L. Jon Wertheim. *Sports Illustrated*, July 7–14, 2014, 94.

17 As he was writing…: Angelo Pizzo. Lydia Wilen and Joan Wilen, 158.

"someone who lives in the state…": Michael Koryta. "20 questions for Angelo Pizzo. You can go home again." *Bloom*, August/September 2006, 42.

"Everywhere we went…": Scott L. Miley.

But Anspaugh asserted…: "Field for location of movie 'Hoosiers' thinned to 4 towns." *Indianapolis Star*, September 5, 1985.

18 Another difficulty was…: David T. Friendly. "Few sports films make a hit." *Los Angeles Times*, August 14, 1986; Travis Vogan. "Interview with David Anspaugh, Filmmaker." *International Journal of Sport Communication*, vol. 4, no. 4, December 2011, 446, 447; http://www.si.com/more-sports/video/2014/07/02/where-are-they-now-angelo-pizzo.

"How do you…": Lynn Houser. "Ten years after Hoosiers." *Bloomington (IN) Herald-Times*, September 15, 1996, D1.

One of them…: Greg Rice, 32.

"I knew what would happen": David Davis, 156–157.

"the only way to truly protect…": Gary Linehan. "Writer creates on Tulloch shore." (Sonora, CA) *Union Democrat*, June 24, 1994, 21.

19 "They claimed…": Scott L. Miley.

"the environment is as important…": Nelson Price. "Arts awards honor Indiana filmmaker, cellist, others."

Pizzo and Anspaugh also were certain…: David Anspaugh. Interviewed by Farrell Roth and Lon Harris. *This Week in Movies*. YouTube, December 11, 2010.

"Having grown up here…": "'Hoosiers' creator feared it would be a flop." *Evansville (IN) Courier*, November 17, 1996, A14.

"In Hollywood…": Gary Linehan.

"From the start…": Mike Pearson.

"I got to the point…": Angelo Pizzo. Lydia Wilen and Joan Wilen, 158.

"any film by its nature…": Anthony Schoettle. "Lights, camera, history. Movie about first Indy 500 ready for green flag." *Indianapolis Business Journal*, vol. 29, no. 46, January 12–18, 2009, 1.

"A lot of passion…": Program from the world premiere of *Hoosiers*, October 10, 1986.

20 Daly regarded his…: Kevin Phinney. "Rogue or Robin Hood?" *Premiere*, July 1990.

DeHaven called Daly…: Ibid.

Daly was moved…: Angelo Pizzo. Interviewed by Mickey Maurer.

Unlike most of the other producers…: Angelo Pizzo. Interviewed by the author August 18, 2012.

a $12 million budget…: Mike Pearson.

Although Anspaugh was relieved…: Frank Gray.

The first story…: Ibid.

Chapter 2

21 In late March…: "Miracle of Milan may be in movie." *Indianapolis Star*, March 28, 1985, 60.

The filmmakers needed…: Bruce C. Smith. "School was made for the movies . . . until bulldozers rolled in." *Indianapolis Star*, April 14, 1985, 1A.

The organization…: Lindel Hutson. "State film commission 'slow.'" *Indianapolis Star*, February 25, 1984, 32.

It was estimated…: "Hollywood, Ind.?" *Indianapolis Star*, December 2, 1986, 25.

The producers of *Breaking Away*…: *Indianapolis Star*, January 8, 1982, 22.

"We've tried…": Norm Bess. "Smile, folks! You just might be in 'Hoosiers.'" *Indianapolis News*, September 25, 1985, 22.

The movie was expected…: Scott L. Miley. "It's back to Hollywood, but will Hollywood come back?" *Indianapolis Star*, December 15, 1985, 6B.

"We've been waiting…": Norm Bess.

22 Ironically, Milan…: Bruce C. Smith.

They toured…: "Miracle of Milan may be in movie."

In April…: Bruce C. Smith; Angelo Pizzo. Interviewed by Andy Hunsucker and Jason Thompson. *A Place for Film: The IU Cinema Podcast*, episode 28, April 8, 2011.

Pizzo, Anspaugh...: Steve Bell. "Fast breaking away. Plans for a basketball movie stir up an early epidemic of Hoosier Hysteria." *Indianapolis Monthly*, October 1985, 70; David Anspaugh. Interviewed by Andy Hunsucker and Jason Thompson. *A Place for Film: The IU Cinema Podcast*, episode 28, April 8, 2011.

Location manager...: Rick Schmidlin. Interviewed by the author February 8, 2010.

"You have to be careful...": Steve Bell, 70.

23   The retired...: "Richmond basketball guard may get a shot at stardom." *Indianapolis Star*, August 25, 1985, 1C.

And after reading...: Peg Mayhill. Interviewed by the author August 27, 2009.

During a late-summer...: "List of small towns sites for 'Hoosiers' film cut." *Indianapolis Star*, September 5, 1985, 36.

24   Officials in Nineveh...: Dean George. "Nineveh flirting with cinema glory. School one of 5 finalists for 'Hoosiers' site." *Indianapolis Star*, September 9, 1985, 26.

Upon learning...: Ibid.

School representatives...: Jim Slater. "Small towns are gym-dandy locations for basketball movie." UPI, *Indianapolis News*, September 10, 1985, 24.

The film crew thought...: Alberta White. "Linden, New Richmond are hoping to go to the movies." *Crawfordsville (IN) Journal Review*, September 5, 1985, 1.

"We walked into...": *Hoosiers*. 2005. Audio commentaries (DVD). MGM Home Entertainment LLC.

25   Pizzo said it was evident...: Robert Reed. "Screenwriter: Don't get too caught up in detail; enjoy movie." *Knightstown (IN) Tri-County Banner*, November 12, 1986, 1.

Nichols declared...: "Knightstown's preview of 'Hoosiers' sold out; drawing set for free tickets." *Knightstown (IN) Tri-County Banner*, November 5, 1986, 16.

The producers pledged...: Jim Slater.

Anspaugh explained...: David Anspaugh. Interviewed by Andy Hunsucker and Jason Thompson.

Nichols and art director...: Alberta White. "Linden, New Richmond are hoping to go to the movies."; Wilma Lewellyn. Interviewed by the author November 16, 2015; Alberta White. "New Richmond looking good." *Crawfordsville (IN) Journal Review*, September 6, 1985, 1; Susan Headden. "Director casts about for 'Hoosiers' extras." *Indianapolis Star*, September 29, 1985, 1B; Alberta White. "New Richmond gearing up for part in film." *Crawfordsville (IN) Journal Review*, September 9, 1985, 1.

26   Filming would begin...: Alberta White. "New Richmond looking good."

27   A barbershop in nearby Linden...: Roger Kunkel. Interviewed by the author.

Every newspaper...: Scott L. Miley. "Hickory dickory dock, town turns back the clock. New Richmond goes '50s for filming of 'Hoosiers.'" *Indianapolis Star*, November 30, 1985, 1; Sam Stall. "Hoosiers hysteria." *Indianapolis Monthly*, November 1986, vol. 10, no. 3, 84.

"You have no idea...": Kathy Matter. "'Hoosiers' pairs basketball, redemption." *Lafayette (IN) Journal and Courier*, November 9, 1986, C1.

In the town's museum...: Alberta White. "New Richmond gearing up for part in film."

The set decorators...: Alberta White. "Sun brightens stars' spirits." *Crawfordsville (IN) Journal Review*, December 4, 1985, 9.

"They dirtied things a bit...": Scott L. Miley. "Hickory dickory dock, town turns back the clock. New Richmond goes '50s for filming of 'Hoosiers.'"

"They tore it up...": Alberta White. "Sun brightens stars' spirits."

Karen Galvin...: Norm Bess.

28 Two meetings were held...: Alberta White. "Overflow crowd attends meeting about movie." *Crawfordsville (IN) Journal Review*, September 17, 1985, 1.

The townspeople were warned...: Alberta White. "Excitement building for movie." *Crawfordsville (IN) Journal Review*, September 24, 1985, 1.

Contemplating the number...: Emily M. Smith. "New Richmond awaits 'Hoosiers.'" *Lafayette (IN) Journal and Courier*, September 1985; Emily M. Smith. "Movie role bewilders town. New Richmond gets ready for Hollywood." *Lafayette (IN) Journal and Courier*, September 17, 1985.

Byron Alexander...: "New Richmond residents come out for casting call." *Crawfordsville (IN) Journal Review*, September 30, 1985, 1.

permanent extras: Scott L. Miley. "It's back to Hollywood, but will Hollywood come back?"

They would play...: Norm Bess; Alberta White. "Excitement building for movie."

29 Applicants had...: Fred D. Cavinder. "Little Hickory continues to grow in basketball lore." *Indianapolis Star*, May 6, 1990, B4; Susan Headden; Alberta White. "Many residents earn roles in 'Hoosiers.'" *Crawfordsville (IN) Journal Review*, October 15, 1985, 1.

They were informed...: Roger Kunkel. Interviewed by the author.

A woman from Lafayette...: Emily M. Smith. "Hoosiers: extras worry about image." *Lafayette (IN) Journal and Courier*, October 16, 1985, A1.

"One of the people...": Scott L. Miley. "Movie creators goal of authenticity has some real Hoosiers' on defensive."

"very sensitive...": Aaron Baker. "The Indiana movie Hoosiers." *The Ryder Magazine*, December 1986, 16.

"I happen to love...": Scott L. Miley. "Movie creators goal of authenticity has some real Hoosiers' on defensive."

30 Casting sessions...: Scott L. Miley. "Knightstown recreates past to lend authenticity to film." *Indianapolis Star*, November 20, 1985, 27; Janet Helms. "Shirts helped chamber cash in." *New Castle (IN) Courier Times, National Road Edition*, 1995; Lisa Pfenninger. "'Doc Buggins' crazy about Gene Hackman, Dennis Hopper."

The movie's costumers...: Peg Mayhill. Interviewed by the author.

Said one crew member...: "How to land role in 'Hoosiers.'" *Knightstown (IN) Tri-County Banner*, October 10, 1985, 2.

Everyone was issued...: Robert Reed. "K'town says hello to Hollywood. Residents flood call for extras." *Knightstown (IN) Tri-County Banner*, October 17, 1985, 1.

31 "About 60 percent...": Kellie Edwards. "Film hopefuls out to give something extra. Lebanon residents try to pass as 'Hoosiers.'" *Indianapolis News*, October 14, 1985, 13.

"We will be going...": David Penticuff. "2,000 answer casting call for a chance to be in 'Hoosiers.'" *New Castle (IN) Courier-Times*, October 14, 1985, 1.

Old vehicles...: Alberta White. "Cameras roll on 'Hoosiers.'" *Crawfordsville (IN) Journal Review*, October 18, 1985, 1.

Mike Hendrickson: Tim Baker. "'50s return. Nineveh gets 'new' old look for 'Hoosiers.'" *Johnson County (IN) Daily Journal,* October 28, 1985, 1.

After conducting a wide...: Darryll Baker. E-mail communication, December 29, 2012.

32   Costumers Mary Weir...: Kellie Edwards; Alberta White. "Many residents earn roles in 'Hoosiers.'"

The female extras...: Kellie Edwards; "Extra! Extra! Extras needed." *Hendricks County (IN) Guide Gazette,* November 5, 1985, 1.

"find out real fast...": David Penticuff.

33   As the extras pulled together...: Frank Espich. "Fashion goes old school. Franklin woman loves to share the vintage life." *Indianapolis Star,* March 10, 2013, G1; Jane Anderson, interviewed by the author February 23, 2016; William Jackson. "She's picking out clothes for movie's stars." *Muncie (IN) Star,* October 5, 1985, 1A.

The Huskers' home and away...: Jerry Graff. "'Hoosiers' uniforms will be the real McCoy ... almost." *Indianapolis News,* October 23, 1985, 50.

Anderson decided to change...: Dana Hunsinger Benbow. "The fascinating tale of the 'Hoosiers' Hickory uniforms." *Indianapolis Star,* November 5, 2015.

The design...: Jane Anderson, interviewed by the author.

34   background artists: *Hoosiers.* 2005. Audio commentaries (DVD).

"place is as powerful...": Bill Kauffman. "Hoops. Hoosiers. Hollywood. Home." *The American Enterprise,* vol. 17, no. 2, March 2006, 41.

"the details in any film...": *Hoosiers.* 2005. Audio commentaries (DVD).

Chapter 3

35   Jack Nicholson...: David Anspaugh. Interviewed by the author January 13, 2010; Bonnie Britton. "Secrets behind the scenes. Heartland film panel reveals who might have starred in famous role." *Indianapolis Star,* October 31, 1994, D1; Robert Reed. "It's a wrap. 'Hoosiers' filming ends in K-town." *Knightstown (IN) Tri-County Banner,* December 19, 1985, 5; Program from the world premiere of *Hoosiers,* October 10, 1986; Mike Pearson. "How 'Hoosiers' got from script to filming." *Bloomington (IN) Sunday Herald-Times,* November 17, 1985, D1; Aaron Baker. "The Indiana movie Hoosiers." *The Ryder Magazine,* December 1986, 16.

he agreed to a salary...: Aleene MacMinn. "Morning report: legal file." *Los Angeles Times,* May 11, 1989.

36   "sometimes it can be...": Steve Bell. "Fast breaking away. Plans for a basketball movie stir up an early epidemic of Hoosier Hysteria." *Indianapolis Monthly,* October 1985, 72.

"From the moment I saw...": Richard Lormand. "'Hoosiers' is a memory trip for Hackman." Reuters, *Dallas Morning News,* March 13, 1987.

"I was walking home...": Todd Webb. "Hackman on familiar ground with 'Hoosiers.'" *The Oklahoman,* February 20, 1987.

improvisational theater: Michael Norman. "Hollywood's uncommon everyman." *New York Times,* March 19, 1989.

"almost purely on story...": Darlene Arden. "Hackman: critic to his film past." New York Times Syndicate, *Ocala (FL) Star-Banner,* July 16, 1988, TVWeek 4.

"it tells an interesting story…": Barbara Paskin. "Gene Hackman: The Common Man." *Films and Filming*, issue no. 365, May 1986.

37 "a very competitive man…": Richard Lormand.

Pizzo and Anspaugh learned…: Evan West. "Basketball diary." *Indianapolis Monthly*, vol. 27, no. 8, March 2004, 132.

"We interviewed, read…": Mark Turner. "Hoosiers: An Interview with Director David Anspaugh." Epinions.com, March 16, 2005.

Pizzo said he and Anspaugh were confident…: Aaron Baker.

Hopper was drawn…: Martin Jasicki. "Hopper's role has familiar ring to it." *Terre Haute (IN) Tribune-Star*, November 14, 1986, C1.

"I know about how…": Elena Rodriguez. *Dennis Hopper: A Madness to His Method*. New York: St. Martin's Press, 1988, 165.

38 "his own story…": Program from the world premiere of *Hoosiers*.

Christine Lahti…: Angelo Pizzo. Interviewed by the author November 24, 2009; David Anspaugh. Interviewed by the author January 5, 2010.

"never fulfills her destiny…": Dan Yakir. "Barbara Hershey: an understated talent." *Spectravision Satellite Program Guide*, April 1988.

"fiercely proud…": *Hoosiers* pressbook.

"quite a few problems…": "'Home team' has a Hoosier flavor." *Indianapolis News*, October 14, 1985, 3.

"I have never…": Program from the world premiere of *Hoosiers*.

39 she was looking forward…: Mike Pearson. "Hoosier hysteria: The movie. Pizzo's film gets small-town authenticity in Indiana locations." *Bloomington (IN) Sunday Herald-Times*, November 17, 1985, D1.

"That's the jerk…": Steve Wulf. "Three-sport star." *ESPN The Magazine*, November 29, 2010, 89.

Gloria Dorson…: Mike Pearson. "Hoosier hysteria: The movie."

Sam Smiley…: Sandra Knipe. "Angry ref is Smiley." *Evansville (IN) Courier*, November 14, 1986, 17.

Michael O'Guinne…: Rita Rose. "Indiana actor pleased with small role in 'Hoosiers.'" *Indianapolis Star*, November 30, 1986, 2E.

Some of the supporting roles…: Scott L. Miley. "'Hoosiers' happenings. Mellencamp may do soundtrack for movie." *Indianapolis Star*, December 1, 1985, 7B.

Selected as one…: Jeff Hutson. "Johnson County men call the shots in film." *Johnson County (IN) Daily Journal*, November 13, 1986, 11.

40 Rich Komenich…: Scott L. Miley. "'How'd you do it?' Reporter plays himself in 'Hoosiers' movie." *Indianapolis Star*, November 3, 1985, 1B; Jim Gordon. *Merrillville (IN) Post-Tribune*, November 11, 1986, A1.

very opposed to the idea…: Scott L. Miley. "'Hoosiers' introduce their starting lineup. Basketball movie's cameras will soon begin rolling." *Indianapolis Star*, October 15, 1985, 1.

"You can't fake…": Lynn Houser. "Ten years after Hoosiers." *Bloomington (IN) Herald-Times*, September 15, 1996, D1.

"There was resistance…": *Hoosiers* pressbook.

41 They would earn...: "Would-be stars shoot for roles in 'Hoosiers' basketball movie." *Evansville (IN) Courier*, August 27, 1985, 11.

Those trying out...: Ibid; Dan Carpenter. "They're cashing in that round, orange ticket to Hollywood." *Indianapolis Star*, August 27, 1985, 17.

"The primary requirement...": "Would-be stars shoot for roles in 'Hoosiers' basketball movie."

"This state loves...": Dan Carpenter.

The young men were asked...: Jim Hopkins. "Bellmont grad hustles to part in 'Hoosiers.'" *Decatur (IN) Daily Democrat*, October 9, 1985.

In the first half...: Dan Carpenter.

"thought Maris had sex appeal": Spyridon Stratigos. Interviewed by the author August 24, 2013.

42 At the end of the evening...: Evan West, 133.

Ball State University junior...: Mark Bennett. "Anniversary of movie 'Hoosiers' brings back memories for Greene County native who played Ollie." *Terre Haute (IN) Tribune-Star*, June 5, 2006.

He had averaged...: Scott L. Miley. "Back to reality for 'Hickory' players." *Indianapolis Star*, November 9, 1986, 1E.

It had been the best year...: Mark Alesia. "'Shot' survives test of time." *Indianapolis Star*, February 15, 2004, C1.

written about in *Sports Illustrated*...: See Bruce Newman. "Back home in Indiana. From Bippus to Birdseye, from Holland to Peru, Indiana's game is basketball, otherwise known as Hoosier Hysteria." *Sports Illustrated*, February 18, 1985.

Kent Poole's high school...: Nelson Price. "Kent Poole. Sometimes he acts, but mostly he farms." *Indianapolis News*, June 10, 1989, A7; Scott L. Miley. "Back to reality for 'Hickory' players."; Leslie Collins. "Hoosiers: fact & fiction. Decade after movie, 'Husker' Poole coaches girls, farms outside Advance." *Indianapolis Star*, January 22, 1997, Inside 1; Mike Beas. "Once a Husker . . . always a Husker. Sixteen years ago, Kent Poole & Co. ran the ol' picket fence at 'em in the movie 'Hoosiers.'" *Lebanon (IN) Reporter*, July 18, 2002, 10.

In the final game...: John Shaughnessy. "Art may imitate life for ex-Warsaw player." *Indianapolis Star*, October 11, 1985, 31.

43 Hollar read about...: Greg Rice. "DePauw student brings real championship experience to the movie set in Hoosiers." *Alumnus* (DePauw University), volume 50, issue 2, Winter 1986, 32.

One of the hopeful actors...: Scott L. Miley. "'Hoosiers' introduce their starting lineup; Jim Hopkins.

Brad Long...: Scott L. Miley. "Back to reality for 'Hickory' players."

At 23...: Brett Halbleib. "Good memories — and gum flavor — stick with 'Hoosier.'" *Indianapolis Star*, March 12, 2005, S1.

Scott Summers...: Scott L. Miley. "'Hoosiers' introduce their starting lineup."

44 "I tried to get...": Judy Thorburn. "Vegas Happenings." *Las Vegas Round the Clock*. February 18, 2007.

As they got closer...: David Anspaugh. Interviewed by the author July 23, 2016.

Hollar's many trips…: Steve Hollar. Interviewed by Dick Gordon. "The Making of Hoosiers." American Public Media. WUNC 91.5, North Carolina Public Radio. April 1, 2011.

Finally, after six rounds…: Dan Carpenter; Bob Cook. "Kick Out the Sports!" *Flak*, May 24, 2004; Mike Pearson. "'There's a lot involved in making movies.'" *Bloomington (IN) Sunday Herald-Times*, November 17, 1985, A1.

One day in early October…: Steve Hollar. Interviewed by Dick Gordon.

When he was contacted…: John Shaughnessy. "Art may imitate life for ex-Warsaw player."

On October 14…: Scott L. Miley. "'Hoosiers' introduce their starting lineup."

45   "I immediately felt…": Evan West, 133.

"So much of who he is…": David Anspaugh. Interviewed by Andy Hunsucker and Jason Thompson. *A Place for Film: The IU Cinema Podcast*, episode 28, April 8, 2011.

unofficial leader: Tim Baker. "Captain. Brad Long to lead 'Hoosiers' team." *Johnson County (IN) Daily Journal*, October 14, 1985, 1.

"They told me…": Rev Mengle. "Long's life. A new job, impending wedding and movie role." *Johnson County (IN) Daily Journal*, December 5, 1985, 1.

"As far as I'm concerned…": Scott L. Miley. "Back to reality for 'Hickory' players."

"I think it's fine…": Mike Ellis. "Brownsburg blossoms with movie hopefuls. Hundreds dress parts in 'Hoosiers' auditions." *Indianapolis News*, October 21, 1985, 14.

"read about one kid…": John J. Shaughnessy. "Crossroads connections. People whose faith guides them through crises are the focus of 'Hoosiers' writer Pizzo's work." *Indianapolis Star*, March 5, 2005, B1.

"I think what they like…": Chris Pruett. "Schencks to appear on screen in 'Hoosiers.'" *Linton (IN) Daily Citizen*, October 15, 1985, 1.

This was unsurprising…: Dan Carpenter.

"Nobody wanted to be Ollie": Mark Bennett.

After conducting auditions…: Angelo Pizzo. Interviewed by the author August 18, 2012; Mike Leonard. "Buddies: Filmmakers Angelo Pizzo and David Anspaugh. Back in Bloomington where it all began." *Bloom*, October/November 2014, 88.

46   Like the other Huskers…: David Neidorf. Interviewed by the author May 20, 2016.

Along with the cheerleaders…: Tim Baker. "Long learning new way to play for movie role." *Johnson County (IN) Daily Journal*, October 23, 1985, 1; Marcia Duke. Interviewed by the author August 16, 2012.

Pizzo borrowed the character surnames…: Angelo Pizzo. Interviewed by the author August 18, 2012.

After accepting roles…: Scott L. Miley. "Back to reality for 'Hickory' players."

47   Schenck and Poole left…: Scott L. Miley. "'Hoosiers' introduce their starting lineup."; Leslie Collins.

Long was forced…: Scott L. Miley. "Back to reality for 'Hickory' players."

To help them…: Lynn Houser.

Summers called…: Mike Ellis.

"To me…": Leslie Collins.

"I'm just kind of stunned…": Scott L. Miley. "'Hoosiers' introduce their starting lineup."

Chapter 4

49   "The newly formed…": Mark Bennett. "Anniversary of movie 'Hoosiers' brings back memories for Greene County native who played Ollie." *Terre Haute (IN) Tribune-Star*, June 5, 2006.

They needed…: Mike Reilley. "Celluloid hero. His smooth jumper captures the moment in 'Hoosiers.'" *Los Angeles Times*, April 21, 1994.

Technical advisor…: Spyridon Stratigos. Interviewed by the author August 24, 2013.

Hired to instruct…: Steve Bell. "Fast breaking away. Plans for a basketball movie stir up an early epidemic of Hoosier Hysteria." *Indianapolis Monthly*, October 1985, 70; Mike Pearson. "Hoosier hysteria: The movie. Pizzo's film gets small-town authenticity in Indiana locations." *Bloomington (IN) Sunday Herald-Times*, November 17, 1985, D1.

"shouldn't do fancy moves…": Scott L. Miley. "'Hoosiers' happenings. Mellencamp may do soundtrack for movie." *Indianapolis Star*, December 1, 1985, 7B.

"I've worked hard…": Mike Ellis. "Brownsburg blossoms with movie hopefuls. Hundreds dress parts in 'Hoosiers' auditions." *Indianapolis News*, October 21, 1985, 14.

"You have to…": Greg Rice. "DePauw student brings real championship experience to the movie set in Hoosiers." *Alumnus* (DePauw University), volume 50, issue 2, Winter 1986, 33.

Hollar hoped…: Grady Tate. "Hoosier hysteria. Fans gather to celebrate 1986 film." *Connersville (IN) News Examiner*, April 12, 2016.

the art of acting: Skip Stogsdill. "'It was Dentyne.'" *Sharing the Victory* (Fellowship of Christian Athletes), March/April 1988, 2.

50   Brad Boyle said Anspaugh…: Lorrie Hamrick. "'Bigger perspective' on life gained from film." *Decatur (IN) Daily Democrat*, November 27, 1985.

"That's how they…": Greg Rice.

"Rade and I have a lot in common.": Kirby Sprouls. "Steve Hollar goes to Hollywood…er, Indianapolis." *Warsaw (IN) Times-Union*, January 7, 1986, 1A.

truly fit his personality: Lynn Houser. "Ten years after Hoosiers." *Bloomington (IN) Herald-Times*, September 15, 1996, D1.

"I did play…": Tim Baker. "Captain. Brad Long to lead 'Hoosiers' team." *Johnson County (IN) Daily Journal*, October 14, 1985, 1.

"I don't feel I'm cocky": Clark Spencer. "Theaters are now his court." *Wichita (KS) Eagle-Beacon*, March 13, 1987, 1C.

"in a word, dumb": *Hoosiers* screenplay, revised draft, October 13, 1985.

"The producers told us…": Lorrie Hamrick.

"dumbfounded": Lynn Houser. "Ten years after Hoosiers."

51   David Neidorf remarked…: David Neidorf. Interviewed by the author May 20, 2016.

"You're somewhat limited…": Paul Willistein. "Gene Hackman is once again at center court." *The (Allentown, PA) Morning Call*, March 1, 1987.

Hackman put the Huskers…: Brad Long. Interviewed by the author July 10, 2013.

In return, the Huskers assisted…: Kirby Sprouls.

"Just remember…": Dan Patrick. "'Hoosiers' captures madness." March 1, 2001. http://espn.go.com/talent/danpatrick/s/2001/0301/1119482.html.

"there are only so many...": Bob Cook. "'Hoosiers' turns 25." *Forbes*, November 21, 2011.

"talked about going to...": Garret Mathews. "'Hoosiers' spirit lives on, two decades after its release." *Evansville (IN) Courier & Press*, June 11, 2006, B3.

"If [acting isn't]...": "'Hoosiers' actor fights for child." *Indianapolis Star*, April 24, 2005, A3.

"a no-bull guy...": Garret Mathews.

Eventually Hollar figured out...: Steve Hollar. Interviewed by Dick Gordon. "The Making of Hoosiers." American Public Media. WUNC 91.5, North Carolina Public Radio. April 1, 2011.

52   "Gene was pretty intense...": Evan West. "Basketball diary." *Indianapolis Monthly*, vol. 27, no. 8, March 2004, 256.

"You can imagine...": Lynn Houser. "A tough loss." *Indianapolis Monthly*, October 2006, 168; Ibid.

"You have a perception...": Nelson Price. "Kent Poole. Sometimes he acts, but mostly he farms." *Indianapolis News*, June 10, 1989, A7.

"He has a rural quality...": Lynn Houser. "Ten years after Hoosiers."

Anspaugh noticed that...: *Hoosiers*. 2005. Audio commentaries (DVD).

"The directors and everybody...": Scott L. Miley. "Movie creators goal of authenticity has some real Hoosiers' on defensive." *Indianapolis Star*, December 1, 1985, 1B.

Anspaugh didn't work...: David Anspaugh. Interviewed by the author July 23, 2016.

53   Hackman admitted that he...: Angelo Pizzo. Videoconference at the Challenger Learning Center, Brownsburg, Indiana, March 3, 2009.

One example was...: *Hoosiers* screenplay, revised draft.

Pizzo had never dealt...: David Anspaugh. Interviewed by the author July 23, 2016.

"The first time...": Kirby Sprouls.

54   "Coach, we're gonna...": *Hoosiers* screenplay, September 24, 1985.

When Pizzo heard...: Aaron Baker. "The Indiana movie Hoosiers." *The Ryder Magazine*, December 1986, 16; Kathy Matter. "'Hoosiers' pairs basketball, redemption." *Lafayette (IN) Journal and Courier*, November 9, 1986, C1.

"I try to work out...": Alberta White. "The 'stars' come out in Hickory, Indiana." *Crawfordsville (IN) Journal Review*, October 24, 1985, 1.

"taking a leap of faith...": Angelo Pizzo. Interviewed by the author November 12, 2012.

"I felt I was ready...": Bettelou Peterson. "Hill Street, Miami Vice 'too good for their own good'?" KNT News Service, May 31, 1985.

"I've done [*Hill Street* episodes]...": Scott L. Miley. "Movie creators goal of authenticity has some real Hoosiers' on defensive."

"the long scenes...": Bettelou Peterson.

55   state of semi-panic: David Anspaugh. Interviewed by the author January 5, 2010.

The night before...: David Anspaugh. Interviewed by Farrell Roth and Lon Harris. *This Week in Movies*. YouTube, December 11, 2010.

"a tornado...": Scott L. Miley. "Hickory dickory dock, town turns back the clock. New Richmond goes '50s for filming of 'Hoosiers.'" *Indianapolis Star*, November 30, 1985, 1.

"There are a lot more…": Susan Headden. "Director casts about for 'Hoosiers' extras." *Indianapolis Star*, September 29, 1985, 1B.

"It's not uncommon…": Sandra J. Flint. "'Hoosiers' films in New Richmond." *479 Newsletter*, October 1985.

"The film's helped…": "State star-struck. On location with 'Hoosiers.'" *Electric Consumer*, vol. 35, no. 6, December 1985.

56 Deputy town marshal…: Doug Hunt. "New Richmond's movie memories recalled." *Crawfordsville (IN) Journal Review*, September 9, 2001; Ibid.

To the souvenir…: Scott L. Miley. "Hickory dickory dock, town turns back the clock."

Other items for sale…: Ibid; Susan Headden.

About 6 a.m.…: Sam Stall. "Hoosiers hysteria." *Indianapolis Monthly*, November 1986, vol. 10, no. 3, 84; Debbie Burns. "Take one. A Danville family prepares its home for the silver screen." *Indianapolis Monthly*, vol. 9, no. 3, November 1985, 16.

Before filming began…: Alberta White. "Cameras roll on 'Hoosiers.'" *Crawfordsville (IN) Journal Review*, October 18, 1985, 1.

57 Then it began raining…: Alberta White. "New Richmond thinks Hackman super as movie begins filming." *Crawfordsville (IN) Journal Review*, October 19, 1985, 1.

58 The cast and crew returned…: Alberta White. "The 'stars' come out in Hickory, Indiana."

On hand that day…: David Neidorf. Interviewed by the author.

Also present was…: Alberta White. "The 'stars' come out in Hickory, Indiana."

"I'm not the kind of director…": David Anspaugh. Interviewed by Andy Hunsucker and Jason Thompson. *A Place for Film: The IU Cinema Podcast*, episode 28, April 8, 2011.

At the end of each filming day…: Roger Kunkel. Interviewed by the author.

59 New Richmond grocery…: Scott L. Miley. "Hickory dickory dock, town turns back the clock."

"It was interesting…": Doug Hunt.

Fannie Stephens…: Alberta White. "New Richmond couple's pictures a surprise for Hackman." *Crawfordsville (IN) Journal Review*, October 19, 1985, 1.

"They are so…": Scott L. Miley. "Hickory dickory dock, town turns back the clock."

Casting director…: Ibid.

"like people did…": Robert Reed. "Filming for the 'big screen' gets closer." *Knightstown (IN) Tri-County Banner*, October 10, 1985, 1.

"I love shooting…": Joe Hodes. "Going for the Cup: Interview with screenwriter Angelo Pizzo." PLAYBACK:stl, August 31, 2003.

60 "Wabash County": Tim Baker. "'50s return. Nineveh gets 'new' old look for 'Hoosiers.'" *Johnson County (IN) Daily Journal*, October 28, 1985, 1.

"I like to have the writer…": David Anspaugh. Interviewed on Spike. "The Game of Their Lives: interview with director David Anspaugh," April 13, 2005, http://www.spike.com/video/game-of-their-lives/2668849.

"he gives you…": David Anspaugh. Interviewed by the author January 13, 2010.

However, the production got off...: Angelo Pizzo. Interviewed by the author November 27, 2009; David Anspaugh. Interviewed by the author January 5 and 13, 2010.

61 Hackman didn't go easy...: Angelo Pizzo. Videoconference.

At the beginning of one...: David Anspaugh. Talk at the IU Cinema, April 7, 2011.

Pizzo and Anspaugh perceived...: Angelo Pizzo. Interviewed by the author November 27, 2009; Angelo Pizzo. Talk at the IU Cinema, April 7, 2011; David Anspaugh. Interviewed by the author January 5, 2010; Evan West, 256.

"At any given time...": "State star-struck. On location with 'Hoosiers.'"

62 "Anything like this...": Dean A. George. "Nineveh to participate in 'Hoosiers' movie." *Edinburgh (IN) Tri-County Enterprise*, October 2, 1985, 1.

Although location manager...: "Nineveh will host film crew." *Johnson County (IN) Daily Journal*, September 11, 1985, 1; Tim Baker. "Action! Nineveh school could host film." *Johnson County (IN) Daily Journal*, September 5, 1985, 1; Jeff Owen. "Educational era comes to end." *Greenwood (IN) News*, May 29, 1986, 1.

Darlene Dugan: Tim Baker. "Film helps Nineveh relive 'old times.'" *Greenwood (IN) News*, October 3, 1985, 1.

Bruce Lucas: Ibid.

The crew prepared...: Rosemarie Sylvester. "'Hoosiers.' Nineveh prepared for cameras." *Johnson County (IN) Daily Journal*, October 19, 1985, 1.

Some outdoor scenes...: Tim Baker. "'50s return. Nineveh gets 'new' old look for 'Hoosiers.'"

Members of the drama club...: Scott L. Miley. "Knightstown recreates past to lend authenticity to film." *Indianapolis Star*, November 20, 1985, 2; *Edinburgh (IN) Tri-County Enterprise*, October 30, 1985, 1.

"We spent hours...": "State star-struck. On location with 'Hoosiers.'"

63 Because school was in session...: Tim Baker. "Roll 'em." *Johnson County (IN) Daily Journal*, October 29, 1985, 3.

When Norman enters Cletus's office...: Angelo Pizzo. Interviewed by the author August 18, 2012.

One disadvantage...: Scott L. Miley. "It's back to Hollywood, but will Hollywood come back?" *Indianapolis Star*, December 15, 1985, 6B.

The crew made a few changes...: Tim Baker. "'50s return. Nineveh gets 'new' old look for 'Hoosiers.'"

64 "I was nervous...": Evan West, 258.

a look at the original script...: *Hoosiers* screenplay, September 24, 1985.

Pizzo described...: Angelo Pizzo. Interviewed by the author August 18, 2012.

The problems between...: Tim Baker. "'Hoosiers' crew gone." *Johnson County (IN) Daily Journal*, October 30, 1985, 1.

According to the director...: David Anspaugh. Interviewed by the author January 5, 2010.

"I depend on energy...": Darlene Arden. "Hackman: critic to his film past." New York Times Syndicate, *Ocala (FL) Star-Banner*, July 16, 1988, TVWeek 4.

Supporting actor Chelcie Ross...: Chelcie Ross. Interviewed by the author August 26, 2014.

65   "I had never worked…": Darlene Arden.

a confluence of energy: Angelo Pizzo. Interviewed by the author November 27, 2009 and August 18, 2012; David Anspaugh. Interviewed by the author January 13, 2010.

"I don't need a lot of help…": Elena Rodriguez. *Dennis Hopper: A Madness to His Method*. New York: St. Martin's Press, 1988, 166.

"wonderful sort of gray…": Fred Murphy. Interviewed by the author January 31, 2016.

"That kind of gloomy…": Evan West, 256.

Anspaugh agreed…: Lynn Houser. "Ten years after Hoosiers."

Chapter 5

67   "a really difficult movie…": Scott L. Miley. "Movie creators goal of authenticity has some real Hoosiers' on defensive." *Indianapolis Star*, December 1, 1985, 1B.

"film all day…": Garret Mathews. "'Hoosiers' spirit lives on, two decades after its release." *Evansville (IN) Courier & Press*, June 11, 2006, B3.

Assistant directors…: Herb Adelman. Interviewed by the author January 29, 2010; Harvey Waldman. Interviewed by the author January 26, 2010.

One result…: David Anspaugh. Interviewed by the author January 5, 2010.

Pizzo conceded…: Angelo Pizzo. Interviewed by the author November 27, 2009.

On one occasion…": David Anspaugh. Interviewed on Spike. "The Game of Their Lives: interview with director David Anspaugh," April 13, 2005, http://www.spike.com/video/game-of-their-lives/2668849.

"banged heads": David Anspaugh. Interviewed by the author January 13, 2010.

"We have our squabbles": Michael Koryta. "Pizzo getting a kick out of latest movie." *Hoosier Times* (Bloomington, IN), August 17, 2003.

Supporting actor Chelcie Ross…: Bonnie Britton. "Too clean, frustrated filmmakers claim." *Indianapolis Star*, December 1, 1996, 16.

As fatigue set in…: Angelo Pizzo. Interviewed by the author November 27, 2009.

68   On Sundays…: David Anspaugh. Interviewed by the author January 13, 2010; Herb Adelman. Interviewed by the author; Rick Schmidlin. Interviewed by the author February 8, 2010.

Schmidlin had considered…: David Saunders. "'Hoosiers' to play in old Knightstown gym." *New Castle (IN) Courier-Times*, September 7, 1985, 1.

Instead, one classroom…: Mike Pearson. "Hoosier hysteria: The movie. Pizzo's film gets small-town authenticity in Indiana locations." *Bloomington (IN) Sunday Herald-Times*, November 17, 1985, D1.

"There have been some…": "Knightstown likes being in movie." *Crawfordsville (IN) Journal Review*, November 19, 1985, 11.

As had happened…: Lisa Pfenninger. "'Doc Buggins' crazy about Gene Hackman, Dennis Hopper."; Dell Ford. "Cameras roll for filming of 'Hoosiers.'" *Fort Wayne (IN) Journal Gazette*, November 10, 1985, 1D; Dick Leakey. Interviewed by the author October 13, 2009; Bob Reed. "Hackman likes it in small town Indiana; stays busy." *Knightstown (IN) Tri-County Banner*, November 7, 1985, 3; Wilma Lewellyn. Interviewed by the author February 14, 2010.

69   The narrow street next to…: Alberta White. "'Hoosiers' nearing finish." *Crawfordsville (IN) Journal Review*, December 3, 1985, 1; Alberta White. "The 'stars' come out in Hickory, Indiana." *Crawfordsville (IN) Journal Review*, October 24, 1985, 1.

The film crew managed…: Alberta White. "Mehanry knows the real 'score' on Hoosiers." *Crawfordsville (IN) Journal Review*, October 7, 1985, 1; "State star-struck. On location with 'Hoosiers.'" *Electric Consumer*, vol. 35, no. 6, December 1985.

70   In the first scene…: Scott L. Miley. "'How'd you do it?' Reporter plays himself in 'Hoosiers' movie." *Indianapolis Star*, November 3, 1985, 1B; Bob Reed. "Academy turns into movie set." *Knightstown (IN) Tri-County Banner*, November 7, 1985, 1; Zaenger. "Performers add state flavor to basketball film." *Fort Wayne (IN) News-Sentinel*, November 10, 1986, 1D.

The extras were surprised…: Dell Ford.

The large group of extras…: Bob Reed. "Academy turns into movie set."; Scott L. Miley. "Knightstown recreates past to lend authenticity to film." *Indianapolis Star*, November 20, 1985, 27.

71   "I was all nerves…": Chelcie Ross. Interviewed by the author August 26, 2014.

When the Huskers struggled…: Brad Long. Interviewed by the author July 10, 2013.

Long improvised…: Ibid.

The screenplay offers a clue…: *Hoosiers* screenplay, revised draft, October 13, 1985.

72   "I wanted an image…": Zaenger. "'Hoosiers' co-producer regrets having to cut Indiana scenes." *Fort Wayne (IN) News-Sentinel*, November 14, 1986, 1D.

it was Anspaugh's idea…: *Hoosiers*. 2005. Audio commentaries (DVD). MGM Home Entertainment LLC.

As a painter…: David Anspaugh. Interviewed by the author January 13, 2010.

Recalled Roger Hamilton, Jr.…: Janet Helms. "Ten years later, Hamilton still dreams." *New Castle (IN) Courier Times, National Road Edition*, 1995.

Lieutenant Governor John Mutz…: "Mutz celebrates birthday in Knightstown on movie set." *Knightstown (IN) Tri-County Banner*, November 7, 1985, 1; "Field for location of movie 'Hoosiers' thinned to 4 towns." *Indianapolis Star*, September 5, 1985.

73   Husker David Neidorf didn't enjoy…: Mike Beas. "Know when to fold 'em. 'Hoosiers' actor goes from poker pro to stay-at-home dad." *Johnson County (IN) Daily Journal*, September 15, 2011, B1.

"It had kind of…": Fred Murphy. Interviewed by the author January 31, 2016.

Anspaugh had planned…: David Anspaugh. Visit to the Hoosier Gym, Knightstown, Indiana, March 20, 2013.

74   Dale Basham, a teacher…: Rodney Richey. "Union City: school of the stars." *Muncie (IN) Star*, November 16, 1985, 1A.

75   When at one point…: "The genesis of 'Hoosiers.'" *Muncie (IN) Star*, November 24, 1985, D1.

76   One special group…: "Knightstown likes being in movie."

Knowing that most…: Bob Reed. "School to screen 'student actors.' See need to limit movie activity." *Knightstown (IN) Tri-County Banner*, October 31, 1985, 1; David Saunders. "Filming of 'Hoosiers' causes problems for 7 KHS band members." *New Castle (IN) Courier-Times*, December 3, 1985, 3.

Other local students…: Brian Hulse. Interviewed by the author January 3, 2010; Ross Wells. Interviewed by the author January 6, 2010.

Before filming...: Mike Pearson. "Hoosier hysteria: The movie."

The basketball plays were staged.... Fred Murphy. Interviewed by the author.

"into almost scenes...": Ibid.

To amuse themselves...: Mike Reilley. "Celluloid hero. His smooth jumper captures the moment in 'Hoosiers.'" *Los Angeles Times*, April 21, 1994; Garret Mathews.

77   Maris Valainis noted...: Lynn Houser. "A tough loss." *Indianapolis Monthly*, October 2006, 168; Evan West. "Basketball diary." *Indianapolis Monthly*, vol. 27, no. 8, March 2004, 256.

"Being an extra...": Herb Adelman. Interviewed by the author.

Extras casting assistant...: Alberta White. "Many residents earn roles in 'Hoosiers.'" *Crawfordsville (IN) Journal Review*, October 15, 1985, 1.

IUPUI senior Marcia Wright...: Marcia Duke. Interviewed by the author August 16, 2012.

"We had anywhere from 200...": Paul Willistein. "Gene Hackman is once again at center court." *The (Allentown, PA) Morning Call*, March 1, 1987.

78   "They had choreographed...": Keith Roysdon. "Hoosiers cut hair, don '50s attire to appear as extras in 'Hoosiers.'" *Muncie (IN) Evening Press*, November 21, 1985, 11.

"We were all dying...": Lorrie Hamrick. "'Bigger perspective' on life gained from film." *Decatur (IN) Daily Democrat*, November 27, 1985.

During breaks in the action...: Tim Baker. "Long learning new way to play for movie role." *Johnson County (IN) Daily Journal*, October 23, 1985, 1.

"With the Steadicam...": Fred Murphy. Interviewed by the author.

David Neidorf said the Oscar winner...: David Neidorf. Interviewed by the author May 20, 2016.

Steve Hollar noticed...: Steve Hollar. Interviewed by Dick Gordon. "The Making of *Hoosiers*." American Public Media. WUNC 91.5, North Carolina Public Radio. April 1, 2011.

79   Hackman also could be a prankster: Peg Mayhill. Interviewed by the author August 27, 2009.

All 324 students...: Rodney Richey. "Union City: school of the stars."; Keith Roysdon.

For the scene: Terry Mikesell. "Controlled madness in crowd scenes." *Richmond (IN) Palladium-Item*, November 16, 1985, A3.

80   After lunch that day...: Rodney Richey. "Hoosiers — the movie." *Muncie (IN) Star*, November 24, 1985, D1.

This scene was one of Anspaugh's...: *Hoosiers*. 2005. Audio commentaries (DVD).

"that sense of...": "The genesis of 'Hoosiers.'"

"In many of these farming communities...": Angelo Pizzo. Interviewed by Andy Hunsucker and Jason Thompson. *A Place for Film: The IU Cinema Podcast*, episode 28, April 8, 2011.

81   Because she had been chosen...: Wilma Lewellyn. Interviewed by the author February 14, 2010 and February 21, 2016.

Offered a role...: Spyridon Stratigos. Interviewed by the author August 24, 2013.

"I knew the kind of play": Joe Shearer. "Corn-fed classic. Writer Angelo Pizzo shares some secrets from 'Hoosiers.'" *Indianapolis Star*, March 17, 2005, INtake 24.

82 The "fence" was a four-man screen…: Bob Hammel. *Hoosiers Classified: Indiana's Love Affair with One-Class Basketball.* Indianapolis: Masters Press, 1997, 126.

"We liked it so much…": Kyle Neddenriep. "He was Shooter. Pizzo says Hopper's role was centerpiece of 'Hoosiers.'" *Indianapolis Star*, June 2, 2010, B2.

83 "I've been going…": Evan West, 258.

In the locker room scene…: Bob Cook. "'Hoosiers' turns 25." *Forbes*, November 21, 2011.

Later, during the regional game…: *Hoosiers.* 2005. Audio commentaries (DVD).

"These people aren't…": Program from the world premiere of *Hoosiers*, October 10, 1986.

The young men were…: Alberta White. "'Hickory Huskers' a hit at media showing of 'Hoosiers.'" *Crawfordsville (IN) Journal Review*, October 31, 1986, 1.

Anspaugh noted that…: Mary Beth Moster. "… and the story of Hoosiers." *Indianapolis Magazine*, January 1986, 78.

84 To the slogan…: Scott L. Miley. "Knightstown recreates past to lend authenticity to film."; Dick Leakey. Interviewed by the author; "Knightstown likes being in movie."

After the majority…: Robert Reed. "Movie continues to give school board a major headache." *Knightstown (IN) Tri-County Banner*, December 5, 1985, 1; David Saunders. "Filming of 'Hoosiers' causes problems for 7 KHS band members."

85 Veteran stage actor Sam Smiley…: "After 'Hoosiers.' Stage actor Smiley learned from being in a movie." *Bloomington (IN) Sunday Herald-Times*, November 9, 1986, D1.

"take it easy…": Sandra Knipe. "Angry ref is Smiley." *Evansville (IN) Courier*, November 14, 1986, 17.

Greg Eckstein…: Ben Smith. "Ecksteins enjoy 'movie magic.'" *Anderson Daily Bulletin*, December 13, 1985, 10.

Eckstein's father…: Colleen Steffen. "Ordinary Hoosiers made movie special." *Muncie (IN) Star Press*, February 20, 2004, special section 12.

86 Appearing as a benchwarmer…: Todd Baxter. Interviewed by the author January 16, 2015.

"They hit me…": Steve Hollar. Interviewed by the author June 8, 2013.

His lawyer advised…: Angelo Pizzo. Interviewed by the author November 12, 2012.

During the location scouting…: Mike Ellis. "Brownsburg already getting recognition as site for movie." *Indianapolis News*, October 7, 1985, 14; Grant Flora. "'Hoosiers' to shoot at College Ave. gym." *Brownsburg (IN) Guide*, September 26, 1985, 1.

87 "I was never as tired…": Alberta White. "'Hoosiers' filming continues." *Crawfordsville (IN) Journal Review*, October 25, 1985, 1.

So on those dates…: "Extras needed for 'Hoosiers.'" *Crawfordsville (IN) Journal Review*, November 6, 1985, 2.

Because the Huskers had not…: David Neidorf. Interviewed by the author.

88 Neidorf described the fight…: Ibid.

Sixth-grader Shane Headlee…: Shane Headlee. Interviewed by the author January 26, 2010.

Pizzo may have had…: *Hoosiers* screenplay, revised draft, October 13, 1985.

89 Harvey Waldman was uneasy…: Scott L. Miley. "Taking an educational recess: 750 students become 'Hoosiers.'" *Indianapolis Star*, November 23, 1985, 1; "Extras still

needed for local shooting of 'Hoosiers' film." *Lebanon (IN) Reporter*, November 23, 1985, 1.

"It is really exciting…": Teresa Fisher. "Shooting under way in community of 'Hoosiers' film actor Kent Poole. Local students serve as extras." *Lebanon (IN) Reporter*, November 22, 1985, 1.

"It has really been work…": Ibid.

"The spectators got to see…": Jeff Moster. Interviewed by the author February 5, 2010; Ross Flint. "Two lines made many memories." *Lebanon (IN) Reporter*, July 11, 2006.

90   "a terrific basketball player…": Angelo Pizzo. Interviewed by Bill Littlefield. *Only A Game*, "Indiana Basketball Hall of Fame honors 'Hoosiers,'" WBUR, December 1, 2012, http://onlyagame.wbur.org/2012/12/01/indiana-honors-hoosiers-movie.

Gary Long: John Laskowski with Stan Sutton. *John Laskowski's Tales from the Hoosier Locker Room*. Champaign, IL: Sports Publishing LLC, 2003, 58.

91   While they were still…: Teresa Fisher. "'Hoosiers' crew to film on downtown square tonight." *Lebanon (IN) Reporter*, November 26, 1985, 1.

92   Coach Dale's journey…: Roger Kunkel. Interviewed by the author.

John & Calverts: "State star-struck."

This 96-year-old…: "Fire destroys church shown in 'Hoosiers.'" *Indianapolis Star*, January 11, 1994, B5; "Arson at church puzzles both congregation, police." *Indianapolis News*, January 11, 1994, E2; Susan Schramm. "Their faith stands the test of fire." *Indianapolis Star*, January 17, 1994, C1.

The 91-year-old…: Lynn Tharp. Interviewed by the author January 24, 2010; Sharon Louks. Interviewed by the author February 10, 2010.

93   Senior citizen Faye Wolf…: Emily M. Smith. "Movie extras devote time to 'Hoosiers.'" *Lafayette (IN) Journal and Courier*, November 24, 1985, B1.

Ten-year-old Daniel Louks…: Daniel Louks. Interviewed by the author April 19, 2010.

Hackman's place…: Ibid.

94   This scene helped Maris…: "Shooting star." *Indianapolis Monthly*, January 1986, 10.

Teammate David Neidorf complimented…: Evan West, 258.

Hackman became impatient…: Sharon Louks. Interviewed by the author.

First assistant director…: Herb Adelman. Interviewed by the author.

One day in September…: "These folks caught 'Hoosiers' hysteria." *Electric Consumer*; Scott L. Miley. "Greenwood theater throws party for national release of 'Hoosiers.'" *Indianapolis Star*, February 27, 1987, 18; Mike Ellis. "Hollywood magic transforms their house." *Indianapolis News*, July 30, 1986, 43.

95   Debbie Burns told…: Debbie Burns. "Take one. A Danville family prepares its home for the silver screen." *Indianapolis Monthly*, November 1985, 16.

The home actually…: Jody Whicker. Interviewed by the author May 10, 2010.

In the scene where Shooter…: David Anspaugh. "Doug Loves Movies" podcast, hosted by Doug Benson, June 4, 2016; *Hoosiers*. 2005. Audio commentaries (DVD).

Two more scenes…: Jody Whicker. Interviewed by the author.

96   Whicker chose…: Ibid.

The exterior shots…: Roger Kunkel. Interviewed by the author January 23, 2010.

Location manager…: Rick Schmidlin. Interviewed by the author.

97 One of Schmidlin's…: Todd Harper. "Wishard marks 25 years since nursing school closed." Press release from Wishard health services, September 6, 2005.

98 To prepare for the scene…: David Neidorf. Interviewed by the author.

The image of the sun…: Fred Murphy. Interviewed by the author.

internalize his anxiety: David Anspaugh. Interviewed by the author January 5, 2010.

One night, while viewing…: Lynn Houser. "'Hoosiers' No. 1 after 20 years. Pizzo, Anspaugh never set out to make a 'sports' movie for the ages." *Bloomington (IN) Herald-Times*, June 21, 2006.

99 "no one can translate…": Nelson Price. "Pair plots next moves. 2 filmmakers took 'Rudy' to White House." *Indianapolis News*, October 25, 1993, B1.

After that night…: David Anspaugh. Interviewed by the author January 5, 2010.

When the cast and crew…: Alberta White. "'Hoosiers' nearing finish."; Scott L. Miley. "Hickory dickory dock, town turns back the clock. New Richmond goes '50s for filming of 'Hoosiers.'" *Indianapolis Star*, November 30, 1985, 1; Alberta White. "Sun brightens stars' spirits." *Crawfordsville (IN) Journal Review*, December 4, 1985, 9; Nancye Hawes. "'Hoosiers'—real people living a legend." *Anderson (IN) Sunday Herald*, November 16, 1986, 22.

100 After they finished the scene…: David Neidorf. Interviewed by the author.

101 Byron Alexander's store…: Alberta White. "New Richmond looking good." *Crawfordsville (IN) Journal Review*, September 6, 1985, 1.

"Part of it…": *Hoosiers*. 2005. Audio commentaries (DVD).

He served as a buffer…: David Anspaugh. Interviewed by the author January 5, 2010.

Pizzo described DeHaven…: Angelo Pizzo. Interviewed by the author August 18, 2012.

"during this entire movie…": *Hoosiers*. 2005. Audio commentaries (DVD).

"every day I thought…": Mike Pearson. "Emotional 'Hoosiers' stands test of time." (Tucson) *Arizona Daily Star*, March 10, 2005.

Anspaugh said that during…: David Anspaugh. Interviewed by the author January 5, 2010.

"It's not just…": Steve Bell. "Fast breaking away. Plans for a basketball movie stir up an early epidemic of Hoosier Hysteria." *Indianapolis Monthly*, October 1985, 72.

Maris Valainis overheard…: Mike Reilley.

According to Pizzo…: Angelo Pizzo. Interviewed by Andy Hunsucker and Jason Thompson.

Recalling the production…: Judy Thorburn. "Vegas Happenings." Las Vegas Round the Clock. February 18, 2007.

102 The two lead actors…: Elena Rodriguez. *Dennis Hopper: A Madness to His Method*. New York: St. Martin's Press, 1988, 165.

But Hopper said…: Mary Beth Moster. "Rehabilitated actor recalls idol James Dean." *Indianapolis Star*, March 15, 1987, p. 5E.

"Hopper was our champion…": Angelo Pizzo. Interviewed by the author August 18, 2012.

"A lot of actors don't…": David Anspaugh. Interviewed by the author July 23, 2016.

"The local community...": Robert Reed. "Screenwriter: Don't get too caught up in detail; enjoy movie." *Knightstown (IN) Tri-County Banner*, November 12, 1986, 1.

Chapter 6

103 When it was built in 1928...: http://en.wikipedia.org/wiki/Hinkle_Fieldhouse; http://butlersports.cstv.com/trads/butl-hinkle.html; David J. Bodenhamer and Robert G. Barrows (eds.). *The Encyclopedia of Indianapolis*. Bloomington, IN: Indiana University Press, 1994, 682.

"To have a 15,000-seat arena...": "ESPN Classic to Air Documentary About Butler's Hinkle Fieldhouse." February 2, 2006. Horizon League website.

The Fieldhouse was designed...: David J. Bodenhamer and Robert G. Barrows.

Playing at Butler...: "ESPN Classic to Air Documentary About Butler's Hinkle Fieldhouse."

104 they were Anspaugh's idea: *Hoosiers*. 2005. Audio commentaries (DVD). MGM Home Entertainment LLC.

This spontaneous tribute...: Brad Long. E-mail communication, March 30, 2014.

105 "if we wanted to believe...": Evan West. "Basketball diary." *Indianapolis Monthly*, vol. 27, no. 8, March 2004, 257.

"Being an alcoholic...": Elena Rodriguez. *Dennis Hopper: A Madness to His Method*. New York: St. Martin's Press, 1988, 164.

The Fieldhouse had changed...: Scott L. Miley. "Moviemakers are offering deal to draw a crowd." *Indianapolis Star*, December 5, 1985, 80.

Fortuitously...: Scott L. Miley. "Knightstown recreates past to lend authenticity to film." *Indianapolis Star*, November 20, 1985, 27.

The group of New Richmond...: Roger Kunkel. Interviewed by the author January 23, 2010.

106 A press conference...: "Press conference to promote attendance of extras for movie." *Crawfordsville (IN) Journal Review*, December 2, 1985, 9; Alberta White. "'Hoosiers' nearing finish." *Crawfordsville (IN) Journal Review*, December 3, 1985, 1; Scott L. Miley. "Moviemakers are offering deal to draw a crowd."; "Bodies needed." *Indianapolis Star*, December 1, 1985, 2E; "Attention, Hoosiers: *Hoosiers* wants you!" *Indianapolis Star*, December 1, 1985, 6B; "Movie all cast except for 15,000 fans." *Indianapolis Star*, December 4, 1985, 56.

Producer Carter DeHaven...: "Hoosier History: The Truth Behind the Legend." 2004. MGM Home Entertainment LLC.

Anspaugh recalled...: David Anspaugh. Interviewed by Farrell Roth and Lon Harris. *This Week in Movies*. YouTube, December 11, 2010.

"We thought our careers...": "Hoosier History: The Truth Behind the Legend."

Crowd member Jody Whicker...: Jody Whicker. Interviewed by the author May 10, 2010.

The few extras...: Rev Mengle. "Hoosiers come through, just like the film." *Johnson County (IN) Daily Journal*, December 7, 1985, 1.

107 Close-ups of the newspapermen...: Roger Kunkel. Interviewed by the author; Wilma Lewellyn. Interviewed by the author February 14, 2010.

Performing the national anthem...: Greg Demmitt. "Singers on movie soundtrack." *Frankfort (IN) Times*, June 7, 1986, 5.

The filmmakers tried...: Scott L. Miley. "Filming set for basketball game after few show for crowd scenes." *Indianapolis Star*, December 6, 1985, 32.

But a crane operator...: *Hoosiers*. 2005. Audio commentaries (DVD).

An assistant to Lieutenant Governor...: Dick Denny. "Rockets, Huskers both are winners at Hinkle." *Indianapolis News*, December 7, 1985, 10.

108 They waited in long lines...: Scott L. Miley. "Moviemakers are offering deal to draw a crowd."

Women were asked...: Christy Huston. Interviewed by the author November 6, 2009.

The filming didn't cease...: Roger Kunkel. Interviewed by the author; Herb Adelman. Interviewed by the author January 29, 2010; Scott L. Miley. "5,000 at filming of 'Hoosiers' movie." *Indianapolis Star*, December 7, 1985, 15.

109 The filmmakers later learned...: *Hoosiers*. 2005. Audio commentaries (DVD); Scott L. Miley. "5,000 at filming of 'Hoosiers' movie."; "Hoosiers state finals filming." *Danville (IN) Republican*, December 5, 1985, 7; "Poole on team in movie." *Jamestown (IN) Press*, October 17, 1985, 1.

Well-known sports broadcaster...: Zaenger. "Gates in 'Hoosiers' movie." *Fort Wayne (IN) News-Sentinel*, December 4, 1985, D10; Bud Gallmeier. "'Hoosiers' director happy to be back home in Hilliard country." *Fort Wayne (IN) News-Sentinel*, June 13, 1988, C1.

110 "an homage...": Bill Simmons. Page 2. ESPN.com. October 18, 2002. http://sports.espn.go.com/espn/page2/story?page=simmons/021018.

Player number 45...: Richard Robinson. Interviewed by the author October 8, 2011.

111 Wood feared...: Hank Nuwer. "Hoosiermania." *Saturday Evening Post*, March 1, 1987.

Assistant director Harvey Waldman...: Jody Whicker. Interviewed by the author.

Growing impatient...: David Anspaugh. Interviewed by the author January 5, 2010; *Hoosiers*. 2005. Audio commentaries (DVD); Evan West, 258; Herb Adelman. Interviewed by the author.

112 Brad Long agreed...: Rick Morwick. "Whiteland man was part of cinematic underdog story." *Johnson County (IN) Daily Journal*, April 1, 2010, A6.

Although Steve Hollar...: Steve Hollar. Interviewed by Dick Gordon. "The Making of *Hoosiers*." American Public Media. WUNC 91.5, North Carolina Public Radio. April 1, 2011.

Interestingly, the screenplay...: *Hoosiers* screenplay, revised draft, October 13, 1985.

113 Pizzo said he wrote...: Angelo Pizzo. Interviewed by the author November 12, 2012.

The result was...: David Anspaugh. Interviewed by the author January 13, 2010.

This time students...: Robert Reed. "It's a wrap. 'Hoosiers' filming ends in K-town." *Knightstown (IN) Tri-County Banner*, December 19, 1985, 5.

Throughout the movie's production...: David Anspaugh and Angelo Pizzo. Interviewed by Andy Hunsucker and Jason Thompson. *A Place for Film: The IU Cinema Podcast*, episode 28, April 8, 2011.

114 "a vociferous and unrelenting...": Mary Beth Moster. "*Hoosiers* in the heartland." *Indianapolis Magazine*, September 1986, 17.

"I'm going to fight...": Angelo Pizzo, 159; Scott L. Miley. "It's back to Hollywood, but will Hollywood come back?" *Indianapolis Star*, December 15, 1985, 6B.

"If Andy's happy...": Scott L. Miley. "Movie creators goal of authenticity has some real Hoosiers' on defensive." *Indianapolis Star*, December 1, 1985, 6B.

Chapter 7

115 As soon as...: Angelo Pizzo. Interviewed by the author November 27, 2009.

Anspaugh felt...: David Anspaugh. Interviewed by the author January 5, 2010.

"It's too damn long.": Bonnie Britton. "A 'Hoosier' homecoming. Movie's makers will attend the reunion at Heartland Festival." *Indianapolis Star*, November 6, 1996, D1.

Film distributor Orion...: Scott L. Miley. "Movie shot in Indiana in editing process." *Indianapolis Star*, February 7, 1986, 44; Michelle Kinsey. "A legend returns. 2-disc edition of Indiana high school basketball classic has documentary, deleted scenes." *Muncie (IN) Star Press*, March 4, 2005, 1C; Zaenger. "'Hoosiers' co-producer regrets having to cut Indiana scenes." *Fort Wayne (IN) News-Sentinel*, November 14, 1986, 1D; Mike Pearson. "Sneaking a look at 'Hoosiers' happenings." *Bloomington (IN) Sunday Herald-Times*, July 6, 1986, D1.

116 "once you've written...": Mike Pearson. "Hoosier hysteria: The movie. Pizzo's film gets small-town authenticity in Indiana locations." *Bloomington (IN) Sunday Herald-Times*, November 17, 1985, D1.

117 Pizzo said he didn't want...: Angelo Pizzo. Interviewed by the author November 12, 2012.

118 tedious and long: David Anspaugh. Interviewed by the author.

"a terrific editor...": Peter Tonguette. "He shoots; he cuts. Picture editors collaborate with cinematographers." *Editors Guild Magazine*, vol. 2, no. 5, September/October 2013.

"actually propelled the story...": Fred Murphy. Interviewed by the author January 31, 2016.

"there's enough basketball...": John D. Miller. "Real-life legend inspires Indiana-made film." *South Bend (IN) Tribune*, November 9, 1986, G1.

Also, the filmmakers...: "Surfers give OK to film about 'Hoosiers.'" *Indianapolis Star*, July 10, 1986, 51.

119 "John never played...": Bill Kauffman. "Hoops. Hoosiers. Hollywood. Home." *The American Enterprise*, vol. 17, no. 2, March 2006, 40.

"They didn't think...": David Morgan. *Knowing the Score: Film Composers Talk About the Art, Craft, Blood, Sweat, and Tears of Writing for Cinema*. New York: HarperEntertainment, 2000, 78.

Goldsmith agreed to view...: Alan Siegel. "Scoring an underdog: The story behind *Rudy*'s enduring soundtrack." *Sports Illustrated* Extra Mustard, si.com, December 6, 2013.

"We got a score...": Mary Beth Moster. "*Hoosiers* in the heartland." *Indianapolis Magazine*, September 1986, 17.

For a comprehensive review of the *Hoosiers* soundtrack, see http://www.filmtracks.com/titles/hoosiers.html.

Before Hackman came in...: David Anspaugh. Interviewed by the author.

120 After trimming and deleting...: The material in this section is drawn from the following: Angelo Pizzo. E-mail communication, April 18, 2016; "Surfers give OK to film

about 'Hoosiers.'"; "'Hoosiers' creator feared it would be a flop." *Evansville (IN) Courier*, November 17, 1996, A14; Mike Pearson. "Emotional 'Hoosiers' stands test of time." (Tucson) *Arizona Daily Star*, March 10, 2005; Lynn Ford. "Mild hysteria accompanies 'Hoosiers' premiere." *Indianapolis Star*, November 11, 1986, 1; Mike Pearson. "Sneaking a look at 'Hoosiers' happenings."; Angelo Pizzo, interviewed by the author August 18, 2012.

121 "We're working…": Scott L. Miley. "Movie shot in Indiana in editing process."

"The thing is…": Mike Pearson. "Hoosier hysteria: The movie."

After the triumphant…: "Surfers give OK to film about 'Hoosiers.'"

A little later…: Ibid.

"had always sought…": Mike Pearson. "Sneaking a look at 'Hoosiers' happenings."

"We are holding back…": Scott L. Miley and Rita Rose. "'Hoosiers' film release date pushed back to January." *Indianapolis Star*, August 28, 1986, 19.

122 "In the movie business…": Ibid.

Orion announced…: Scott L. Miley. "'Hoosiers' to premiere at Circle in November." *Indianapolis Star*, September 12, 1986, 39.

Pizzo asserted that a successful Indiana premiere: Bonnie Britton.

Orion wanted to test *Hoosiers*…: Nina Darnton. "At the movies: in New York, a late start on 'Hoosiers.'" *New York Times*, February 27, 1987, C6.

And even if *Hoosiers* did do well…: Angelo Pizzo. Interviewed by the author August 18, 2012.

tremendous doubt…: Angelo Pizzo. Interviewed by Peter Noble Kuchera. *Profiles*, WFIU HD1, June 25, 2006.

123 "This is a movie…": Robert Reed. "Screenwriter: Don't get too caught up in detail; enjoy movie." *Knightstown (IN) Tri-County Banner*, November 12, 1986, 1.

In October 1984…: Mike Medavoy and Josh Young. *You're Only as Good as Your Next One: 100 Great Films, 100 Good Films, and 100 for Which I Should Be Shot*. New York: Pocket Books, 2002, 132. This book contains an interesting account of the history of Orion Pictures.

"Orion spent less…": Mike Medavoy and Josh Young, 196.

Oliver Stone's…: Ibid, 139.

124 review-based marketing campaign: Ibid, 140.

$6 million budget: http://www.imdb.com/title/tt0091763/business.

The resulting reviews…: Henry Sheehan. "'Hoosiers.'" *The Hollywood Reporter*, October 14, 1986, 3; Todd McCarthy. "Hoosiers." *Variety*. October 15, 1986, 21; Bruce Williamson. *Playboy*, November 1986, 24; Cathleen Schine and David Denby. "Hoosiers." *McCall's*, November 1986, 161; Edwin Miller. "Movie of the month." *Seventeen*, October 1986, 84; *Siskel & Ebert*. November 8, 1986.

Pizzo trusted that…: Angelo Pizzo. E-mail communication, August 1, 2014.

125 "I have a real…": Scott L. Miley. "Movie creators goal of authenticity has some real Hoosiers' on defensive." *Indianapolis Star*, December 1, 1985, 1B.

Pizzo mainly hoped…: Angelo Pizzo. Interviewed by the author November 27, 2009.

"Andy and I…": Scott L. Miley. "Movie creators goal of authenticity has some real Hoosiers' on defensive."

Chapter 8

127 In the fall...: Scott L. Miley. "Back to reality for 'Hickory' players." *Indianapolis Star*, November 9, 1986, 1E.

But Anspaugh and Pizzo...: Bonnie Britton. "A 'Hoosier' homecoming. Movie's makers will attend the reunion at Heartland Festival." *Indianapolis Star*, November 6, 1996, D1; Bill Kauffman. "Hoops. Hoosiers. Hollywood. Home." *The American Enterprise*, vol. 17, no. 2, March 2006, 42; Dale Stevens. "Unusual marketing may make 'Hoosiers' a hit." *Indianapolis Star*, January 10, 1987, 17; Lynn Houser. "Overtime. A decade after its premiere, the movie Hoosiers still grips Indiana's soul." *Indianapolis Monthly*, vol. 20, no. 2, October 1996, 68; Evan West. "Basketball diary." *Indianapolis Monthly*, vol. 27, no. 8, March 2004, 258.

The almost-1,800-seat venue...: David J. Bodenhamer and Robert G. Barrows (eds.). *The Encyclopedia of Indianapolis*. Bloomington, IN: Indiana University Press, 1994, 425–426; http://wikimapia.org/1060408/Hilbert-Circle-Theatre.

128 By the 1970s...: http://wikimapia.org/1060408/Hilbert-Circle-Theatre.

The world premiere...: Scott L. Miley. "'Hoosiers' to premiere at Circle in November." *Indianapolis Star*, September 12, 1986, 39.

Tickets would cost...: Program from the world premiere of *Hoosiers*, October 10, 1986.

the nearby Columbia Club...: Jim Gordon. *Merrillville (IN) Post-Tribune*, November 11, 1986, A1; Rosemarie Sylvester. "Long enjoys 'Hoosiers' second time around." *Greenwood (IN) News*, November 13, 1986, 1.

The get-together was like a homecoming...: Rosemarie Sylvester.

the filmmakers would hit a home run: David Anspaugh. Interviewed by the author January 5, 2010.

One by one...: Lynn Ford. "Glitzy gala excites Indy at 'Hoosiers' world premiere." *Indianapolis Star*, November 11, 1986, 1; Alberta White. "Hoosiers love 'Hoosiers.'" *Crawfordsville (IN) Journal Review*, November 11, 1986, 1.

35 New Richmond residents: Roger Kunkel. Interviewed by the author January 23, 2010.

three carloads of people: Peg Mayhill. Interviewed by the author September 18, 2009.

129 "I watched the crowd...": Brian Settle. "'Indywood.' 'Hoosiers' has formal premiere." *Indianapolis News*, November 11, 1986, 1.

"Heck, if it...": Greg Guffey. *The Greatest Basketball Story Ever Told: The Milan Miracle* (50th Anniversary ed.). Bloomington, IN: Indiana University Press, 2003, 24.

The viewers went crazy...: Angelo Pizzo. Interviewed by the author November 24, 2009.

"cried three times...": Lynn Ford. "'Hoosiers' creating early hysteria." *Indianapolis Star*, November 11, 1986, 8.

"something so familiar...": Peg Mayhill. Interviewed by the author.

The Huskers...: Robert Reed. "Screenwriter: Don't get too caught up in detail; enjoy movie." *Knightstown (IN) Tri-County Banner*, November 12, 1986, 1; "'It's hard to choose a favorite scene.'" *Bloomington (IN) Sunday Herald-Times*, November 9, 1986, D1; Rosemarie Sylvester. "Long enjoys 'Hoosiers' second time around." *Greenwood (IN) News*, November 13, 1986, 1; "Film has redeeming values, says Mutz." *Indianapolis Star*, August 28, 1986, 20.

130 "there's nothing more magical...": Bonnie Britton. "Pizzo 'back home again' for award. Producer and screenwriter is in Indiana for the Governor's Arts Awards presentations today." *Indianapolis Star*, February 21, 1995, D1.

For the film's director...: David Anspaugh. Interviewed by the author.

"If we can get...": Lynn Ford. "'Hoosiers' creating early hysteria."

"I would be lying...": Ibid.

But he believed...: "No 'Hoosiers' sequel, says David Anspaugh." *Bloomington (IN) Herald-Telephone*, June 15, 1988, A1.

Three marketing consultants...: Pat H. Broeske. *Los Angeles Times*, November 16, 1986.

The celebration didn't end...: Alberta White.

131 A few towns...: Robert Reed. "The glitter and the goodness meet as 'Hoosiers' makes its local debut." *Knightstown (IN) Tri-County Banner*, November 19, 1986, 1; Robert Reed. "Screenwriter: Don't get too caught up in detail; enjoy movie."

Especially gratifying...: Angelo Pizzo. E-mail communication, March 2, 2010.

On Indiana's premiere day...: Lynn Ford. "'Hoosiers' a smash—at least in Indiana." *Indianapolis Star*, November 15, 1986, 25.

132 The movie was playing...: "'Hoosiers' tops $200,000 mark again." *Lafayette (IN) Journal and Courier*, November 26, 1986, A1.

In Vincennes...: "'Hoosiers' opens here Friday." *Vincennes (IN) Sun-Commercial*, November 9, 1986, Life Along the Wabash 9.

Milan residents...: "Hoosiers look back at 'Hoosiers.'" *Indianapolis Star*, March 1987; Greg Guffey, 139.

In Franklin...: Jim Jachimiak. "Film opens to cheers in county." *Johnson County (IN) Daily Journal*, November 15, 1986, 1.

Hoosiers didn't face...: http://www.the-numbers.com/charts/weekly/1986/19861114.php.

Hoosiers grossed...: http://www.imdb.com/title/tt0091217/business; John D. Miller. "'Hoosiers' grosses $225,000 in first week-end." *Fort Wayne (IN) Journal Gazette*, November 23, 1986, 4C; Rich Davis. "'Hoosiers' scoring lots of points in local theaters." *Evansville (IN) Courier*, December 2, 1986, 16; "'Hoosiers' tops $200,000 mark again."

The judgments about *Hoosiers*...: The material in this section is drawn from the following: Rita Rose. "There's more to 'Hoosiers' than basketball." *Indianapolis Star*, October 31, 1986, 41; David Mannweiler. "'Hoosiers' has what it takes." *Indianapolis News*, November 11, 1986, 12; Janet Helms. "'Hoosiers' was okay, but no great flick." *Knightstown (IN) Tri-County Banner*, November 19, 1986, 17; Jim Gordon. "'Hoosiers' hoops it up for Indiana basketball." *Merrillville (IN) Post-Tribune*, February 20, 1987; Sandra Knipe. "'Hoosiers' is sports movie, and a great one." *Evansville (IN) Courier*, November 14, 1986, 17; Reggie Hayes. "Remembering the Milan Miracle. Radio announcer Bob Chase recalls golden moment of 50 years ago." *Fort Wayne (IN) News-Sentinel*, February 20, 2004, 1A; Bob Hammel. Foreword in Greg Guffey, xxvii, xxix, xxx; Bob Knight with Bob Hammel. *Knight: My Story*. New York: Thomas Dunne Books, 2002, 261.

134 The *Indianapolis Star* invited...: "3 experts say 'Hoosiers' has winning touch." *Indianapolis Star*, November 10, 1986, 29.

135 The Milan townspeople...: Greg Guffey, xx, 23, 24; Ibid.

136 Amidst the excitement…: Mike Chappell. "'Hoosiers' stars cry foul on NCAA ruling." *Indianapolis Star*, November 21, 1986, 1; "NCAA says 'Hoosiers' stars ineligible." UPI, *Logansport (IN) Pharos-Tribune*, November 21, 1986, 9.

DePauw University basketball coach…: Dave Kitchell. "Little movie fun costs players." *Kokomo (IN) Tribune*, November 20, 1986, 1.

All five college hoopsters…: Mike Chappell. "Players benched three games for role in movie." *Indianapolis Star*, November 27, 1986, 59.

137 "I'm just very…": Mike Chappell. "'Hoosiers' stars cry foul on NCAA ruling."

A week later…: Mike Chappell. "Players benched three games for role in movie."

Hollar had to wait…: Mike Chappell. "'Hoosiers' fame will cost DePauw cager 5% of pay." *Indianapolis Star*, December 23, 1986, 1.

According to Pizzo…: Angelo Pizzo. Interviewed by the author August 18, 2012.

His plan paid off…: Sheila Benson. "Stand up and cheer for 'Hoosiers.'" *Los Angeles Times*, December 11, 1986.

Another positive review…: Myron Meisel. "Hoosiers." *The Film Journal*, vol. 90, January 1987, 42.

138 Encouraged by the favorable…: Mike Pearson. "'Hoosiers' going strong, headed for national release." *Bloomington (IN) Sunday Herald-Times*, January 18, 1987, D1.

That same month…: http://www.sundance.org/festivalhistory/; David Anspaugh. Interviewed by the author.

"In my mind…": Mike Pearson.

The national premiere…: Sandra Knipe. "Hoosiers. 'Miracle of Milan' was inspiration, but movie's not just about sports." *Evansville (IN) Courier*, November 7, 1986, B14.

Then it was moved…: Dale Stevens.

Joel Resnick…: Nina Darnton. "At the movies: in New York, a late start on 'Hoosiers.'" *New York Times*, February 27, 1987, C6.

139 After playing…: Dale Stevens.

By the end of February…: Nina Darnton.

The movie's performance…: http://www.the-numbers.com/charts/weekly/1987/19870227.php.

Contrary to what…: Mike Pearson.

More good news…: Rita Rose. "Oscar nominations boost for state?" *Indianapolis Star*, February 15, 1987, 2E.

"His role in *Hoosiers*…: Scott L. Miley. "I.U.'s Hoosiers put Hollywood's Oscar in backseat." *Indianapolis Star*, March 31, 1987, 6.

140 But the American Federation…: Ibid. For more on this controversy, see David Mannweiler. "'Hoosiers' score makes musicians unionist see red." *Indianapolis News*, March 30, 1987, 25.

Hoosiers debuted as the number 5…:
http://www.the-numbers.com/charts/weekly/1987/19870227.php;
http://www.imdb.com/title/tt0091763/business;
http://www.imdb.com/title/tt0093629/business;
http://www.imdb.com/title/tt0093409/business;
http://www.the-numbers.com/charts/index1987.php.

141 A film industry…: Rich Davis.

The movie reviews that rolled in…: The material in this section and its subsections is drawn from the following: Richard Schickel. "Knight-Errant." *Time*, February 9, 1987, 74; Rita Kempley. *Washington Post*, February 27, 1987; Janet Maslin. "Film: Gene Hackman as a coach in 'Hoosiers.'" *New York Times*, February 27, 1987, C10; Gene Siskel. "Flick of the Week: 'Hoosiers' suffers from its sentiment." *Chicago Tribune*, February 27, 1987; Dave Kehr. "'Hoosiers' works magic with a predictable story." *Chicago Tribune*, February 27, 1987; David Ansen. "Easy dribbler: The craft of basketball." *Newsweek*, February 9, 1987, 73; Henry Sheehan. "'Hoosiers.'" *The Hollywood Reporter*, October 14, 1986, 3; Paul Attanasio. *Washington Post*, February 27, 1987; Bruce Newman. "Another beauty out of Indiana." *Sports Illustrated*, February 2, 1987; Myron Meisel. "Hoosiers." *The Film Journal*, vol. 90, January 1987, 42; Roger Ebert. "'Hoosiers' sports winning intensity." *Chicago Sun-Times*, February 27, 1987; Todd McCarthy. "Hoosiers." *Variety*, October 15, 1986, 21; Sheila Benson. "Stand up and cheer for 'Hoosiers.'" *Los Angeles Times*, December 11, 1986; David Sterritt. *Christian Science Monitor*, March 6, 1987; Steve Vineberg. "Net difference. Hoosiers rolls off the rim." *Boston Phoenix*, March 3, 1987, Arts & Entertainment 5; Scot Haller. "Picks and pans review: *Hoosiers*." *People*, February 23, 1987; David Anspaugh. Interviewed by the author July 23, 2016; Angelo Pizzo. E-mail communication, May 10, 2016.

142 many of the scenes selected…: Bonnie Britton. "A 'Hoosier' homecoming."; "New 'Hoosiers' DVD includes '54 title game." *Fort Wayne (IN) Journal Gazette*, March 4, 2005, 1B; Michelle Kinsey. "A legend returns. 2-disc edition of Indiana high school basketball classic has documentary, deleted scenes." *Muncie (IN) Star Press*, March 4, 2005, 1C.

144 Monday, March 30…: Scott L. Miley. "I.U.'s Hoosiers put Hollywood's Oscar in backseat."; Bob Hammel and Kit Klingelhoffer. *The Glory of Old IU*. Sagamore Publishing, 2000, 193.

Chapter 9

147 Its final total box office…: http://www.imdb.com/title/tt0091217/business.

"*The Terminator*…": Mike Medavoy and Josh Young. *You're Only as Good as Your Next One: 100 Great Films, 100 Good Films, and 100 for Which I Should Be Shot*. New York: Pocket Books, 2002, 196.

"The movie generated…": Linda Thomas. "Angelo Pizzo: beyond 'Hoosiers.'" *Bloomington (IN) Herald-Times*, October 13, 1989, D5; Angelo Pizzo. Interviewed by the author November 27, 2009.

"I don't think…": Linda Thomas.

"As much as I'm proud of it…": Ibid.

148 "If someone called…": Mike Pearson. "'There's a lot involved in making movies.'" *Bloomington (IN) Sunday Herald-Times*, November 17, 1985, A1.

When he returned to Lyons…: Mark Bennett. "Anniversary of movie 'Hoosiers' brings back memories for Greene County native who played Ollie." *Terre Haute (IN) Tribune-Star*, June 5, 2006.

"All the guys…": Lynn Houser. "Movie changed lives of Hoosier actors." *Bloomington (IN) Herald-Times*, September 15, 1996, D4; Lynn Houser. "Ten years after Hoosiers." *Bloomington (IN) Herald-Times*, September 15, 1996, D1.

"I wouldn't say…": Lynn Houser. "Movie changed lives of Hoosier actors."

"I was at a Dodgers game…": Evan West. "Basketball diary." *Indianapolis Monthly*, vol. 27, no. 8, March 2004, 259.

"I was in a line…": Brian D. Smith. "Where are they now? Maris Valainis. Star of *Hoosiers*." *Indianapolis Monthly*, vol. 22, no. 13, July 1999, 125.

Valainis appreciated…: Kyle Neddenriep. "'Hoosiers' brings together Indiana legends, those who told their story." *Indianapolis Star*, April 10, 2016.

149 Anspaugh had no control…: David Anspaugh. Interviewed by the author January 13, 2010.

Bobby Plump said he's never…: Mike Lopresti. "George Mason's run is deja vu for Indiana hoops hero." *USA Today*, March 30, 2006.

In April 2006…: Mark Bennett.

150 One of the more surprising references…: Phil Bronstein. "The Man Who Killed Osama bin Laden … Is Screwed," *Esquire*, March 2013.

151 "To me, the greatest…": Lynn Houser. "'Hoosiers' No. 1 after 20 years. Pizzo, Anspaugh never set out to make a 'sports' movie for the ages." *Bloomington (IN) Herald-Times*, June 21, 2006.

"Next to the world premiere…": Nelson Price, 226; "Nyet for net film?" *Merrillville (IN) Post-Tribune*, February 16, 1988, B2.

152 At the fifth and last…: "'Hoosiers' cast, crew 'hoop' it up with reunion. *Merrillville (IN) Post-Tribune*, October 1, 1990.

153 "I never imagined…": Amy Bartner; "Beloved movie 'Hoosiers' is honored twenty years later with a nine-day celebration." Press release from the Hoosier Gym.

154 The night before these games…: Jim Peters. "Portage, Valpo, Wheeler to experience 'Hoosiers' up close and personal." *The Times of Northwest Indiana*, January 7, 2016.

Pizzo attributes it…: Angelo Pizzo. Interviewed by the author November 24, 2009; David Anspaugh. Interviewed by the author January 5, 2010.

"I think for a movie…": Angelo Pizzo. In Lydia Wilen and Joan Wilen. *How to Sell Your Screenplay: A Realistic Guide to Getting a Television or Film Deal*. Garden City Park, NY: Square One Publishers, 2001, 160.

He speculated that…: Angelo Pizzo. Interviewed by Peter Noble Kuchera. *Profiles*, WFIU HD1, June 25, 2006.

"the movies that are made today…": Lynn Houser. "Overtime. A decade after its premiere, the movie *Hoosiers* still grips Indiana's soul." *Indianapolis Monthly*, vol. 20, no. 2, October 1996, 70.

"I felt good…": Darlene Arden. "Hackman: critic to his film past." New York Times Syndicate, *Ocala (FL) Star-Banner*, July 16, 1988, TVWeek 4.

155 "I took the film…": Michael Hainey. "Eighty-one years. Seventy-nine movies. Two Oscars. Not one bad performance." *GQ*, June 2011, 173.

Ten years after…: Bonnie Britton. "A 'Hoosier' homecoming. Movie's makers will attend the reunion at Heartland Festival." *Indianapolis Star*, November 6, 1996, D1.

The DVD reportedly…: Mike Leonard. "'Hoosiers' gets a new spin on ESPN." *Bloomington (IN) Herald-Times*, July 19, 2005.

As a special feature…: Michelle Kinsey. "A legend returns. 2-disc edition of Indiana high school basketball classic has documentary, deleted scenes." *Muncie (IN) Star Press*, March 4, 2005, 1C; "New 'Hoosiers' DVD includes '54 title game." *Fort Wayne (IN) Journal Gazette*, March 4, 2005, 1B.

Some fans…: "New 'Hoosiers' DVD includes '54 title game."

The idea to put…: http://sports.espn.go.com/espn/page2/story?page=simmons/040629.

He wrote about…: Michelle Kinsey.

156 The original negatives: Angelo Pizzo. Interviewed by the author November 12, 2012.

"Some of those scenes…": Michelle Kinsey; "New 'Hoosiers' DVD includes '54 title game."

Pizzo explained that the scene where Buddy…: *Hoosiers*. 2005. Deleted scenes commentaries (DVD). MGM Home Entertainment LLC.

157 "She hates me and Angelo": Bonnie Britton. "A 'Hoosier' homecoming."; "New 'Hoosiers' DVD includes '54 title game."

"I about fell…": Harvey Waldman. Interviewed by the author January 26, 2010.

"I wanted to show…": "New 'Hoosiers' DVD includes '54 title game."

158 "I was disappointed…": Herb Adelman. Interviewed by the author January 29, 2010.

Five years into…: Alexander Wolff. "Class struggle." *Sports Illustrated*, December 2, 2002.

159 only 22,820 fans…: Kyle Neddenriep. "Is a new format for Indiana's high school basketball tournament on the horizon?" *Indianapolis Star*, September 26, 2013.

"disdain and disgust": John Carlson. "'Hoosiers' writer says film is about character." *Muncie (IN) Star Press*, February 20, 2004, special section 12.

Anspaugh felt the same…: Phil Bloom. "Indiana move to multi-class basketball saddens Anspaugh." *Fort Wayne (IN) Journal Gazette*, September 19, 1996, 4B.

"I have very…": Angelo Pizzo. Online chat with HeraldTimesOnline.com, March 6, 2007.

"Hollywood spent millions…": Phil Bloom.

"My heart says…": Lynn Houser. "Overtime," 71.

"[Single-class basketball]…": Mark Schlabach. "In Indiana, basketball is in a sad state. Once a source of pride, the game is losing its place in Hoosier hearts." *Washington Post*, January 15, 2005, A1; Angelo Pizzo. Online chat with HeraldTimesOnline.com.

160 In the fall of 2013…: Kyle Neddenriep. "Is a new format for Indiana's high school basketball tournament on the horizon?"

About 200 cast and crew…: Evan West, 128.

Pizzo described filmmaking…: Bonnie Britton. "State rarely plays itself on-screen. Officials: Weak tax perks can send Indiana-centric films out of state." *Indianapolis Star*, July 5, 2006, A1.

To capitalize on the momentum…: "Mutz: 'Hoosiers' $2.5 million will lead push for more films." *Knightstown (IN) Tri-County Banner*, November 19, 1986, 16.

161 "In *Hoosiers*, the vast majority…": Angelo Pizzo. Online chat with HeraldTimesOnline.com.

"The economic benefits…": Ibid.

Other states spent…: Journalist John Ketzenberger lamented the fact that, of the many scenes filmed on location for *Public Enemies*, the 2009 John Dillinger biopic, only one was shot in Indiana. Two of the movie's real-life events that took place in Indiana were filmed in Wisconsin instead, which offered good tax incentives. See John Ketzenberger. "This time, opportunity escapes." *Indianapolis Star*, July 2, 2009, A2.

In 2002 Louisiana…: Stephanie Goldberg. "States use tax incentives to draw film work from Hollywood." http://www.cnn.com/2010/SHOWBIZ/Movies/02/24/tax.incentives/index.html?hpt=Sbin. Georgia, another state with a generous film incentives program, attracted Oscar-winning blockbuster *The Blind Side*.

162 "At the very moment…": Media advisory, February 14, 2008.

"The incentives for production included…": For more information on the benefits of attracting film companies to a state, see Christopher Lloyd. "Are we rolling yet? Indiana's conservative incentive program so far has failed to attract filmmakers to the state." *Indianapolis Star*, August 17, 2008, Indy Sunday 5–12.

"*Breaking Bad* put New Mexico on the map…": Mary Milz. "Indy-based 'The Fault in Our Stars' filmed in Pittsburgh." WTHR.com, June 9, 2014.

"This was the kind…": Ibid.

In 2016, the Indiana Media…: Annie Ropeik. "Indiana film industry zooms in on tax break proposal." WFYI, July 29, 2016; The Indiana Media Production Alliance, http://indianamedia.org/cms/.

163 "After the success of the movie…": David Anspaugh. Interviewed by Farrell Roth and Lon Harris. *This Week in Movies*. YouTube, December 11, 2010.

"did lousy at the box office…": Thomas P. Wyman. "Another Angelo Pizzo film to focus on Indiana sport." Associated Press, September 7, 1996.

Although they didn't consider…: Angelo Pizzo. Interviewed by Andy Hunsucker and Jason Thompson. *A Place for Film: The IU Cinema Podcast*, episode 28, April 8, 2011; Marc D. Allan. "Governor honors filmmaker. 'Hoosiers' director wins one of seven arts awards." *Indianapolis Star*, February 6, 1991, B11.

Pizzo said both *Hoosiers* and *Rudy*…: Bonnie Britton. "Pizzo 'back home again' for award. Producer and screenwriter is in Indiana for the Governor's Arts Awards presentations today." *Indianapolis Star*, February 21, 1995, D1.

164 Anspaugh said he and Pizzo…: Brian Meyer. *Fort Wayne (IN) Journal Gazette*, July 9, 1993.

Unlike *Hoosiers*, Anspaugh said…: David Anspaugh. Interviewed by Andy Hunsucker and Jason Thompson. *A Place for Film: The IU Cinema Podcast*, episode 28, April 8, 2011.

"significantly not the movie…": David Davis. "Kicked! How the IU grads who created *Hoosiers* and *Rudy* got beaten in *The Game of Their Lives*." *Indianapolis Monthly*, vol. 28, no. 9, April 2005, 250.

"It was a great disappointment": Angelo Pizzo. Interviewed by Peter Noble Kuchera.

"toxic environment…": Bill Kauffman. "Hoops. Hoosiers. Hollywood. Home." *The American Enterprise*, vol. 17, no. 2, March 2006, 42.

"soul-bruising place": Michael Koryta. "20 questions for Angelo Pizzo. You can go home again." *Bloom*, August/September 2006, 40.

"you don't talk about anything…": David Davis, 250.

"You go to dinner…": Eric Harper. "Angelo Pizzo: Screenwriter and film producer." MavenStar Consulting blog, March 23, 2013.

165 "there was stratification…": Bill Kauffman, 42.

"I was never cut out…": Mike Leonard. "Buddies: Filmmakers Angelo Pizzo and David Anspaugh. Back in Bloomington where it all began." *Bloom*, October/November 2014, 95.

"It's bothered me…": David Davis, 157, 250.

"Usually, I'm tortured…": Bailey Loosemore. "'Hoosiers' author returns home to Bloomington." *Indiana Daily Student* (Indiana University), November 30, 2009.

"I'm not disciplined…": Angelo Pizzo. Interviewed by Mickey Maurer. *Mickey's Corner*, JCC Indianapolis, January 16, 2008.

"a deeper place…": Michael S. Maurer. *19 Stars of Indiana: Exceptional Hoosier Men.* Indianapolis: IBJ Media, 2010, 219.

When the idea for *Rudy*…: Andrew Tallackson. "Creator of sports movies gives glimpse into process." *Michigan City (IN) News Dispatch*, October 12, 2003.

he feared becoming pigeonholed…: Angelo Pizzo. Interviewed by the author November 12, 2012.

166 One of his favorite scripts…: Nelson Price. "Pair plots next moves. 2 filmmakers took 'Rudy' to White House." *Indianapolis News*, October 25, 1993, B1.

"I can't do another team sport…": Michael Koryta, 41.

"It's a miracle…": David Hackett. "Bloomington screenwriter still follows bouncing ball." *Bloomington (IN) Herald-Times*, March 24, 2001.

But he never…: Angelo Pizzo. Interviewed by the author November 27, 2009.

He likened writing…: Linda Thomas.

"I just wanted the opportunity…": Laura Rice. "'My All American' is all about Texas football." Texas Standard, October 26, 2015.

"Early on, I was nervous.": Gail Werner. "Q&A with local filmmaker Angelo Pizzo. His new movie, My All American, opens November 13." *Indianapolis Monthly*, November 4, 2015.

"I always wanted…": Video clip with Angelo Pizzo. http://www.youtube.com/watch?v=MYLmWMbATxE.

"The works that I do…": Andrew Tallackson.

167 During their graduate-school days…: "Hoosier headliners: Stars of Indiana: David Anspaugh." *Fort Wayne (IN) Journal Gazette*, October 5, 2003, 2E.

"If we had…": *Hoosiers*. 2005. Audio commentaries (DVD). MGM Home Entertainment LLC.

"*Hoosiers* was a great experience…": Marc D. Allan.

"I don't know how…": "Hoosier History: The Truth Behind the Legend." 2004. MGM Home Entertainment LLC.

"It wasn't as though…": Mark Turner. "Hoosiers: An Interview with Director David Anspaugh." Epinions.com, March 16, 2005.

168 "I never did think…": Lynn Houser. "'Hoosiers' No. 1 after 20 years."

"about fathers and sons…": David Davis, 250.

"it is a good movie…": Lynn Houser. "Ten years after Hoosiers."

"the fans cheered…": David Anspaugh. Visit to the Hoosier Gym, Knightstown, Indiana, March 20, 2013.

"I will never make…": Lynn Houser. "'Hoosiers' No. 1 after 20 years."

"to tell stories that touched us…": Shawn Donnelly. "Angelo Pizzo's 10 Rules for Making a Classic Sports Movie." Made Man, November 12, 2015.

When the writer/producer…: Angelo Pizzo. Interviewed by the author November 24, 2009.

"I look at all the faces…": *Hoosiers*. 2005. Audio commentaries (DVD).

What he admires…: Angelo Pizzo. Interviewed by the author November 12, 2012.

169 "Certain scenes I still enjoy.": Dan Carpenter. "Writer of 'Hoosiers' takes up pen again." *Indianapolis Star*, June 16, 1987, 31.

Chapter 10

172 doesn't like to analyze…: Angelo Pizzo. Interviewed by Peter Noble Kuchera. *Profiles*, WFIU HD1, June 25, 2006.

During production…: Mike Pearson. "How 'Hoosiers' got from script to filming." *Bloomington (IN) Sunday Herald-Times*, November 17, 1985, D1.

173 A few people warned…: David Anspaugh. Interviewed by the author January 13, 2010.

"When things got really stressful…": David Anspaugh. Interviewed by the author July 23, 2016.

"David's like a brother": David Davis. "Kicked! How the IU grads who created *Hoosiers* and *Rudy* got beaten in *The Game of Their Lives*." *Indianapolis Monthly*, vol. 28, no. 9, April 2005, 156.

174 "David and I really did…": Theresa Badovich. "'Hoosiers' to open at theaters throughout Indiana today." *Exponent* (Purdue University), November 14, 1986, 11.

"to show the state off…": Kathy Matter. "'Hoosiers' pairs basketball, redemption." *Lafayette (IN) Journal and Courier*, November 9, 1986, C1.

"very intent on…": Peg Mayhill. Interviewed by the author August 27, 2009.

"have taken the tired…": Paul Attanasio. *Washington Post*. February 27, 1987.

"The first shots…": James Berardinelli. ReelViews. 2006. http://www.reelviews.net/reelviews/hoosiers.

175 Key second assistant…: Harvey Waldman. Interviewed by the author January 26, 2010.

"No one can question…": *Hoosiers* pressbook, Orion, 1986.

"The actors actually…": Pete Croatto. ContactMusic.com. 2004. http://www.contactmusic.com/movie-review/hoosiers_1.

"attention to detail…": David Davis. "Kicked! How the IU grads who created *Hoosiers* and *Rudy* got beaten in *The Game of Their Lives*." *Indianapolis Monthly*, vol. 28, no. 9, April 2005, 157.

"Unabashedly sentimental…": Leonard Pierce. The Screengrab. June 27, 2008.

"In New Richmond, a ghost town…": Scott L. Miley. "Movie creators goal of authenticity has some real Hoosiers' on defensive." *Indianapolis Star*, December 1, 1985, 1B.

176 "Beneath the clichés…": Paul Attanasio.

"Yes, it's replete…": Evan West, 128.

"Rather than being…": Jeffrey Lyons. *Jeffrey Lyons' 101 Great Movies for Kids*. New York: Fireside, 1996, 97.

"The characters are neither…": Todd McCarthy. "Hoosiers." *Variety*. October 15, 1986, 21.

NOTES

"By laconically contrasting...": Richard Schickel. "Knight-Errant." *Time*. February 9, 1987, 74.

"tells its story...": A.O. Scott. *New York Times*. http://video.nytimes.com/video/2009/03/02/movies/1194837942383/critics-picks-hoosiers.html.

177 "Unlike most sports flicks...": Tom Carson. "'Hoosiers': slam dunk." *GQ*, March 2005.

"a world where character...": Michael L. Peterson. "*Hoosiers* and the Meaning of Life." In Jerry L. Walls and Gregory Bassham (eds.). *Basketball and Philosophy: Thinking Outside the Paint*. Lexington, KY: The University Press of Kentucky, 2007, 267.

179 Michael L. Peterson wrote...: Ibid.

180 Pizzo has a fondness...: "The genesis of 'Hoosiers.'" *Muncie (IN) Star*, November 24, 1985, D1.

"The early '50s...": Mike Penner. "Inspiration Points." *Los Angeles Times*, February 20, 2004, D-1.

"there's a fine line...": Angelo Pizzo. Interviewed by Peter Noble Kuchera.

"Whereas most other...": Jeffrey Lyons, 97.

"Pizzo's script...": Pete Croatto.

"The brilliance of Angelo...": David Anspaugh. Interviewed on Spike. "The Game of Their Lives: interview with director David Anspaugh," April 13, 2005, http://www.spike.com/video/game-of-their-lives/2668849.

181 "*Hoosiers* isn't really...": "Movies and March madness." *Chicago Tribune*, March 1, 2013.

183 "Jumpin'" Johnny Wilson...: Thomas R. Graham and Rachel Graham Cody. *Getting Open: The Unknown Story of Bill Garrett and the Integration of College Basketball*. Bloomington, IN: Indiana University Press, 2008, 193.

"performance is letter perfect...": James Berardinelli.

184 "Hackman anchors the movie...": Paul Attanasio.

"Hackman creates an entire...": Myron Meisel. "Hoosiers." *The Film Journal*, vol. 90, January 1987, 42.

"Whenever the schmaltz...": Scott Tobias. The Onion A.V. Club. March 8, 2005. http://www.avclub.com/review/hoosiers-10987.

"I was totally...": Dan Yakir. "Barbara Hershey: an actress, not a 'personality.'" *Boston Globe*, February 22, 1987, 77.

"comprise wonderful examples...": Myron Meisel.

"the kind of actor...": Mike Pearson. "'There's a lot involved in making movies.'" *Bloomington (IN) Sunday Herald-Times*, November 17, 1985, A1.

"I have trouble with direction...": Gene Hackman. *Larry King Live*, CNN, July 7, 2004.

"I learned a lot...": David Anspaugh. Interviewed by the author July 23, 2016.

185 "She stays with her convictions.": Myra Forsberg. "Barbara Hershey: in demand." *New York Times*, March 29, 1987.

"one of the most appealing...": Dave Kehr. "'Hoosiers' works magic with a predictable story." *Chicago Tribune*, February 27, 1987.

Hershey worked on...: Myra Forsberg.

"Out of all...": Alberta White. "'Hickory Huskers' a hit at media showing of 'Hoosiers.'" *Crawfordsville (IN) Journal Review*, October 31, 1986, 1.

"I really didn't think of...": Angelo Pizzo. http://sportsradiointerviews.com, June 4, 2010.

"The performance in *Hoosiers*...": Peter L. Winkler. *Dennis Hopper: The Wild Ride of a Hollywood Rebel.* Fort Lee, NJ: Barricade Books, 2011, 248.

186 "Hopper brings some fresh...": Richard Schickel.

"In creating Shooter...": Paul Attanasio.

"I did the part...": Lynn Ford. "'Hoosiers' creating early hysteria." *Indianapolis Star*, November 11, 1986, 8.

One of the favorite scenes...: Elena Rodriguez. *Dennis Hopper: A Madness to His Method.* New York: St. Martin's Press, 1988, 166.

"Hopper strikes just the right note...": Robert Spuhler. DVD Talk. March 1, 2005. http://www.dvdtalk.com/reviews/14677/hoosiers/.

Actor James Dean...: Mary Beth Moster. "Rehabilitated actor recalls idol James Dean." *Indianapolis Star*, March 15, 1987, 5E.

187 Anspaugh appreciated Hopper's humility: John Seasly. "'Hoosiers' in 60 seconds." *Indiana Daily Student* (Indiana University), April 10, 2011.

"project stoic...": Jeffrey Lyons, 96–97.

"acquit themselves admirably": James Berardinelli.

"After [several] miserably fraudulent...": Steve Vineberg. "Net difference. Hoosiers rolls off the rim." *Boston Phoenix*, March 3, 1987, Arts & Entertainment 5.

"They were terrific kids...": Todd Webb. "Hackman on familiar ground with 'Hoosiers.'" *The Oklahoman*, February 20, 1987.

His character's minimalist...: *Hoosiers* screenplay, revised draft, October 13, 1985.

Pizzo said if he had known...: Alberta White.

"All of us exceeded...": Mike Beas. "Good at being bad. 'Ollie,' now enjoying life as farmer, had to hide basketball skills in film." *Johnson County (IN) Daily Journal*, September 22, 2011, B1.

188 Reviewer David Mannweiler...: David Mannweiler. "'Hoosiers' has what it takes." *Indianapolis News*, November 11, 1986, 12.

"timeless and thought-provoking...": Holly E. Ordway. DVD Talk. March 17, 2002. http://www.dvdtalk.com/reviews/3530/hoosiers/.

189 "By refusing to compromise...": Shaun O'L. Higgins and Colleen Striegel. *Movies for Leaders: Management Lessons from Four All-Time Great Films.* Spokane, WA: New Media Ventures, Inc., 1999, 28.

190 "a difficult mix...": Randy Williams. *Sports Cinema 100 Movies: The Best of Hollywood's Athletic Heroes, Losers, Myths, and Misfits.* Pompton Plains, NJ: Limelight Editions, 2006, 306.

"Everything about him...": John Clemens and Melora Wolff. *Movies to Manage By.* Chicago: Contemporary Books, 1999, 76.

191 "It's never clear...": Henry Sheehan. "'Hoosiers.'" *The Hollywood Reporter*, October 14, 1986, 3.

Hoosiers devotee: "'Sports Guy' rips on 'Hoosiers.'" ABC News *Nightline*, June 9, 2011.

Barry Locke: Barry Locke. "'Hoosiers' myth: Norman Dale takedown." ESPN.com Page 2, November 14, 2011.

192 "In the regional finals…": Drew White. "Defending Coach Dale." *Michigan City (IN) News Dispatch*, February 19, 2013.

193 "a welcome blend…": Randy Williams, 306.

Pizzo viewed Shooter…: Angelo Pizzo. Interviewed by Mickey Maurer. *Mickey's Corner*, JCC Indianapolis, January 16, 2008.

195 "Without Shooter…": Norman K. Denzin. *Hollywood Shot by Shot: Alcoholism in American Cinema*. Aldine Transaction, 1991, 213.

196 "by involving Shooter…": Roger Ebert. "'Hoosiers' sports winning intensity." *Chicago Sun-Times*. February 27, 1987.

197 "the film offers simple…": Norman K. Denzin, 214.

"a love story…": Paul Attanasio.

"seemingly tossed in…": John Nesbit. Old School Reviews. March 9, 2002.

Deborah Tudor believed…: Deborah Tudor. "Hoosiers. The race, religion, and ideology of sports." *Jump Cut: A Review of Contemporary Media*, no. 33, February 1988, 2–9.

198 "the rehabilitation of his heart": Roger Ebert.

Pete Croatto said…: Pete Croatto.

"initial dislike…": Deborah Tudor.

201 never give other people…: Hank Nuwer. Interview with Angelo Pizzo.

"You get the sense…": Mitchell Hattaway. DVD Talk. March 13, 2007. http://www.dvdtalk.com/reviews/27123/hoosiers/.

Longtime Boone County…: Sharon Louks. Interviewed by the author February 10, 2010.

202 "The test of this genre…": Stanley Kauffmann. "Stanley Kauffmann on Films: From Two Americas." *The New Republic*, April 6, 1987, 26.

"It's very simple…": Pete Croatto.

203 And even though tiny Swayzee…: Kyle Neddenriep. "The game that wouldn't end: 9 overtimes." *Indianapolis Star*, March 13, 2010, A1.

"a release point": "The genesis of 'Hoosiers.'"

"One of the best…": John Nesbit.

"there is a passion…": Roger Ebert.

204 "It was very special…": Stuart Levine. "Rick Fox: The Gold Standard: How the movies—past and present—changed our lives." *Variety*, January 5, 2007.

"the rise of high school…": Troy D. Paino. "Hoosiers in a Different Light: Forces of Change v. the Power of Nostalgia." *Journal of Sport History*, vol. 28, no. 1, Spring 2001, 65.

"If a culture's…": Dayna B. Daniels. "You Throw Like a Girl: Sport and Misogyny on the Silver Screen." *Film & History*, vol. 35, no. 1, May 2005, 33.

"The team operates…": Aaron Baker. *Contesting Identities: Sports in American Film*. University of Illinois Press, 2006, 12.

"In these farming…": "The genesis of 'Hoosiers.'"

205 "this isn't the sort of film…": James Berardinelli.

"Audiences would feel…": John Nesbit.

"Nobody could imagine…": "Hoosier History: The Truth Behind the Legend." 2004. MGM Home Entertainment LLC.

"To this day, I don't know…": Todd Shanesy. "Two area men involved in real life 'Hoosiers' legend." *Spartanburg (S-C) Herald-Journal*, April 4, 2010.

206 "Long ago I put…": http://www.odu.edu/ao/instadv/quest/RememberingTheLosses.html.

"My husband was never a loser": Brian Settle. "'Indywood.' 'Hoosiers' has formal premiere." *Indianapolis News*, November 11, 1986, 1.

"hoped that by making…": Rodger Sherman. "'Hoosiers' sucks." SB Nation, July 28, 2015.

Philip Martin stated…: Philip Martin. "As rousing a male weepie as has ever been committed to film." (Little Rock) *Arkansas Democrat-Gazette*, November 25, 2002.

207 "An all-black team from the city…": Aaron Baker, 33.

"The 1954 game…": Troy D. Paino, 73.

"attempted to render invisible…": Ron Briley. "Basketball's Great White Hope and Ronald Reagan's America: *Hoosiers* (1986)." *Film & History*, vol. 35, no. 1, May 2005, 14.

"the film clearly functions…": *TV Guide*. http://www.tvguide.com/movies/hoosiers/review/101215.

Said filmmaker Spike Lee…: Spike Lee. *Best Seat in the House: A Basketball Memoir*. New York: Crown Publishers, 1997, 149.

Some members of the African-American community…: "Would-be stars shoot for roles in 'Hoosiers' basketball movie." *Evansville (IN) Courier*, August 27, 1985, 11; Ron Mader. "'Home team' sought for movie. Film crew wants basketball players." *Indiana Daily Student* (Indiana University), August 27, 1985, 15.

Crispus Attucks: Some people feel that, both in the 1950s and in the decades after, the Crispus Attucks story was not as celebrated as the Milan Miracle. Attucks was created in 1927 as a high school for black students only during an unfortunate period in Indiana history in which some politicians and other power brokers pushed racial segregation and separatism. So the Attucks teams' state championships were more than sports victories; they were triumphs over racism. The Attucks teams have not been forgotten. Randy Roberts wrote about them in *But They Can't Beat Us: Oscar Robertson and the Crispus Attucks Tigers*. They are covered in a chapter of *Hoosiers: The Fabulous Basketball Life of Indiana* (2nd ed.) by Phillip M. Hoose. Robertson discussed his high school days in his autobiography, *The Big O: My Life, My Times, My Game*. The 1955 and 1956 Attucks teams, several Attucks players, and their coach were inducted into the Indiana Basketball Hall of Fame. Some of the players, including Robertson, had their jerseys retired and displayed at Conseco Fieldhouse in 2009. Crispus Attucks High School, which has been integrated since 1967, has its own museum. Filmmakers Betsy Blankenbaker, Spike Lee, and Ted Green made documentaries about the Tigers' tale. And Senator Dan Coats (R-Ind.) honored the 1955 team in a speech to the Senate in 2015. The Attucks story is an important one in the history of Indiana basketball, and it continues to hold special meaning for Hoosiers, especially for African-Americans and the city of Indianapolis.

208 "the racial makeup…": Scott Tobias.

"In the climax…": Mark Royden Winchell. *God, Man and Hollywood: Politically Incorrect Cinema from The Birth of a Nation to The Passion of the Christ*. Intercollegiate Studies Institute, 2008, 313.

"Every principal character…": John J. Shaughnessy. "Crossroads connections. People whose faith guides them through crises are the focus of 'Hoosiers' writer Pizzo's work." *Indianapolis Star*, March 5, 2005, B1.

According to the screenwriter…: Angelo Pizzo. Interviewed by the author November 27, 2009.

"a dark film…": Ibid.

"Like a lot of sons…": Gare Joyce. "'We got a memo about a movie auditioning guys 6'2" and under.'" *ESPN The Magazine*, November 29, 2010, 86.

209 "we long for…": Michael L. Peterson, 265.

"overcoming negative feelings…": Ibid.

"saw the value…": Angelo Pizzo. Interviewed by Mickey Maurer.

"demonstrate the human…": Michael L. Peterson, 266.

"redemption does not…": Brant Short and Dayle Hardy Short. "Redemption by Grace: A Rhetorical Analysis of Hoosiers." *The Journal of Religion and Popular Culture*, vol. XIV, Fall 2006.

210 "No one act…": Ibid.

"everybody gets…": Scott L. Miley. "Movie creators goal of authenticity has some real Hoosiers' on defensive." *Indianapolis Star*, December 1, 1985, 1B.

Ollie's winning shots…: Shaun O'L. Higgins and Colleen Striegel, 31.

211 "sameness can be stifling": Michael Koryta. "20 questions for Angelo Pizzo. You can go home again." *Bloom*, August/September 2006, 38.

212 It's important that…: *Hoosiers*. 2005. Audio commentaries (DVD). MGM Home Entertainment LLC.

The protagonists must…: Angelo Pizzo. Interviewed by the author.

"You don't grow…": Hank Nuwer. Interview with Angelo Pizzo.

213 "You notice a sense…": Bob Cook. "'Hoosiers' turns 25." *Forbes*, November 21, 2011.

"The idea of the power…": Michael Koryta. "Filmmaker Pizzo turns his lens to soccer." *Bloomington (IN) Herald-Times*, April 18, 2005.

215 "It's not enough…": Angelo Pizzo. Interviewed by Peter Noble Kuchera.

"individuals succeeding…": Angelo Pizzo. Interviewed by Randy Williams. *WGA's Written By*, October 2005.

"The appeal…": Joe Hodes. "Going for the Cup: Interview with Screenwriter Angelo Pizzo." PLAYBACK:stl, August 31, 2003.

Anspaugh related a story…: David Anspaugh. Interviewed by Andy Hunsucker and Jason Thompson. *A Place for Film: The IU Cinema Podcast*, episode 28, April 8, 2011.

"what's great about…": Philip Martin.

216 "conformity and loss…": Ron Briley, 16.

Aaron Baker said…: Aaron Baker, 33.

Pat Graham believed…: Pat Graham. *Chicago Reader*.

Deborah Tudor thought…: Deborah Tudor.

"I wanted to have the church…": John J. Shaughnessy.

217 Deborah Tudor theorized…: Deborah Tudor.

218 "creates the unthreatening…": John Clemens and Melora Wolff, 90–91.

219 When the coach agrees…: Shaun O'L. Higgins and Colleen Striegel, 33–34.

220 Clemens and Wolff...: John Clemens and Melora Wolff, 79, 92.

One quality of this...: Ken Blanchard. *Leading at a Higher Level* (Revised and Expanded ed.). Upper Saddle River, NJ: FT Press, 2010, 275, 285.

221 "By the end of the movie...": Shaun O'L. Higgins and Colleen Striegel, 33–34.

"sport is traditionally seen...": Dayna B. Daniels, 33.

Because she temporarily...: Ron Briley, 18.

222 "sports movie tradition...": Bill Simmons. "Evil women of sports movies." http://sports.espn.go.com/espn/page2/story?page=simmons/040629.

When Pizzo shared...: Mike Penner.

"have a personal...": Angelo Pizzo. In Lorian Tamara Elbert. *Why We Write: Personal Statements and Photographic Portraits of 25 Top Screenwriters*. Beverly Hills, CA: Silman-James Press, 1999, 209.

"I hope as a writer...": Bonnie Britton. "Pizzo 'back home again' for award. Producer and screenwriter is in Indiana for the Governor's Arts Awards presentations today." *Indianapolis Star*, February 21, 1995, D1.

223 "will probably be for me...": Mark Turner. "Hoosiers: An Interview with Director David Anspaugh." Epinions.com, March 16, 2005.

"the grandfather...": Mitchell Hattaway.

"I think the movie...": Greg Guffey. *The Greatest Basketball Story Ever Told: The Milan Miracle* (50th Anniversary ed.). Bloomington, IN: Indiana University Press, 2003, 25.

Epilogue

225 Anspaugh described...: "Hoosier History: The Truth Behind the Legend." 2004. MGM Home Entertainment LLC.

Movie reviewer...: A.O. Scott. *New York Times*. http://video.nytimes.com/video/2009/03/02/movies/1194837942383/critics-picks-hoosiers.html.

226 In his review...: Jim Gordon. "'Hoosiers' hoops it up for Indiana basketball." *Merrillville (IN) Post-Tribune*, February 20, 1987.

Index

years and numbers

60 Days In, 161
1951 Indiana state tournament, 110
1953 Indiana state tournament, 9
1954 Indiana state tournament, 3, 9, 110–111, 133, 158, 206
1955 Indiana state tournament, 110
1956 Indiana state tournament, 110
1957 Indiana state tournament, 110
1959 Indiana state tournament, 88
1981 Indiana state tournament, 225
1981 NCAA Division I tournament, 7
1982 Indiana state tournament, 42
1984 Indiana state tournament, 42, 43, 225
1985 Indiana state tournament, 42
1987 NCAA Division I tournament, 144–145
1990 Indiana state tournament, 202
2006 NCAA Division I tournament, 149
2010 NCAA Division I tournament, 149

A

Abernethy, Tom, 46
Academy Awards, 3, 35, 64, 123–125, 137, 139, 140, 144–145, 161, 173, 187, 239
    1987 ceremony, 124, 144–145
    Hoosiers nominations, 139–140, 144–145
Academy of Motion Picture Arts and Sciences, 140, 239
accents, 30, 52
Act 1 Model and Talent Agency, 39
actors
    Huskers, 40–46, 133, 187–188
    main, 35–39, 183–187
    supporting, 39–40, 188, 221
Adams Theater (Decatur), 4–5
Adelman, Herb, 67, 68, 74, 77, 94, 108, 112, 158
Advance, Indiana, 47
advertisements, 139, 160, 238, 239
Adweek, 160
Alexander, Byron, 27–28, 55–56, 101
Allen, Woody, 38

American Federation of Musicians Local 47, 140
American Film Institute, 151
Amo, Indiana, 98
Anderson Highland High School, 85
Anderson, Jane, 33
anniversaries, *Hoosiers*
    1st, 152
    5th, 152
    10th, 152, 155
    20th, 153
    25th, 153
    30th, 168
Ansen, David, 141–142
Anspaugh, David
    childhood, 4–5
    college
        IU, 5–6, 14–15
        USC, 15, 167
    directing
        approach to, 16, 54–55, 58, 60–61, 67, 73, 94, 99
        quality of, 65, 99, 137, 143, 176
    Directors Guild of America Award, 15
    early career, 15, 116
    Emmys, 15
    family, 5
    friendship with Angelo Pizzo, 4–6, 16, 54, 60, 67, 98–99, 163–164, 173
    high school, 5
    later career and life, 147, 163–165
    life philosophy, 167
    opinions
        on Hackman, Gene, 53, 64, 184
        on Hershey, Barbara, 53, 144
        on *Hoosiers*, 16, 130, 138, 142–143, 154, 167–168, 223
        on Hopper, Dennis, 53, 187
        on Huskers, 83
    producing, 15
    working with the actors, 49–50, 52–53
Apocalypse Now, 38
Arcadia, Indiana, 89
Arkansas Democrat-Gazette, 206
Armed & Famous, 161
Armstrong, Richard, 85

Artcraft Theatre (Franklin), 132
Aspen, Colorado, 14
Attanasio, Paul, 142, 144, 174, 176, 184, 186, 197
Attucks High School (Indianapolis). *See* Crispus Attucks High School
auditions. *See* casting
authenticity, 19, 21, 26–27, 29, 31, 33, 40, 49, 75, 141, 164, 174–176, 185, 206, 226
autographs, 56, 68, 69, 72, 77, 81, 132, 153
Avon Theater (Lebanon), 91
away game (Cedar Knob), 85–86, 95, 191

B

"(Back Home Again in) Indiana", 80
Baker, Aaron, 204, 207, 216
Baker, Daren, 135
Baker, Eric, 43, 46
Baker, Jesse "Jack", 32
Ball State University, 42, 43, 127
bands. *See* pep bands
barber. *See* Rooster (barber)
barbershop, 26, 27, 58, 61
barbershop scenes, 99, 100, 134, 189, 193, 201, 202, 211, 216, 217
Barnes, Jimmy, 205
barns, 92, 96, 98, 175, 176
baseball, 4, 166
Basham, Dale, 74, 78
basketball
    1950s style of play, 49, 175
    defense, 134, 201–202, 216
    dunking, 49
    four passes before a shot, 12, 134, 180, 199, 213–214
    games. *See* games
    Indiana tournament. *See* state tournament
    jump shot, 42, 49
    meanings of, 202–208
    multiclass, 158–160
    offense, 134
    one-class, 3, 158–160
    picket fence play, 81–82
    players. *See* Huskers, players
    set shot, 49, 62
    stalling, 110–111
Batesville, Indiana, 49, 132

Baxter, Todd, 86
Bellamy, Walt, 3
Bellmont High School (Decatur), 43
Ben-Hur, 4
Benson, Sheila, 137, 144
Berardinelli, James, 174, 183, 187, 205
Berg, A. Scott, 14
Bergman, Ingmar, 4
Bethesda Christian School (Brownsburg), 43
Bird, Larry, 86
Birdseye, 60
Bishop Chatard High School (Indianapolis). *See* Chatard High School
Blanchard, Ken, 220–221
Bloomington, Indiana, 3–5, 6, 8, 21, 22, 39, 46, 60, 86, 131, 153, 165
    Bloomington South High School, 6
    Indiana Theater, 4, 131
    Indiana University, 3–4, 39, 46, 79, 86, 90, 134, 144–145
    Princess Theater, 4
    University High School, 4, 46
    Von Lee Theatre, 5
Blue Chips, 160
Blue Velvet, 139–140
Bochco, Steven, 15
Boling, Lisa, 47
Bonnie and Clyde, 35
Boone, Al, 27, 55, 59
Boone County, 92
Boston Phoenix, 144, 187
Boswell, Joe, 57, 246
Bowman, Jim, 63
box office receipts
    Indiana, 132, 139
    national, 139–141, 147
Boyle, Bob, 43, 91
Boyle, Brad, 43, 45, 46, 48, 50–51, 78, 82, 91, 127, 159
    acting, approach to, 50
    casting, 43, 45
    later life, 127
Boyle, Dan, 43
Brazil, 164
Breaking Away, 3, 8, 21, 167
Breaking Bad, 162
Breaking Down the Bars, 161
Briley, Ron, 207, 215–216, 221–222
Broad Ripple High School (Indianapolis), 108

Broderick, Matthew, 40
Bronstein, Phil, 150
Brown, Janet, 28
Brownsburg Elementary School, 25
Brownsburg, Indiana, 25, 31, 43, 86–88
  Bethesda Christian School, 43
  Brownsburg Elementary School, 25
  Chamber of Commerce, 86
  College Avenue Gym, 25, 87, 242
  selection as filming site, 25, 86–87
Bruveris, Jill, 129
Bryant, Hallie, 208
Buddy. *See* Walker, Buddy
budget, 20, 54, 55, 113, 119, 222
Buggins, Doc, 30
Bull Durham, 148
Buñuel, Luis, 4
Burns, Bob, 94
Burns, Debbie, 94–96
buses
  school, 60, 63, 100
  team, 31–32, 99, 100, 107, 176, 203, 216, 234–235
Butcher, Rade, 44, 45, 46, 50, 78, 79, 85, 117, 135, 188, 199, 214
Butcher, Rollin, 188, 190, 211
Butcher, Whit, 45, 50, 85, 178, 179, 188, 199
Butler Fieldhouse. *See* Hinkle Fieldhouse
Butler University, 103, 149–150
  basketball team (Bulldogs), 149–150
  Hinkle Fieldhouse, 1, 23, 103–105, 211, 243
Butlerville, Indiana, 22
Butte, Glenn, 129, 223

C

call sheet, 237
Cameron, James, 20
Camp Atterbury, 63
Camp Short, 96
Canada, filming in, 19
Canterbury Hotel, 47
caravan scene, 98, 99–100, 117, 157, 175, 203, 244
Carlson, Ken, 26, 29, 41–42, 45, 59, 112, 136
Carnegie, Tom, 109
cars, 31, 63, 99–100
  driven by Norman, 57, 92, 106, 107
Carson, Tom, 177

casting
  extras, 28–31
  Huskers, 40–46
  main actors, 35–39
  supporting actors, 39–40
Casucci, Mike, 61
Casucci, Yvette, 61
catering, 21, 27, 58, 69, 100, 161
Cedar Knob game, 25, 85, 95, 107, 156, 191, 242
Center Grove High School (Greenwood), 43
change, 188–189, 199, 211–213
character names, 13, 46, 104–105, 176
Chariots of Fire, 18
Chase, Bob, 133
Chatard High School (Indianapolis), 41, 108, 112
cheerleaders, 34, 46, 77, 152, 221
  Hickory, 46
    Harris, Nancy, 46, 108
    Loetta, 46, 157, 214
    Robling, Laura, 46, 52, 157
    Schenck, Libbey, 46, 88
  opposing, 46, 77
    Trout, Teresa, 46
    Wright, Marcia, 77
cheers, 46, 74, 75, 79, 104, 109, 120, 131, 168, 171
Cheren, Robert, 121–122
Chestnut, Bill, 43, 46
Chicago, 39, 46, 161
Chicago Sun-Times, 142, 174
Chicago Tribune, 141, 185
Chitwood, Jimmy, 44, 45, 63, 64, 82, 93, 96, 112–113, 117–118, 177–178, 179, 180, 183, 190, 191–192, 194–195, 197, 198, 199, 200–201, 204, 210–211, 214, 217–222
Chorney, Jo-Ann, 26, 59
Christian Science Monitor, 144
churches
  in background, 96
  opening credits, 92
  town meeting, 92–93
Cinderella story, 135, 149, 225
cinematography, 65, 73, 76, 78, 92, 99, 108, 143, 176
Circle Theatre (Indianapolis), 127–130
  history, 127–128
Clapp, Mark, 56, 59
Clark, Cheri, 245

Clark, Kyle, 23
Clemens, John, 190, 218, 220
Clements, Alan, iv
Cletus. *See* Summers, Cletus
cliché, 7, 113, 125, 141, 142, 176, 198
closing credits, 105, 135
clothing. *See* costumes
coach. *See* Dale, Norman
coaches, opposing, 39, 85, 90–91, 110
Coal Creek Middle School (Montgomery County), 100
Cofield, Brad, 43, 46
Collector's Edition DVD, 155–158, 181
College Avenue Gym (Brownsburg), 25, 87, 242
Color of Money, The, 132
colors, school, 33, 229
Columbia Club, 128, 130
community, 10, 102, 123, 164, 165, 168, 188, 202–203, 214–215
conflict
    as a plot point, 10, 38
    during filming, 55, 60–61, 64–65, 94, 101–102, 111–112
Connersville, Indiana, 74
consolidation, school, 25, 62, 203
continuity people. *See* permanent extras
controversies, 26, 29, 84–85, 129, 135, 136–137, 140
Conversation, The, 35, 183
Cook, Bill, 22
Cook, Bob, 213
Cool Hand Luke, 38
Costa Mesa, California, 120
costumes
    basketball players, 33–34, 172
    cast, 34, 95, 96
    cheerleaders, 34
    extras, 30–33, 72, 74, 79, 83, 87, 106, 107, 108, 109, 175
Craft, Ray, 109
Crawfordsville, Indiana, 57, 70
creative control, 19–20, 165, 173
credits
    closing, 105, 135
    opening, 92, 149, 156, 174–175, 182, 190
Crispus Attucks High School (Indianapolis), 110, 183, 206, 207–208, 284
critical response to *Hoosiers*
    audience, 120–121, 129–132, 138

Indiana, 132–135
international, 151
national, 124–125, 137–138, 141–144, 174
Croatto, Pete, 175, 180, 198, 202
Crocodile Dundee, 132, 140
Crowe, Betty, 206
Crowe, Ray, 110, 206
Cruise, Tom, 163
Curious Case of Benjamin Button, The, 161

D

dailies, 50, 73, 96, 98
Dale, Norman
    coaching ability, 191–192
    friendship with Shooter, 13, 195–197
    personality, 12, 64, 117, 188–192, 196–198
    relationship with Myra, 13, 64, 133, 135, 142, 157, 193, 197–199, 209
Daly, John, 19–20, 113, 137, 173, 193
Dalzell, Mike, 39, 61, 93
Daniels, Dayna B., 204, 221
Daniels, Mitch, 161–162
Danville, Illinois, 36, 59
Danville, Indiana, 95, 98
David and Goliath, 7, 149, 158, 174, 208
day players, 29–30, 160
Days of Thunder, 163
Dean, James, 38, 186
Decatur, Indiana, 4–5, 20, 43, 60, 86, 153
    Adams Theater, 4–5
    Bellmont High School, 43
    Decatur High School, 5
Deer Lick game. *See* sectional game
defense, 134, 201–202, 216
DeHaven, Carter, 19–20, 24, 101, 106, 114, 119, 121
deleted scenes, 55, 115–116, 121, 129–130, 142, 149, 155–158, 181, 202, 211, 244
    on DVD, 155–157
Denzin, Norman K., 195–196, 197
DePauw University, 43, 127, 136–137
    basketball team, 127, 137
Dewitt, Wil, 39, 93, 108
dialog, 50, 53–54, 61, 119, 134, 181, 201, 218, 221
Dillon, Matt, 40
DiMaggio, Joe, 166

diner, 99–100
Dinsmore farm, 98, 158, 244
director's cut, 155–156
distribution, 121–124, 138–139, 151, 173
"Do Lord", 107
Doc Buggins. *See* Buggins, Doc
Dodge City, Kansas, 38
Donovan, Billy, 149
Dorson, Gloria, 39, 97, 108, 241
Doty, Reverend, 39, 108, 216
driving scenes, 57, 92, 107, 182
Dugan, Darlene, 62
Dugger game, 74, 81–82, 205, 214
Dugger, Indiana, 60
Dunsmore, Ed, 70
Duvall, Robert, 35
DVD, 155–158, 181

E

Eakland, William "Fleet", 31, 56
East Park Cinema (Evansville), 132
Easy Rider, 38
Ebert, Roger, 125, 142, 143, 196, 198, 203
Eckstein, David, 85
Eckstein, Greg, 85, 136–137
economic benefits
　of film production, 21, 160–162
　of *Hoosiers* to Indiana, 160
Edinburgh, Indiana, 153
editing, 49, 115–118, 120, 121, 142, 143, 155, 181
　rough cut, 115, 119, 120, 156
Egyptian Theatre (Park City, Utah), 138
Eight Men Out, 160
El Cid, 4
Elizaville Baptist Church, 92–93, 241
Elizaville Christian Church, 93
Elizaville, Indiana, 92, 98
Elkhart, Indiana, 153
ESPN.com, 150, 155, 175, 191, 222
Esquire, 150
E.T., 138
Evansville Courier, 133
Evansville, Indiana, 132
Everett. *See* Flatch, Everett
extras, 19, 58, 62–63, 65, 70, 73–77, 87, 89, 99, 100, 106–109
　assisting the crew, 76, 96
　casting, 28–31

costumes, 30–33, 74, 79, 83, 87, 106, 107, 108, 109
hairstyles, 32–33, 74
impact on film, 102, 168, 173, 175
lack of, 31, 105–108
pay, 29, 58, 106, 136
permanent, 28–30, 58–59, 74, 77, 81, 84, 93, 106, 128
students, 62–63, 74–77, 79, 89, 100, 113
　missing school, 76, 84, 89

F

Fairland, Indiana, 62
faith, 4, 54, 99, 106, 112, 132, 163, 198, 208, 209, 210–211, 212, 219
Falling from Grace, 160
family, 88, 90–91, 123, 168, 199, 214
Farlow, Jay, 70
farm scenes, 92, 96–97, 98, 157–158, 211, 244
farming, 9, 28, 29, 31, 33, 38, 42, 47, 80, 117, 127, 148, 167, 176, 178, 181, 185, 204, 208
Fault in Our Stars, The, 162
fencerow scene, 96–97
Ferazza, Mark, 132
Fiddler, Carolyn, 59
fight songs
　Hickory, 74–75, 128
　Linton, 90
film incentives bill (HEA 1388), 161–162
Film Journal, The, 137–138
filming locations, 21–26, 231, 238
　Amo, 98
　Avon Theater, 91
　Boone County, 92
　Brownsburg, 25, 86–88
　Cedar Knob, 85–86
　churches
　　opening credits, 92
　　town meeting, 92–93
　College Avenue Gym, 25, 86–88
　driving scenes, 57, 92
　Elizaville, 92–94
　Hendricks County, 94, 96, 98
　Hickory, 23, 25–26, 55–59, 99–101
　high school, 23–24, 61–64
　Hinkle Fieldhouse, 103–113
　home gym, 23–25, 68–83

homes, 94–97
hospital, 97–98
Indianapolis, 85–86, 97–98, 103–113
Knightstown, 23–25, 68–83
Lebanon, 88–91
Memory Hall, 25, 88–91
Montgomery County, 23–24, 92
New Richmond, 23, 25–26, 55–59, 99–101
Nineveh, 23–24, 61–64
opening credits, 92
regional game, 88–91
sectional game, 86–88
state-finals game, 103–113
Stilesville, 92
Terhune, 92
Wishard Nursing Museum, 97–98
filming sites. *See* filming locations
final scene, 72, 182, 203, 204
financing, seeking, 16–20, 35
fire truck, 100
Fitzpatricks, The, 7
Flannery, Kathy, 31
Flatch, Everett, 13, 46, 51, 98, 100, 148, 192, 198, 200, 205, 209, 212, 214
    relationship with Shooter, 13, 51, 200, 205, 209, 220–221
Flatch, Wilbur "Shooter"
    alcoholism, 13, 37, 192, 195, 196
    friendship with Norman, 13, 195–197
    personality, 37–38, 188, 192–193, 196, 199
    rehabilitation/sobriety, 37, 97, 105, 192–193, 196, 211, 214, 215
    relationship with Everett, 13, 192, 196, 205, 209, 220–221
Fleener, Myra
    personality, 13, 38, 142–143, 193–195, 197–199
    relationship with Norman, 13, 133, 135, 142, 157, 193, 197–199, 209
Fleener, Opal, 39, 58, 117, 181, 188, 190, 219, 221
floatin' (Cletus), 63
Floyds Knobs, Indiana, 86
football, 5, 12, 13, 163, 166
forgiveness, 177, 209
Fort Wayne, Indiana, 4, 70, 133, 136
Fort Wayne Journal-Gazette, 20
Fox, Rick, 204
Franklin, Indiana, 33, 39, 60, 132

Freel, William, 68, 76
French Connection, The, 35
French Lick, Indiana, 86
Fresh Horses, 147, 148

G

Galvin, Karen, 21–23, 27
Game of Their Lives, The, 164
games, 229
    away (Cedar Knob), 85–86, 107, 156, 191, 242
    home, 73–83, 241
    regional (Jasper), 83, 86, 88–91, 191–192, 200, 210, 243
    sectional (Deer Lick), 86–88, 104
    state (Butler Fieldhouse), 102, 103–113, 190–192, 197, 205–206, 219–220, 243
Gardner, Willie, 208
Garner, Bob, 246
Garrett, Bill, 110
Gary Roosevelt High School, 207
Gates, Hilliard, 109–110
gender issues, 221–222
George. *See* Walker, George
Georgia, 162
Giant, 38, 39, 186
Gibson, Derek, 19
Glowacki, Joe, 74
Going All the Way, 160
Golden Globes, 123, 187, 238
Goldsberry, Tom, 79, 80
Goldsmith, Jerry, 119
    Academy Award nomination, 139, 144–145
    controversy, 140
Goodwill, 33, 79
Gordon, Jim, 133, 226
Gorrell, Ken, 39–40
Gould, Todd, 103
GQ, 177
grace, 189, 209–210, 218
Graham, Pat, 216
Grantham, Louise, 63
Gray, Lyda, 59
Greenfield, Indiana, 131
Greenwood, Indiana, 33, 43
Grinstead, Herman "Snort", 9
Guiding Light, The, 93
gyms
    away, 25, 85, 95, 242

INDEX 293

home, 23–25, 69, 240, 241
    regional, 25, 31, 88–89, 107, 243
    sectional, 25, 31, 87, 104, 242
    state, 103–105, 243

H

Hackman, Gene
    acting
        approach to, 36, 51–53, 64, 78–79, 184
        quality of, 143–144, 183–184
    casting, 35
    early life, 36
    opinions
        on Anspaugh, David, 60–61
        on *Hoosiers*, 36–37, 65, 101–102, 120, 154–155
        on Huskers, 51, 120, 187
        on Norman, 37
    personality, 51–52, 59, 61, 64–65, 68–69, 71, 78–79, 85
    reasons for appearing in *Hoosiers*, 36, 154–155
    salary, 35–36
Hager, Eddie, 69
hairstyles, 32–33, 48, 74, 143
Haller, Scot, 144
Hamilton Heights High School (Arcadia), 89
Hamilton, Roger Jr., 72
Hammel, Bob, 134
Hannah and Her Sisters, 38
Hard Rain, 160
Harlem Globetrotters, 166, 183, 207
Harris, Nancy, 46, 108
Harrison, Ann, 21
harvest scene, 98, 157–158, 211, 244
Hattaway, Mitchell, 201, 223
Hayes, Woody, 12
HEA 1388 (film incentives bill), 161–162
Headlee, Shane, 88
Heartland Film, 162
Heartland Film Festival, 152
Heaven's Gate, 101
Hee Haw, 39
Hemdale Film Corporation, 19–20, 114, 128, 139
Hendricks County, 94, 96, 98
Hendrickson, Mike, 31
Henry County, 23, 29, 68

Hershey, Barbara
    acting
        approach to, 38–39, 52, 185
        quality of, 144, 184, 185
    casting, 38
    early life, 38
    opinions
        on Anspaugh, David and Pizzo, Angelo, 61, 157
        on Hackman, Gene, 39, 184
        on *Hoosiers*, 157
        on Myra, 38, 185
    personality, 61, 69
Hickory, 10, 26, 60, 214, 215–216
    establishments, 26–27
Hickory (proposed TV series), 163
Hickory Café, 171
Hickory Festival, 152
Hickory Huskers. *See* Huskers
hicks, 29, 53–54, 133, 135, 175, 189
Higgins, Shaun O'L., 189, 210, 219, 221
High Noon, 39
Hill Street Blues, 15, 39, 54–55
Hilton, Charles, 23
Hinkle Fieldhouse, 1, 23, 103–105, 211, 243
    filming in, 103–113
    history of, 103–104
    measuring, 104
Hinkle, Tony, 103
Holland, Indiana, 60, 113
Hollar, Steve, 42–44, 46, 48, 49–53, 67, 69, 77–79, 86, 112, 127, 129, 136–137, 148, 159, 246
    casting, 42–44
    later life, 127, 148
    NCAA sanctions, 136–137
    opinions on Rade, 50
    reaction to *Hoosiers*, 129
Hollywood Reporter, 124, 139, 143, 160, 191, 239
home games, 73–83, 241
home scenes, 94–97, 175
honors, for *Hoosiers*, 139–140, 150–151
Hoosier, meaning of, 17, 191
Hoosier Dome, 202
Hoosier Gym (Knightstown), 153–154, 168, 171, 245
Hoosier Hysteria, 1, 6, 8, 10, 62, 222
Hopper, Dennis
    Academy Award nomination, 139, 144–145, 187, 239

acting
  approach to, 186
  quality of, 37, 125, 139–140, 144, 185–187
addiction/sobriety, 37–38, 105, 186
casting, 37
directing, 38, 102
early life, 38
friendship with James Dean, 186
Golden Globe nomination, 187, 238
LAFCA Award, 187
opinions
  on Anspaugh, David, 65, 67
  on Hackman, Gene, 38
  on *Hoosiers*, 101–102
  on Shooter, 37–38, 105
personality, 65, 69, 102, 185, 187
hospital scenes, 30, 97–98, 186, 209
houses. *See* home scenes
Hudnut, William, 109, 130–131
Hulse, Brian, 84
Hungary, 140
Hushour, Christopher, 74, 246
Huskers (actors),
acting
  learning, 49–51
  quality of, 133, 187–188
basketball playing, 49, 78
  learning 1950s style, 49
Boyle, Brad, 43, 45, 46, 48, 50–51, 78, 82, 91, 127, 159
casting, 40–46, 227
Hollar, Steve, 42–44, 46, 48, 49–53, 67, 69, 77–79, 86, 112, 127, 129, 136–137, 148, 159, 246
  NCAA sanctions, 136–137
later lives, 127, 148
Long, Brad, 43, 45, 47–48, 49–50, 52, 71, 77, 90, 112, 127, 128, 129–130, 132, 148, 159
Neidorf, David, 45–46, 48, 51–52, 58, 73, 78, 87–88, 94, 98, 100, 127, 148, 208, 240
pay, 41
personalities, 77, 83–84, 188
Poole, Kent, 42, 45, 47, 48, 50, 52, 77, 82, 83, 87, 88–89, 127, 129, 148, 240
premiere, world, 128–130
Schenck, Wade, 42, 45, 46–47, 48, 50, 77, 82, 86, 88, 90, 100, 127, 129, 148, 184, 187–188

Summers, Scott, 43, 45, 46–47, 48, 49, 82, 88, 127, 187
Valainis, Maris, 41–42, 44–45, 48, 51, 64, 77, 82, 94, 101, 108, 111–112, 127, 148, 153
Huskers (characters), 2, 10, 13
Buddy, 45, 50, 54, 71, 129–130, 156–157, 179, 199
  rejoining the team, 129–130, 156–157
Everett, 13, 46, 51, 98, 100, 148, 192, 198, 200, 205, 209, 212, 214, 220–221
  relationship with Shooter, 13, 51, 192, 200, 205, 209, 220–221
Jimmy, 44, 45, 63, 64, 82, 93, 96, 112–113, 117–118, 177–178, 179, 180, 183, 190, 191–192, 194–195, 197, 198, 199, 200–201, 204, 210–211, 214, 217–222
Merle, 45, 82, 83, 192, 200, 212–213, 219
Ollie, 45, 46, 50, 83, 86, 90–91, 175, 182, 187, 188, 191, 200, 210–211, 216
personalities, 117, 187, 199–201
Rade, 44, 45, 46, 50, 78, 79, 85, 117, 135, 188, 199, 214
Strap, 45, 179, 187, 191–192, 200, 216
Whit, 45, 50, 85, 178, 179, 188, 199
Hutton, Harry, 132

I

IFC. *See* Indiana Film Commission
IHSAA, 103, 109, 134, 158, 160
improvisation, 44, 57, 71, 78–79, 83
In the Company of Men, 160
incentives bill (HEA 1388), 161–162
incentives, filming, 19, 161–163
Indian Creek High School (Trafalgar), 62
Indiana Basketball Coaches Association, 160
Indiana Central University, 46
Indiana Department of Commerce, 72
Indiana Film Commission, 21–22, 23–24, 27, 72, 87, 127, 160
Indiana General Assembly, 21, 162
Indiana High School Athletic Association. *See* IHSAA

Indiana Media Industry Network
(IMIN), 162
Indiana Media Production Alliance,
162–163
Indiana National Guard, 43, 63, 127
Indiana Pacers, 16, 86, 150
Indiana State Police, 28, 57, 71, 100
Indiana Theater (Bloomington), 4, 131
Indiana University (IU), 3–4, 14, 15, 39,
46, 57, 79, 86, 89, 90, 134, 144–145,
165
   basketball team, 3, 7, 49, 79, 88,
144–145
      1981 NCAA Division I
tournament, 7
      1987 NCAA Division I
tournament, 144–145
   Little 500 bicycle race, 3, 167
   Sigma Nu fraternity, 4, 6
Indiana University–Purdue University
Fort Wayne, 136
Indiana University–Purdue University
Indianapolis. *See* IUPUI
Indianapolis, Indiana
   Broad Ripple High School, 108
   Butler University, 103, 149–150
   Canterbury Hotel, 47
   Chatard High School, 41, 108, 112
   Circle Theatre, 127–130
   Columbia Club, 128, 130
   Crispus Attucks High School, 110,
183, 207–208, 284
   Hinkle Fieldhouse (state-finals
game), 1, 23, 103–113, 211, 243
   Indiana Central University, 46
   Indianapolis 500, 163
   Indianapolis Motor Speedway, 5, 109
   IUPUI, 41, 43, 77, 110
   Marion County General Hospital, 97
   Marshall High School, 110
   Monument Circle, 129
   Ramada Inn Northwest, 47, 98
   St. Luke School, 41
   St. Philip Neri School (Cedar Knob
game), 25, 85, 242
   Southport High School, 90, 128
   Wishard Nursing Museum (hospital
scenes), 97–98
   Wood High School, 183
Indianapolis 500, 163
Indianapolis Magazine, 89
Indianapolis Monthly, 176

Indianapolis Motor Speedway, 5, 109
Indianapolis News, 133, 245
Indianapolis Star, 21, 70, 133, 134, 175,
245
Indianapolis Symphony Orchestra, 128
IU. *See* Indiana University
IUPUI, 41, 43, 47, 77, 110

J

Jameson Camp for children, 128
Jasper game. *See* regional game
Jasper, Indiana, 86, 88
Jimmy. *See* Chitwood, Jimmy
Jobe, Kenny, 107
John & Calverts store, 92
John Marshall High School
(Indianapolis). *See* Marshall High
School
Johnson County, 23
Johnson, Judi, 42
Jones, Oliver, 46
Jostens, 43, 127

K

Kajee Inc., 33
Kauffman, Stanley, 202
Kehr, Dave, 141, 143, 144, 185
Kempley, Rita, 141, 143, 144
Kercheval, Kent, 107
Kilmer, Mervin, 245
King, Larry, 184
King of the Mountain, 37
kissing scene, 53, 96, 142
Klever, Kristine, 62–63
Knight, Bob, 12, 79, 134
Knightstown Elementary School, 24, 25,
68, 153
Knightstown High School, 24–25
Knightstown, Indiana, 23–25, 28, 30, 62,
63, 68–85, 89, 93, 113, 128, 129, 131,
153–154, 168, 171, 174, 236, 240, 241
   Chamber of Commerce, 84
   gym, 23–25, 69, 240, 241
   Hoosier Gym, 153–154, 168, 171,
245
   Knightstown Elementary School, 24,
25, 68, 153
   Knightstown High School, 68, 69,
70, 76
   Morton Memorial High School, 113

school board, 76, 84–85
  selection as filming site, 23–25
Knightstown Tri-County Banner, 133
Knipe, Sandra, 133
Knute Rockne, All American, 164
Koewler, Joe, 132
Kokomo, Indiana, 88
Komenich, Rich, 40
Kunkel, Janice, 55
Kunkel, Ralph, 28
Kunkel, Roger, 28, 245, 246

L

L&M High School (Greene County), 42, 127
La Jolla Playhouse, 38
Lafayette Jefferson High School, 39
Lafayette Square Cinema, 131
Lafferty, Darrin, 107
Lafferty, Dennis, 107
Lahti, Christine, 38
Lawrence of Arabia, 4
leadership, 196, 219–221
League of Their Own, A, 160
Leakey, Dick, 30, 70
Lebanon High School, 88, 89, 201
Lebanon, Indiana, 25, 31, 32, 88–91, 201
  Avon Theater, 91
  Lebanon High School, 88, 89, 201
  Memory Hall, 25, 31, 88–89, 243
Lee, Herbie, 3
Lee, Spike, 207
Leningrad, 151
Lethal Weapon, 140
Levinson, Barry, 185
Lewellyn, Wilma, 26, 55, 69, 81, 129, 245, 246
Lewis, Mick, 43, 46
Liberty Chapel Church, 96
Library of Congress, 150–151
Lincoln High School (Vincennes), 225
Linda's Hickory Tree, 27
Linden, Indiana, 23–24, 27
Linton game. *See* regional game
Linton, Indiana, 86, 90
literalism, 182–183
Little 500 bicycle race, 3, 167
location scouting, 21–26, 86–87, 94–95, 97, 228
locations. *See* filming locations, location scouting

Locke, Barry, 191–192
locker rooms
  Hickory, 25, 54, 73, 80, 83, 171, 190, 213
  regional, 90, 212
  state, 104–105, 109, 212–213
Loetta. *See* Summers, Loetta
Logansport, Indiana, 166
Long, Brad, 43, 45, 47–48, 49–50, 52, 71, 77, 90, 112, 127, 128, 129–130, 132, 148, 159
  casting, 43, 45
  later life, 127
  opinions on Buddy, 50
  reactions to *Hoosiers*, 129, 130
Long, Gary, 3, 90–91
Long, Nancy, 246
looping, 119–120
Los Angeles, 11, 34, 40, 46, 51, 52, 120, 122, 137, 140, 145, 161, 164, 165
Los Angeles Times, 137, 139, 144, 150, 174
Louisiana, 129, 144, 161
Louks, Daniel, 93
Louks, Sharon, 201
Lubin, David, 25
Lucas, Bruce, 62
Lucas, George, 15
Lynch, David, 139
Lynn, Indiana, 74
Lyons game, 81
Lyons, Indiana, 42, 60, 148
Lyons, Jeffrey, 176, 180, 187

M

Madison, 160
Madison, Indiana, 22
main actors. *See* actors
makeup, 32, 108
Malone, Greg, 162
man-to-man defense, 134, 216
Manchester High School (North Manchester), 75
Mandelker, Philip, 7, 14
Mannequin, 140
Mannweiler, David, 133, 188
Mantle, Mickey, 4, 166
Marc, Daniel, 32
Marines, 36
Marion County General Hospital, 97

INDEX

marketing strategy, 121–125, 130, 138–139, 147
Marshall High School (Indianapolis), 110
Martin, Philip, 206–207, 215
Martinsville, Indiana, 10, 159
Mary Tyler Moore Show, The, 7
Mascia, Jeanne, 32
Maslin, Janet, 141, 143
Mayhill, Peg, 23–24, 83, 128, 129, 174
mayor, 39
McCall's, 125
McCarthy, Andrew, 147
McCarthy, Todd, 124, 143, 176
McClain, Dan, 89
McConnell, Tom, 49, 85
McPike, Ollie, 45, 46, 50, 83, 86, 90–91, 175, 182, 187, 188, 191, 200, 210–211, 216
measuring Hinkle Fieldhouse, 104
Medavoy, Mike, 123, 147
media coverage, 20, 23, 44, 106–107, 109, 124–125, 127, 147, 173–174, 245
meet-and-greet scene, 99, 134, 189, 201–202, 211, 216, 217
meeting, town, 92–94, 183–184, 209–210, 216, 218–219, 237, 241
Meharry, Roy, 69–70
Meisel, Myron, 138, 142, 143, 184
Mellencamp, John Cougar, 106, 118–119
Memory Hall (Lebanon), 25, 31, 88–89, 243
Merle. *See* Webb, Merle
Merrillville Post-Tribune, 133, 226
Method acting, 35, 186
Meyers, Stephen, 31
MGM Home Entertainment, 155–156
Miami Vice, 15
Michigan City News Dispatch, 192
Milan High School. *See* Milan Indians
Milan, Indiana, 8–10, 22, 132, 135, 153, 203
  museum, 172
  residents' opinions on *Hoosiers*, 135
Milan Indians, 3, 8–10, 46, 86, 104, 109–111, 118, 129, 132, 158, 172, 205–207, 223
  1953 state tournament, 9
  1954 state tournament, 3, 9, 110–111, 133, 158, 206
  Butte, Glenn, 129, 223

Craft, Ray, 109
Grinstead, Herman "Snort", 9
Plump, Bobby, 9, 111, 135, 149, 159
Schroder, Roger, 110
White, Gene, 9, 135
Wood, Marvin, 8–10, 12, 111, 135
Milan Miracle, 3, 10, 42, 109, 134, 203
Miley, Scott, 70, 175–176
Miller, Mary, 86–87
Mills, Griff, 43, 46, 136–137
minimalism, 180–182, 187, 218–219
ministers, 30, 39. *See also* Doty, Reverend and Purl, Preacher
Mitchell, Indiana, 49
montages, 91, 95, 98, 118, 244
Montgomery County, 22–24, 92
Monument Circle (Indianapolis), 129
Morton Memorial High School (Knightstown), 113
Moscow, 151
Moster, Jeff, 89–90
Moviefone, 151
MTM Enterprises, 7
MTM Productions, 15
multiclass basketball, 158–160
Muncie Central High School, 9, 111, 205–207
Muncie, Indiana, 159
Muncie Southside High School, 74
Murphy, Fred, 57, 65, 73, 76, 78, 99, 118, 143
museums
  Milan, 172
  New Richmond, 27, 55, 59
music. *See* soundtrack
Mutz, John, 72–73, 89, 107–108, 130
My All American, 166

N

names
  character, 13, 46, 104–105, 176
  town, 86
national anthem, 107
National Barber College, 108
National Collegiate Athletic Association. *See* NCAA
National Film Registry, 150
National Guard. *See* Indiana National Guard
National Register of Historic Places, 128
Natural, The, 18, 38, 185

NBA, 154, 207
NCAA
   sanctions for *Hoosiers* actors, 136–137
   tournaments, 7, 144–145, 149
Neidorf, David, 45–46, 48, 51–52, 58, 73, 78, 87–88, 94, 98, 100, 127, 148, 208, 240
   acting, approach to, 51, 94
   casting, 45–46
   later life, 127, 148
   opinions
      on Everett, 51
      on *Hoosiers*, 148, 208
Nemo, Jack, 149
Nesbit, John, 197, 203, 205
New Castle, Indiana, 202
New Mexico, 162
New Palestine, Indiana, 23
New Richmond, Indiana, 23, 25–29, 55–59, 63, 68, 69, 73, 77, 81, 84, 87, 93, 96, 98, 99–101, 106, 128, 129, 152, 157, 168, 171, 175–176, 240, 244, 245
   selection as filming site, 23, 25–26
New Ross, Indiana, 32
New York, 33, 36, 40, 76, 125, 132
New York Daily News, 150
New York Times, 141, 174, 225
Newman, Bruce, 142
Newsweek, 141–142
Nichols, David, 22, 24–26, 94–95, 234–235
Nicholson, Jack, 14–15, 35
Nightmare on Elm Street 3: Dream Warriors, A, 140
Nineveh Elementary School, 24, 25, 132
Nineveh-Hensley-Jackson School Corporation, 24
Nineveh High School, 24, 62
Nineveh, Indiana, 23–25, 61–64, 132, 153
   Nineveh Elementary School, 24, 62, 132
   Nineveh High School, 24, 62
   selection as filming site, 23–24
North Central High School (Indianapolis), 135
North Manchester, Indiana, 75
North Montgomery High School, 100
North Vernon, Indiana, 22
Northgate Cinema (Greenfield), 131

nostalgia, 177, 180, 207, 215
Notre Dame, University of, 163–164

O

objectivity, 11, 101, 176
O'Guinne, Michael, 39, 61
Ohio State University, 12
Old Globe Theatre (San Diego), 38
Ollie. *See* McPike, Ollie
O'Meara, Tim, 118
Omen, The, 140
On Golden Pond, 17
one-class basketball, 3, 158–160
Oolitic game, 39, 77, 79–81, 91, 197
Oolitic, Indiana, 60, 86
Opal. *See* Fleener, Opal
opening credits, 92, 149, 156, 174–175, 182, 190
opponents. *See* players, opposing
opposing coaches. *See* coaches, opposing
opposing players. *See* players, opposing
Oppy, David, 96
Oppy, Joan, 96
Ordway, Holly E., 188
Orion Pictures, 20, 114, 115, 120–125, 128, 130, 132, 137–139, 142, 147, 155–157, 163, 173, 238, 239, 271
Orleans, Indiana, 49
Oscars. *See* Academy Awards
Osgood, Indiana, 22
Outrageous Fortune, 140
overalls, 83, 175

P

Pacers. *See* Indiana Pacers
Paino, Troy D., 204, 207
Painter, Matt, 159
Paris, 15
Park City, Utah, 138
Pasadena Playhouse, 36, 38
Passenger, The, 14
pay. *See* salaries
Pearson, Mike, 181
Pennsylvania, 162
People, 144
pep bands
   Hickory, 76, 84, 100, 175
   Linton, 90
pep rally. *See* pep session

pep session, 70, 183, 190, 198
permanent extras, 28–30, 58–59, 74, 77, 81, 84, 93, 106, 128
Persons, Fern, 39, 58, 96, 188, 221
Peterson, Michael L., 177, 179, 209
Phillips, Michael, 181–182
picket fence play, 81–82
Pierce, Leonard, 175
Pittsburg, Pennsylvania, 162
Pizzo, Andy. *See* Pizzo, Angelo
Pizzo, Angelo
   childhood, 3–4,
   college
      IU, 4–6
      USC, 6–7, 167, 222
   directing, 147, 166
   early career, 7
   family, 3, 165
   friendship with David Anspaugh, 4–6, 16, 54, 60, 67, 98–99, 163–164, 173
   high school, 4
   later career and life, 147, 163–167
   life philosophy, 166–167, 169, 201, 212, 213
   opinions
      on Hackman, Gene, 53
      on Hershey, Barbara, 144
      on *Hoosiers*, 130, 138, 142, 147, 154, 168–169
      on Hopper, Dennis, 65, 139–140, 185
      on Huskers, 83–84, 187
   producing, 19, 60, 116, 163
   screenplay
      inspiration for, 3, 6, 8–10, 12–13
      residents' concerns about, 26, 29
      revising, 14, 53, 55, 115
      writing, 7–14, 50, 112–113
   writing
      approach to, 11, 165, 187, 222–223
      quality of, 14, 16, 19, 60, 137, 142–143, 176–177, 180–181, 201
Platoon, 20, 123–124, 127, 140, 148
Playboy, 125
players, opposing, 46, 85–86, 88, 89–90, 110, 136–137, 205–208
Plump, Bobby, 9, 111, 135, 149, 159
Plymouth High School, 136

Poole, Kent, 42, 45, 47, 48, 50, 52, 77, 82, 83, 87, 88–89, 127, 129, 148, 240
   casting, 42, 45
   later life, 127, 148
   opinions on Merle, 50
   reactions to *Hoosiers*, 129, 148
Porky's, 17
Porter Ridge, 161
Poseidon Adventure, The, 35
poster, 124–125
prayer, 45, 179, 200, 216
Preacher Purl. *See* Purl, Preacher
premieres
   California, 137–138
   Indiana, 122, 131–136
   national, 138–144
   Western states, 138, 139
   world, 127–131
press conferences, 23, 44, 72, 106
press coverage. *See* media coverage
press releases, 124–125, 207, 227
previews, sneak, 124–125, 131
Princess Theater (Bloomington), 4
profits. *See* box office receipts
props. *See* set decoration
publicity. *See* media coverage
Purl, Preacher, 108, 216, 219
Purl, Strap, 45, 179, 187, 191–192, 200, 216
"Purple People Eater, The", 39

R

race issues, 206–208
Rade. *See* Butcher, Rade
radio, listening to, 68, 95
Raging Bull, 18
rain, 57, 64, 65, 91, 98–99
Raisor, Philip, 206
Ramada Inn Northwest, 47, 98
Rambo, 17
Randolph Southern High School (Lynn), 74
Rawhide, 39
Ray. *See* Butcher, Rade
Ray, 161
Rayl, James D. "Jimbo", 88, 90, 136–137
Rayl, James R. "Jimmy", 88
RCA Dome, 149
Rebel Without a Cause, 38, 185, 186
receipts. *See* box office receipts

redemption, 1, 12, 18, 35, 123, 130, 133, 172, 177, 179, 182, 208–210, 212, 215, 218, 222
referees, 39, 85, 91
referendum. *See* town meeting
regional game (Jasper), 83, 86, 88–91, 191–192, 200, 210, 243
relationships, 10, 18, 65, 119, 130, 133, 142, 177, 195–199, 209
release dates
    Indiana, 122
    national, 121–122, 138
religion, 45, 80, 200, 216
reporters, 39, 57, 107, 190, 244
reporters scene, 70
Resnick, Joel, 122, 138
Reverend Doty. *See* Doty, Reverend
reviews. *See* critical response to *Hoosiers*
Reynolds, Burt, 35
Rhodes, Al, 43
Rice, Dennis, 28
Rice, Kemper, 76, 131
Richmond, Indiana, 23
Ricks, Mike, 136–137
Right Stuff, The, 38
Ringwald, Molly, 147
Ripley County, 9
Rising Sun, Indiana, 22
rival teams. *See* players, opposing
Robertson, Bailey, 110, 207–208
Robertson, Oscar, 103–104, 208
Robinson, Richard, 110
Robling, Laura, 46, 52
Rocky, 18, 133
Rodriguez, Elena, 186
Rogers, Alma, 63
Rolling Stone, 151
Rollins (Fla.) College, 136
Rooster (barber), 39, 73, 217
Rose, Rita, 133
Ross, Chelcie, 39, 64–65, 67, 71, 93, 188
rough cut, 115, 119, 120, 156
Rudy, 160, 163–166
running time, 115, 120–121, 142, 156
rushes. *See* dailies
Russia, 151
RVs, 69

S

Sagamore of the Wabash, 130, 206
St. Elsewhere, 15

St. Louis, Missouri, 164
St. Luke School (Indianapolis), 41
St. Philip Neri School (Indianapolis), 25, 85, 242
salaries
    extras, 29, 58, 106
    Hackman, 35–36
    Huskers, 41
San Diego, 38
Sassone, Michael, 108
schedule, 55, 67, 113, 167, 230, 236
Schenck, Libbey, 46, 88
Schenck, Todd, 42
Schenck, Wade, 42, 45, 46–47, 48, 50, 77, 82, 86, 88, 90, 100, 127, 129, 148, 184, 187–188
    casting, 42, 45
    later life, 127, 148
    reaction to *Hoosiers*, 129
Schickel, Richard, 141, 143, 144, 176, 186
Schmidlin, Rick, 22, 26, 59, 62, 68, 96, 97
school bus, 60, 63, 100
school colors, 33, 229
school scenes, 61–64
school songs. *See* fight songs
Schroder, Roger, 110
Schult, Jack, 39
score. *See* soundtrack
scoreboards, 69–70, 105
Scott, A.O., 176–177, 225
screenplay
    early drafts, 10–14, 116–117
    inspiration for, 3, 5–6, 8–10, 12–13
    quality of, 14, 16, 19–20, 60, 124–125, 137, 142–143, 157, 176–177, 180–181, 187, 189, 195, 201
    researching, 9
    residents' concerns about, 26, 29
    revising, 14, 53, 55, 115
    writing, 7–14, 50, 112–113
script. *See* screenplay
SEAL Team 6, 150
sectional game (Deer Lick), 86–88, 104, 242
semifinal. *See* semistate
semistate, 9, 42, 118
senior cords, 91
sequel, 130

set decoration, 26–27, 62–63, 68, 69–70, 87, 93, 94–97, 99–100, 104–105, 232
Seventeen, 125
Seventh Seal, The, 4
Sheehan, Henry, 124, 143–144, 191
Shelbyville, Indiana, 90
Sheridan, Indiana, 92–93
sheriff, 39, 73, 100
Sherman, Rodger, 206
Shift, The, 161
Shively, Debby, 29–30, 32–33, 74, 77, 106
Shively, Ralph "Whitey", 30, 68
Shooter. *See* Flatch, Wilbur "Shooter"
Shore, Jack, 84
Short, Brant, 209–210
Short, Dayle Hardy, 209–210
Showplace Theatre (Vincennes), 132
Shy People, 129
Siegel, Ed, 134
Sigma Nu fraternity, 4, 6, 127
Simmons, Bill, 155–156, 175, 191, 222
Simon, Mel, 16–17
single-class basketball. *See* one-class basketball
Siskel & Ebert, 125
Siskel, Gene, 125, 141, 144
Skidmore, Fred, 122
small-town life, 27–28, 188, 193, 203, 215–216
Smiley, Sam, 39, 85
Smithville, Indiana, 10
smoker pots, 70, 73
sneak previews, 124–125, 131
soccer, 164
Some Kind of Wonderful, 140
songs, school. *See* fight songs
sorghum grinding, 95–96
Sorvig, Greg, 162
soundtrack, 118–119
    Academy Award nomination, 139, 144–145
    controversy, 140
South Bend Central Bears, 104–106, 108, 110, 206–208, 213
South Bend Central High School, 9, 41–42
South Bend, Indiana, 49, 163
Southport High School (Indianapolis), 90, 128
Southwestern College, 43
souvenirs, 56, 84, 101, 160, 171

Soviet Union, 151
Sports Illustrated, 42, 142, 150, 174
sports movies, 10, 18, 133, 150–151, 163–166, 168, 176, 177, 180, 181, 187, 202, 222, 223
Spuhler, Robert, 186
stand-ins, 40, 69, 76, 92, 104, 160
Stanton, Harry Dean, 37
"Star-Spangled Banner, The", 107
Star Wars, 15, 138
State Department of Education, 89
state-finals game (Butler Fieldhouse), 102, 103-113, 190–192, 197, 205–206, 219–220, 243
state tournament, 3, 9, 42, 43, 88, 103, 110–111, 118, 133, 158–160, 205–206, 225, 247
    in *Hoosiers*. *See* tournament games
Steadicam, 78, 80, 241
Steele, Mike, 136
Stephens, Fannie, 59
Stern, Stewart, 185
Sterritt, David, 144
Stilesville, Indiana, 92
Stinesville, Indiana, 10
Stockton, Norman L., 24
Stone, Oliver, 20, 123
Strap. *See* Purl, Strap
Stratigos, Spyridon "Strats", 41, 49, 73, 77, 81, 89–90
Striegel, Colleen, 189, 210, 219, 221
student extras, 62–63, 74–77, 79, 89, 100, 113
    missing school, 76, 84, 89
Summers, Cletus, 39, 63, 94, 96, 100, 108, 117, 156, 157, 202, 214
Summers, Loetta, 46, 157, 214
Summers, Millie, 39, 108, 157, 214, 221
Summers, Scott, 43, 45, 46–47, 48, 49, 82, 88, 127, 187
    acting, approach to, 45
    casting, 43, 45
    later life, 127
Sundance Film Festival, 138
Sunville, 117
Superman, 35, 72
Superman IV, 129
supporting actors. *See* actors
Sutton, Robert, 70
Swan, Robert, 82, 188
Swayzee High School, 203
symbolism, 182–183

T

Tank McNamara, 141
tax breaks, for filming, 19, 161–163
Taylor University, 127
team bus, 31–32, 99, 100, 107, 176, 203, 216, 234–235
team members. *See* Huskers
team members, opposing. *See* players, opposing
teamwork, 49, 213–214
Ten Commandments, The, 4–5
Tender Mercies, 35
Terhune, Indiana, 39, 60, 86, 88, 92, 117, 156
Terminator, The, 20, 123, 147
Terminator 2: Judgment Day, 123
Terms of Endearment, 17
Tesich, Steve, 8
test screening, 120–121, 127
Thompson, John Robert, 39, 61
Thompson, Nancy, 24, 62
Thorntown, Indiana, 42
thrift shops, 33, 79
Time, 141, 174, 186
Time Life Films, 7
Tin Men, 185
Tinder, Bill, 205–206
Tinker, Grant, 7
title, 17, 114, 121, 151
  alternatives, 114, 151–152
Tobacco Road, 29
Tobias, Scott, 184, 208
tournament. *See* NCAA, state tournament, tournament games
tournament games, 86–91, 103–113
town meeting, 92–94, 183–184, 209–210, 216, 218–219, 237, 241
town names, 29–30, 86
Trafalgar, Indiana, 62
Travel-Aires, 107
Triton Central High School (Fairland), 62–63
Tri-West High School (Lizton), 49
Trout, Teresa, 46
Tudor, Deborah, 197, 198, 216, 217–218
Turner, Ken, 135
TV Guide, 207
TV series based on *Hoosiers*, 163
TV version of *Hoosiers*, 149

U

UA Coronet Theatre (Los Angeles), 137
uniforms, basketball, 33–34, 172
Union City Community High School, 79
Unionville, Indiana, 10
United States Film Festival, 138
University High School (Bloomington), 4, 46
University of Illinois, 36
University of Notre Dame, 163–164
University of Southern California (USC), 6–7, 15, 167, 222
Urioste, Frank, 118
USA Today, 150
USC. *See* University of Southern California

V

Valainis, Maris, 41–42, 44–45, 48, 51, 64, 77, 82, 94, 101, 108, 111–112, 127, 148, 153
  acting, approach to, 94
  casting, 41–42, 44–45
  later life, 127, 148
Variety, 124, 139, 143, 160, 167, 174, 176, 239
Variety Club of Indiana, 128
Varynit Garment Factory, 33
vehicles, 31, 63, 99–100, 175, 233
  car driven by Norman, 57, 92, 106, 107
  cars, 31, 63, 99–100
  fire truck, 100
  school bus, 60, 63, 100
  team bus, 31–32, 99, 100, 107, 176, 203, 216, 234–235
Verdi, 86
Vernon, Indiana, 22
Versailles, Indiana, 9, 22
Vevay, Indiana, 22
VHS. *See* videocassette
videocassette, 36, 147
videotaping, 57, 74
Vietnam War, 6, 20, 123, 167
Vincennes, Indiana, 132, 225
  Lincoln High School, 225
Vineberg, Steve, 144, 187
Von Lee Theatre (Bloomington), 5

W

Wabash College, 136
Waldman, Harvey, 31, 67, 74–75, 79, 89, 104, 108–109, 111, 113, 157, 175
Walker, Buddy, 45, 50, 54, 71, 129–130, 156–157, 179, 199
   rejoining the team, 129–130, 156–157
Walker, George, 39, 71, 188, 194
Walking Dead, The, 162
Wanamaker, Indiana, 23
Ward, Sarah, 85
wardrobe. *See* costumes
Warner Bros. Television, 7
Warsaw Community High School, 43
Warsaw, Indiana, 204
Washington Post, 141, 142, 174
Waveland, Indiana, 22
weather, 65, 95, 99–100, 131. *See also* rain
Webb, Merle, 45, 82, 83, 192, 200, 212–213, 219
Weir, Mary, 32
Welker, Skip, 39
Wells, Ross, 63
Wendel, Phil, 43, 136
West, Evan, 176
Westerfeld, Ron, 84–85

Western Boone High School (Thorntown), 42, 89
Whicker, Jody, 95–96, 106
Whit. *See* Butcher, Whit
White, Drew, 192
White, Gene, 9, 135
Widmer, Harold, 28
Williams, Randy, 190, 193
Williamson, Bruce, 125
Wilson, "Jumpin'" Johnny, 183
Winchell, Mark Royden, 208
Winning, 5
Wishard Memorial Hospital, 97
Wishard Nursing Museum, 97–98
Wolf, Faye, 93
Wolff, Melora, 190, 220
Wood High School (Indianapolis), 183
Wood, Marvin, 8–10, 12, 111, 135
Wooley, Sheb, 39, 58, 80, 97, 108, 157
world premiere, 127–131
Wright, Marcia, 77

Y–Z

Yates, Peter, 8
Young, John Sacret, 11

zone defense, 134, 201–202, 216

Made in the USA
Monee, IL
11 April 2023